CONFRONTING POLITICAL ISLAM

CONFRONTING POLITICAL ISLAM

Six Lessons from the West's Past

John M. Owen IV

PRINCETON UNIVERSITY PRESS

Princeton and Oxford

press.princeton.edu

Jacket art: *Sacking Police Station in Naples, Italy, during a riot.* Worms after Cairoli,
published in *L'Illustration,* Journal Universel, Paris, 1860. © Antonio Abrignani/Shutterstock.
Photograph: Egyptians Protest against President Morsi in Sidi Gaber, Alexandria, Egypt,
June 30, 2013. © MidoSemsem/Shutterstock.

ISBN 978-0-691-16314-7

Library of Congress Control Number: 2014947452

British Library Cataloging-in-Publication Data is available

This book has been composed in Minion Pro & ITC Avant Garde Gothic

Printed on acid-free paper ∞

Printed in the United States of America

1 3 5 7 9 10 8 6 4 2

For Malloy, Frances, and Alice

CONTENTS

ILLUSTRATIONS

TABLES

PREFACE

Nearly a century after it first emerged in Egypt, political Islam confronts the world and the world confronts political Islam. Also called Islamism, this potent ideology holds that the billion-strong Muslim community would be free and great if only it were pious—if Muslims lived under state-enforced Islamic law or Sharia, as Muslims have for most of Islamic history. Islamists have long been confronted by Muslims who reject Sharia, and by non-Muslims who press or influence them to reject it. These interlocking confrontations sometimes have been benign, in the sense of parties standing face to face, and sometimes malign, in the sense of parties standing against and even fighting each other. Whether benign or malign, the confrontations continue to matter because they shape not only the lives of Muslims but also the politics of many nations and indeed of the entire world.

Islamism began in the 1920s as a call to Muslims living in modernizing, secularizing societies to return to Sharia, derived from the Quran and various other sacred or authoritative texts of Islam. As they encountered resistance from both militaries and other elites, Islamists became increasingly political, desiring to influence or capture the states that were reshaping their societies so that those states would enforce Sharia. By the 1950s many Islamist movements had been radicalized and were being ruthlessly suppressed by the regimes they had come to hate.

Thanks to the scholarship of scores of experts on Islamic jurisprudence, theology, and history, we know a great deal about Islamism. But most of this scholarship treats this ideology as if it were *sui generis*, unique, to be studied only in isolation. Like any social phenomenon, political Islam does have singular features that may be understood only through deep study. Yet, Islamism is an "ism," an ideology, a plan for ordering common life. As such, it can be compared profitably with other "isms."

No part of the world has generated as many "isms" as the West itself—Europe and the Americas.[1] Although scholars and journalists occasionally draw parallels between the Middle East today and the West in earlier centuries—jihadi terrorists to anarchists around 1900, or the Arab Spring to the European revolutions of 1848—until now no one has attempted a sustained comparison between political Islam and Western ideologies of the past.

This book carries out such a comparison. It begins with the observation, already made by scholars of Islamism, that this complex and robust ideology cannot be understood without reference to the broad ideology to which it is a reaction: secularism. In its original form, secularism in the Muslim world mandated that the laws derive from strictly human reason and experience, and not from divine revelation. Secularism came to Muslim lands in the nineteenth century, at the hands of European colonizers, and in the twentieth, at the hands of authoritarian modernizers such as Mustafa Kemal of Turkey and Reza Pahlavi of Iran. Twentieth-century hard-edged secularism is all but dead in the Middle East today—most Muslims accept that Islam should at least influence law and government—but Islamists still define themselves and struggle against various shades of softer secularism.

In coexisting with its opposite, Islamism is, again, like ideologies in the West's own past. *Confronting Political Islam* builds upon my past scholarly work, especially my 2010 book *The Clash of Ideas in World Politics*,[2] in focusing on ideological contests in Europe and the Americas that stretched across countries and decades, scrambling power relationships and altering expectations and behavior, generating new patterns of conflict and cooperation, befuddling both participants and observers, and finally ending in unexpected times and ways. From the West's own past I sift six broad lessons for policy makers and citizens trying to deal with the prolonged ideological travails in the Middle East.

I am grateful to many people and institutions for helping me conceive of, research, and write this book. The Institute for Advanced Studies in Culture at the University of Virginia provided ideas and criticism—from scholars including James Hunter, Ashley Berner, Josh Yates, Joe Davis, Neslihan Çevik, Chuck Mathewes, and George Thomas—and its genteel intellectual hothouse, Watson Manor. John Moon and the IMR Foundation, Earhart Foundation, and the Smith Richardson Foundation all provided funding that enabled me to devote a scholar's most precious commodity—time—to the book. For invaluable research assistance I thank Bob Kubinec and Malloy Owen. Conversations with Michael Barnett, Peter Katzenstein, Ahmed al-Rahim, Judd Owen, Alexander Evans, and my Politics Department colleagues at the University of Virginia—especially Bill Quandt, Jonah Schulhofer-Wohl, and Jeff Legro—were most helpful. The Centre of International Relations at the University of British Columbia provided me with a place to write and research during the summers. For Map 6.1, I thank Chris Gist.

The Smith Richardson grant enabled me to hold three workshops in Washington, where I tested some of the arguments on academic, military, intelligence, and policy analysts. I thank the Brookings Institution and the Heritage Foundation for hosting those bracing sessions. I also thank those in attendance, especially Michael O'Hanlon, Steve Grand, Nathan Brown, Karim Sadjadpour, Peter Mandaville, Marc Lynch, Charles "Cully" Stimson, Reuel Marc Gerecht, Jim Philips, Lisa Curtis, Peter Henne, and Tim Shah. Special thanks go to Roger Herbert for handling logistics and for offering his own criticism of the manuscript itself.

While he was still a senior editor at Princeton University Press, Chuck Myers was both advocate and critic; without him, this book never would have been written. Eric Crahan at Princeton carried the project through with skill and care. The two manuscript reviewers, Jeremy Pressman and Dan Nexon, helped me see things that I had not and steered me away from some errors in fact and interpretation. Joseph Dahm was a superb copy editor.

My dear family has supported me by being present and by letting me sometimes be absent. For understanding and even enjoying the peculiarities of marriage to an academic, my wife Trish is *sine qua non*. I dedicate this book to our three children, Malloy, Frances, and Alice, who remind me daily that God is good and that a book such as this is worth writing.

CONFRONTING POLITICAL ISLAM

Introduction
It Did Happen Here

History doesn't repeat itself, but it does rhyme.
—*Attributed to Mark Twain*

The Middle East in recent years has been, in some ways, very much as Northwestern Europe was 450 years ago. Then, a wave of insurrection rolled across three Western countries and threatened to break over more. In 1560 the wave struck Scotland; in 1562, France; in 1567, the Netherlands.

Each insurrection was different, because each country was different. Scotland was a relatively isolated land, of rugged terrain and small population, perpetually worried about invasion from its southern neighbor England. France was a great power, with vast farmlands and wealth, its rulers longtime rivals with those of Spain for supremacy in Europe. The Netherlands or Low Countries were small, also relatively prosperous, and directly ruled by Spain. As is always the case, rebels within and across the countries had diverse complaints and motivations.

But the three revolts had much in common. In contrast to the peasant rebellions that sometimes shook parts of early modern Europe, all three were led by nobles—landowning men with titles, trained for war. The Scottish, French, and Dutch nobles all, in a sense, were playing out an old story, fighting back against a monarch trying to centralize power at their expense. In the Scottish and Dutch cases, the monarch was a foreigner: French for the Scots, Spanish for the Dutch. Perhaps most strikingly, the leaders of all three sets of rebellious aristocrats—and probably most of the common men who fought for them—were believers in a Christian creed that was, depending upon one's point of view, either radically new or a faithful retrieval of original Christianity. All were adherents of a branch of Protestantism founded in the preceding decades by the French theologian John Calvin.

That so many rebels in the three countries were Calvinists—or Reformed, as they also were called—was no coincidence. Calvinists held in common a set of doctrines concerning God and man, among which were that a human being could do nothing to save himself but must rely on the mercy of God, and that God had decided on his own volition whom he would save before he created the world. The Reformed also held distinctive beliefs about how the church was to be organized, how the faithful were to live, and how the church and civil authorities or state should relate. Reformed churches did not have bishops and priests, but instead were governed by elders and deacons. Christians were to aim at holy lives, to "make their calling and election sure," in the words of St. Peter.[1] And the community itself was to aim at holiness, with the civil and church authorities separated but the former enforcing the teachings of the latter.

This, then, was not the Calvinism of the Presbyterian Church of Main Street, U.S.A., in the twenty-first century or even the nineteenth. Early modern Calvinism was—like the Catholicism, Lutheranism, and other Christian "isms" of the time—a political ideology as well as a set of religious doctrines. It emerged in a time when the social, political, and economic order of Central and Western Europe was built around, and partly by, the Roman Catholic Church. In medieval Europe the Church—parishes, dioceses, religious orders—owned vast tracts of land that generated huge amounts of wealth. Clergy enjoyed deep influence over princes, nobles, and peasants. The legitimacy of the hierarchical social system depended in part on the imprimatur of the Church. Some bishops, including the popes, ruled large territories and could raise their own armies. In the Europe of the sixteenth century, Calvinism at this time was partly defined as anti-Catholicism, and being anti- or pro-Catholic was as much a political as it was a religious commitment.

That raises a second and related similarity among the Scottish, French, and Dutch revolts: all were directed against Catholic monarchs who were tied to the teachings and institutions of the Church of Rome. These were, on one level, anti-Catholic rebellions. The statements and writings of the leaders are in a particular religious idiom; one 1559 manifesto from the Lords of the Congregation was addressed to "the generation of Antichrist, the pestilent prelates and their shavelings within Scotland," and went on, "We shall begin that same war that God commanded the Israelites to execute against the Canaanites; that is, contract of peace shall never be made, till ye desist from your open idolatry and cruel persecution of God's children. And this we signify unto you in the name of the eternal God, and of His Son, Jesus Christ, whose verity we profess, and evangel we will have preached, and holy sacraments rightly ministrate, so long as God will assist us to gainstand your idolatry."[2] This was not just a peculiar "way of talking," a pious adornment of more mundane concerns. Calvinists in all three countries engaged in bouts of iconoclasm, smashing icons in churches because for them such images were idols, stealing glory that rightly belonged to God. The Calvinists had deep and, it seemed at the time, irreconcilable differences with Catholics.

In yet another sense the three insurrections were not coincidental: Calvinists communicated across national boundaries, encouraging and learning from one another, circulating sermons, tracts, letters, and themselves. Historians refer to a "Calvinist International," a network of Reformed Christians that existed across countries, its nerve center in Calvin's own adopted city of Geneva. Garrett Mattingly writes that "all of them, everywhere, vibrated to any impulse that stirred their connecting web." Andrew Pettegree notes that the Dutch Calvinists were encouraged by the Huguenot rebellion in France: "In the year following the outbreak of fighting in France, Dutch Calvinists . . . began to imitate the provocative and confrontational behavior that had brought French evangelicals such success."[3]

Catholics, too, existed in all of these countries and had a parallel imperative to suppress Calvinism. They too formed a sophisticated network with its chief node in Rome. The revolts and the attempts to suppress them were really part of a single larger phenomenon, a contest that stretched across Northwestern and Central Europe over religion—and not only religion in the modern sense, but in the sense of the time, when church and state were intimate and a country's established religion affected its institutions and way of life and how power and wealth were distributed. The root problem was that Western Christendom was torn by a *legitimacy crisis*, a struggle over the best way to order society. The crisis is seen particularly in the Reformation and Counter-Reformation of the time.

Because the legitimacy crisis was *transnational*, with Catholics sympathizing with one another regardless of homeland, and Calvinists doing the same, it is no surprise that the rulers of many countries had a stake in the outcomes of the revolts. Protestant England and Catholic France intervened in the Scottish rebellion. England did the same to help the French Calvinists (or Huguenots). Later the German state of Palatinate joined the Calvinist side, as Spain did the Catholic. In the Netherlands Spanish troops naturally intervened to put down the Calvinists, and English, Huguenot, and German troops helped the Calvinists. Even the Ottoman sultans—who, as Muslim emperors, had no religious stake in the Reformation—became involved, offering to help Lutherans and Calvinists against the Catholic Habsburgs who ruled so much of Europe.

There is more. In the previous decades similar chain reactions had detonated in the Holy Roman Empire—roughly today's Germany—with Catholics facing off against Lutherans. And well after the 1560s more such chain reactions were to flash through Europe. One in particular was catastrophic: A Calvinist-led revolt in Bohemia led to intervention and counter-intervention that escalated into the horrific Thirty Years' War (1618–48). While that complex struggle was wiping out perhaps one-fifth of Germany's population, the English Civil War (1642–51) broke out. It was these violent civil and international wars that helped Europeans to see their way, begrudgingly, to the religious toleration that Westerners today take for granted.

One of the three revolts of the 1560s failed. In France, the Huguenots and Catholics fought on and off for several decades, often savagely. A stalemate finally was broken in 1593 when Henry IV, Huguenot champion, agreed to convert to Catholicism so as to take Paris unopposed. ("Paris is well worth a mass," Henry was reported to have said.)

But the Scottish and Dutch revolutions succeeded and invented a new thing in Europe: a Reformed realm. The Scottish insurrectionists won quickly and set up a Reformed (Presbyterian) kingdom in 1560. The Dutch had to fight the Spanish for nearly two decades, but in 1585 they set up the United Provinces of the Netherlands, with the Reformed as the established religion. The Calvinists proved adept not only at mobilizing for rebellion but at consolidating and institutionalizing power.

▨ ▨ ▨

That was long ago, and it was Europe. But parts of the Muslim world today, in many respects, bear an uncanny resemblance to that time and place. Over the past century, rulers of many majority-Muslim countries have amassed power by weakening other actors in their societies. Some have extended their influence in foreign countries. Networks of ideologues with nodes in places such as Tehran, Riyadh, and Cairo have sliced across Muslim countries, with members in each monitoring, educating, and encouraging their counterparts in others. Where early modern Europe had its religious massacres, the Middle East has had its terrorism—which has extended into Asia, Africa, Europe, and North America, most catastrophically to New York and Washington on September 11, 2001. And of course, waves of rebellion, suppression, revolution, and foreign intervention have taken place periodically within and across Muslim countries. (Throughout this book I use the term "Middle East," by which I mean the vast region stretching from North Africa into Southwest Asia, even though the ideological struggles I analyze extend into parts of sub-Saharan Africa, South and Southeast Asia, and some cities in Europe and North America.) Sometimes, when a revolution has succeeded, a new regime, proclaiming a return to Islamic roots, has been established.[4]

It is difficult fully to understand what is going on in these Muslim societies. The history, interests, power, ambitions, and beliefs of the various actors, and how those things interact, are exceedingly complex. But we can make some headway, and the most straightforward path is for academic and policy experts on the Middle East or Islam to bring to bear their learning. Experts have been doing just that for many years, in works too numerous to begin to mention here. Deep analysis by scholars who speak and read Arabic, Farsi, Pashto, Urdu, and other languages, who know the histories and cultures intimately, is indispensable to policy makers, students, and citizens trying to make sense of the bewildering and fraught dynamics of the Middle East.

But a second, complementary way to understand the Middle East has barely been undertaken. That way involves taking analytical advantage of the West's own history of ideological conflict. For the story of the rolling revolts across Northwestern Europe in the 1560s is only one of many such stories that have a strangely familiar ring. Here, too, is no coincidence. One important reason why the dynamics of Muslim societies and regions so resemble early modern Europe is that *for at least a century the Middle East has been roiled by a legitimacy crisis—a contest over the best way to order society.* It is not Islam the religion that is generating the problems, any more than Calvinist doctrine per se was sowing discord in early modern Europe. It is rather a deep and prolonged disagreement among Muslims over how far Islam ought to shape the laws and institutions of society.

For a number of decades Muslims have argued, organized, formed networks, rebelled, suppressed, allied, befriended, betrayed, killed, and died for the sake of ideology, or visions of the good life and public order. Muslims have been unable to agree on the basic questions of society. They have been polarized within and across countries, sometimes to the point of civil war, and often to the point where many identify more with foreigners who share their principles than with their fellow citizens who do not. The legitimacy crisis has complicated domestic and international politics, creating alliances and enmities that can be especially vicious and resistant to compromise. The crisis has dramatically affected the interests of the United States and other outside powers at particular junctures: the 1952 Egyptian Revolution, 1979 Iranian Revolution, the 2001 al-Qaeda attacks, most recently the Arab Spring that began in late 2010.[5]

Some writers have drawn analogies between these dynamics and ideological struggles in the West's own past.[6] This book takes that insight much further. It is the first sustained analytical comparison between the Middle East today and various region-wide legitimacy crises in the history of Europe and the Americas—crises that exhibited remarkably similar chains of events. I present lessons about the current upheaval in Muslim societies, and its troubled interactions and interpenetration with the rest of the world, drawn from past ideological struggles in other parts of the globe.

I make two general claims in this book:

1. Understanding political Islam requires understanding its long twilight struggle with secularism.
2. Understanding that Islamist-secularist struggle requires that we understand the origins, dynamics, and ultimate end of similar ideological struggles in the history of the Western world.

Although I describe the content of each ideology—Lutheranism, monarchism, liberalism, Islamism, and so on—I abstract from that content and focus simply on the fact that each ideology was caught in a struggle with one or more alternatives. Content does matter, and these ideologies have varied widely in goals, strategies, and tactics. Radical Calvinists, republicans, and communists never engaged in suicide bombing, as radical Islamists do. Many Islamists appear to want only to be left alone by the non-Muslim world, whereas many Western ideologies have had global ambitions. But I deliberately pass over these important differences because the formal similarities—the fact of ideological competition—are striking and instructive enough for one book. They show that much of what we think about political Islam is wrong.

The Rhyme of History

In the following pages, I draw lessons from three long periods in which Western societies were divided, internally and internationally, over the best way to order society and powerful ideological movements stretched across entire regions, agitating for change and disrupting "normal" domestic and international politics.

The first is the struggle between Catholics and Protestants over which form of Christianity should be established or favored by the state. This contest raged in Western and Central Europe from roughly 1520 until around the 1690s.

The second struggle emerged in the 1770s and endured for a century. In Europe and the Americas people differed deeply over whether the best regime was a monarchy, with a king and subjects, or a republic, where authorities were elected and people were citizens.

The third struggle arose in the 1910s and lasted until the late 1980s. The struggle most familiar to today's readers, it raged among communism, liberalism, and fascism.

In each of these long contests ideologies mutated, and some of the mutations survived and competed with the originals. In the first, Protestantism began as Lutheranism in Germany, quickly developed a Zwinglian version in

Switzerland and Anabaptism in Germany, then a Calvinist version in France, an Anglican one in England, and still other versions elsewhere. Calvinists and Lutherans became serious rivals at certain points. In the second contest, monarchists were divided between absolutists, who maintained that kings had their title to rule directly from God and were constrained only by him, and constitutionalists, who insisted that monarchs must be constrained by representative legislatures. In the third, communists divided into many groups, with Chinese (Maoists) and Soviets falling into a severe rivalry in the 1960s.

The same is true of the Middle East today. Ideological disagreements among Muslims are many and serious, but the most fundamental line is between *secularists* and *Islamists*. The nub of the question is, in a sense, who or what is sovereign in society, and the chief sign of this is the source and content of the law. Islamists insist that law must be *Sharia*, derived from the sacred texts of Islam—the Quran, or direct revelation from Allah to the Prophet Muhammad, and the Hadith, or sayings of the Prophet. Secularists counter that law should derive from human reason and experience, not from Islam (or, for moderate secularists, not from Islam alone).

These two ideologies, secularism and Islamism, originated as negations of one another. Secularism came to the Muslim world with European colonialism in the eighteenth and nineteenth centuries.[7] Many Muslim elites in the Middle East adopted it in the twentieth century precisely because of the power of the European states that had long surpassed and humiliated the Ottoman Empire, generally regarded as the caliphate or universal Islamic polity. The Ottoman Empire was built upon traditional Islamic social and political institutions, and Muslim military and political elites in particular saw secularism as the remedy.

Islamists typically present their ideology not as an "ism" but as simply Islam, the pristine religion of the Prophet. In fact, their belief system has modern features and arose in reaction to secularism, from both European colonizers and Muslim modernists. Early Islamists such as Egypt's Hassan al-Banna (1906–49), British India's Abul Ala Maududi (1903–79), and Iran's Ruhollah Khomeini (1902–89) were convinced that it was hard to live as a pious Muslim under a secular regime, and began to push back in the second quarter of the twentieth century by organizing cultural resistance movements. In the 1950s Islamists became more radical and began advocating, in various ways, for an end to secular regimes and a return to state-enforced Sharia.

From the 1920s through late 1960s, secularism had the whip hand. After the Ottoman Empire's defeat in the First World War, Mustafa Kemal Atatürk (1881–1938) dissolved it, abolished the old caliphate, and founded modern Turkey, the prototypical secular Muslim state that explicitly repudiated the traditional Islamic organization of society and adopted Western norms and practices. Atatürk had admirers and imitators in other Muslim countries. Typically these were military officers and intellectuals who chafed under Western domination and wanted to build modern, independent states. Reza Shah Pahlavi (1878–1944) in Iran was one; Muhammad Ali Jinnah (1876–1948) in Pakistan was another; Gamal Abdel Nasser (1918–70) in Egypt was a third.[8] Nasser and his circle also were influenced by the Syrian intellectual Michel Aflaq (whose background was Christian) and the Ba'athist, or Arab nationalist, movement that he helped found.[9] Nasser's Arab socialism had a following across the Arab world and led to the establishment of Ba'athist regimes in Syria and Iraq. Secularism even threatened the conservative Saudi monarchy, and Egypt and Saudi Arabia fought a Vietnam-like proxy war in Yemen in the 1960s.

The turning point, scholars say in hindsight, came in 1967. Israel's quick and crushing defeat of the armies of Egypt, Jordan, and Syria in the Six-Day War represented a fundamental failure for Nasser and his secularist project. Evidently casting aside Islam and becoming like a Western state was not the way to free Muslim societies from outside domination. An alternative program for success, long opposed to secularism, already enjoyed support among clergy and some lay Muslims.[10] The Muslim Brotherhood propagated their narrative that the real reason behind Muslims' failures was their abandonment of the true religion. "Islam is the solution" became a slogan not of quaint old men but, increasingly, of the young. The Iranian Revolution in 1979, establishing the Islamic Republic, sent shock waves across the Middle East; it was a sign that Islamism was for real. Even secular rulers such as Anwar el-Sadat in Egypt and Zia ul-Haq in Pakistan began to adopt more Islamic slogans and institutions.[11]

French political scientist Gilles Kepel was among the first to note that the Islamic revival has coincided roughly with revivals in Christianity and Judaism. New "fundamentalist" movements across the globe, including in the West, have thwarted the confident predictions of modernization theorists in the 1950s and 1960s that revealed or traditional religion was dying away.[12] Hinduism has joined the general revival, as has (in some places) Buddhism. All of these movements not only falsify the claim that modern technology necessarily brings religious skepticism or indifference but also entail a skepticism or hostility toward secularism itself.[13] Although I return at the book's very end to parallels between America's culture wars and the struggles in the Middle East—particularly how Americans disagree on the goodness and role of traditional institutions that come between individual and state—in this book I limit my focus to Islam and the Middle East. Each of the revival movements in other religions is consequential in specific nations, but none has established a theocratic state in the modern era, nor does any possess the transnational power of Islamism. As Kepel notes, in the West in particular the acceptance of democracy by Christians and Jews has constrained revivalists from violence and from pressing for transformation of the social order.[14] Political Islam is of the greatest global consequence, and so it is to political Islam that we must attend.

The Situation Today

Surveys reveal that, in the second decade of the twenty-first century, most Muslims are neither secularist nor Islamist in any pure sense. Islamism and secularism are what social scientists call ideal types. Atatürk was close to being a pure secularist. "We do not consider our principles as dogmas contained in books that are said to come from heaven," Turkey's founder declaimed in 1937. "We derive our inspiration, not from heaven, or from an unseen world, but directly from life."[15] A pure Islamist would be Sayyid Qutb (1906–66), the Egyptian writer sometimes called the "grandfather of al-Qaeda." "The umma [Islamic world] must be restored to its original form," wrote Qutb, "so that Islam can once again perform its appointed role as leader of humankind. It is essential to excavate this umma buried beneath the rubble accumulated from generations of ideas, practices, and systems entirely unrelated to Islam and the Islamic way."[16]

Most Muslims fall between these two extremes. We have abundant evidence that, at least in the Middle East, the average Muslim is now leaning Islamist. Large majorities in countries such as Jordan, Egypt, and Pakistan want their laws to derive from the Quran and Hadith (or sayings of the Prophet Muhammad). Table 1.1 presents data from a 2012 poll taken by the Pew Research Center.[17]

It is worth asking what answers Christians, Hindus, or adherents of other religions would give to these questions if "Quran" were changed to their

Table 1.1.
How much influence should the Quran have on the laws?

Country	Laws should strictly follow the teachings of the Quran	Laws should follow the values and principles of Islam but not strictly follow the teachings of the Quran	Laws should not be influenced by the teachings of the Quran	Don't know
Egypt	60	32	6	2
Jordan	72	26	1	1
Lebanon	17	35	42	6
Pakistan	82	15	1	2
Tunisia	22	64	12	2
Turkey	17	46	27	10

Source: Pew 2012 Global Attitudes Survey.
Note: Values in the table are percentages of those surveyed.

sacred texts. Perhaps many would at least agree with the statement in the second column, that the "laws should follow the values and principles of" their religion.

What is striking about Table 1.1, however, are the figures in the first column in Egypt, Jordan, and Pakistan, and also the figures in all of the countries if the first two columns are summed. Even in the most secular state in Table 1.1—Lebanon—a slight majority wants the laws either to strictly follow the Quran or to follow Islam's principles. Since Lebanon's population is estimated to be 39 percent Christian,[18] it is a safe bet that most of the 42 percent of Lebanese who want no Islamic influence over the laws are Christians, and hence that the great majority of Lebanese Muslims are not strict secularists. A 2007 poll of four Muslim countries—Morocco, Egypt, Pakistan, and Indonesia—revealed that, on average, three out of four respondents agreed that all Muslim countries should have a strict application of Sharia and "keep Western values out." Two-thirds would prefer a world in which "all Islamic countries [were unified] into a single Islamic state or caliphate."[19] Behind this trend away from secularism and toward Islamism lies a decided shift in recent decades among Arab intellectuals away from hostility to traditional religion and toward an appreciation of Islam's cultural significance for Arabs.[20]

At the same time, recent revolts in Iran, Tunisia, Libya, Egypt, Yemen, and Syria show that most Muslims want democracy or popular rule, thereby departing from what has been mainstream Islamism. As I discuss in later chapters, it is difficult for Westerners to grasp, but today millions of Muslims want both democracy and Islamism and believe they can have both.

In one sense, then, Islamism has already triumphed in the Middle East. The old extreme secularism of the middle twentieth century, in which the state seizes control of the religion so as to eliminate its independent role in public affairs, has retained few followers. In another sense, however, Islamism continues to struggle and encounter resistance to its full ambitions. Muslims continue to disagree over how much influence their religion ought to have over public life and the role of the clergy in government. Today's secularists are those who call for less rather than none. Islamists, meanwhile, differ among themselves over which version of Islam is normative and whether violence and revolution or law and reform are the better routes to Sharia.

Thus the legitimacy crisis continues in various forms—some violent, some peaceful, some open, some hidden—across the Middle East. Well into the second decade of the twenty-first century, in Afghanistan, NATO forces struggled against a remarkably robust set of jihadists. The Taliban (who ruled most of Afghanistan until toppled by U.S. and Afghan forces in October 2001), the Haqqani Network, and others greatly complicated Western efforts to build a stable and friendly Afghanistan. To the immediate east was Pakistan, a country with a secular founding and tradition whose army was deeply penetrated by a powerful Islamist cohort. The Pakistani Taliban virtually ran parts of the country that border Afghanistan. Pakistan's perpetually troubled relations with its giant eastern neighbor India were entangled with its Islamists' militancy. The problem was especially acute because Pakistan has a nuclear arsenal that outsiders estimate at between 90 and 110 warheads.[21]

Lodged between Iraq and Afghanistan is the Islamic Republic of Iran, which enjoyed a remarkable rise in power in the Middle East in the preceding decade. For a number of years it had been on a path to develop nuclear weapons and medium-range missiles; it had deep influence in Syria, Lebanon, and Palestine via ideological networks; it was an avowed enemy of the United States and Israel.

The trouble extended to the southwest. Saudi Arabia, the world's biggest oil producer, was itself an Islamist state. Its Wahhabist form of Sunni Islam gave it the world's strictest form of Sharia. Its longtime cooperation with the United States over oil prices, its generally moderate foreign policy stance, and the legendary profligacy and hypocrisy of many members of its swollen royal family generated a potent radical Islamist opposition. The late Osama bin Laden, responsible for the terrorist attacks of September 11, 2001, had been a leader of this opposition, exiled from Saudi Arabia because he sought the overthrow of the House of Saud.

The Saudis and their wealthy small Gulf Arab neighbors worried about their own domestic terrorist threats, as well as about the expanding power of Iran just across the Persian Gulf. The Saudis' Sunni version of Islamism vied with Iran's Shia-Islamism for supremacy, and that ideological struggle exacerbated the rivalry between the states of Iran and Saudi Arabia themselves. Yemen, the Saudis' impoverished southern neighbor, was torn by a radical Islamist insurrection.

To the northwest, the nascent country of Palestine was cut in two not only by geography: the West Bank was ruled by the secular Palestinian Authority, and Gaza, by the Islamist Hamas. In Lebanon, Hezbollah, a Shia-Islamist group funded by Iran, held sway in the south, bordering Israel, and part of the capital Beirut, alienating Druze, Christians, and other Lebanese. Still farther northward, in Turkey secularists feared that their country was already ruled by closet fundamentalists waiting for the right time to impose Islamic law. The probability was not trivial that at some point the army, guardian of Turkey's secular Kemalist tradition, would carry out a coup d'état. And Syria was being thrashed by a horrific civil war, its secularist regime pitted against a divided and largely jihadi-Islamist opposition. Each side was ruthless and the violence drove millions of refugees, many of them radicalized, into neighboring Jordan, Lebanon, Iraq, and Turkey.

To the southwest, in Africa, some countries were on a knife's edge, others going through civil violence and brutal repression. In less than three years

Egypt had careened from a secular regime to an Islamicizing one (following the 2011 revolution) and back to a secular one (following the 2013 military coup d'état). The Arab Spring of 2010–12 had left Libya under something approaching anarchy. Only Tunisia had come out of the Spring with something like a stable pluralist democracy. To the south, in the Sahel, where Muslim and Christian Africa meet and many adherents of both religions favor making their sacred texts the law of the land, conflicts ignited regularly in Mali, Nigeria, the Central African Republic, and on eastward.[22]

Six Lessons

What can the West's own history of transnational ideological conflict teach us about the struggles of political Islam? To preview what follows, I use the analytical leverage provided by the three historical Western ideological contests to extract six lessons concerning political Islam and secularism today.

Lesson 1: Don't Sell Islamism Short

The imminent demise of political Islam has been declared ever since the ideology emerged in the 1920s. But rumors of Islamism's death are invariably exaggerated. One reason why Westerners discount Islamism is our own secularist bias, which tells us that a backward-looking ideology such as Islamism cannot last. In past ideological struggles, adherents of one ideology likewise have been prone to underestimate the longevity of their foe, precisely because they believe that their own ideology is the wave of the future. This short selling led to bad policies then, and will do so now as well.

Lesson 2: Ideologies Are (Usually) Not Monolithic

Particularly in the wake of the Arab Spring, debate continues to rage over the question of moderate Islamism—in Turkey, Egypt, and so on—and whether outside powers can or should accommodate moderate or pragmatic Islamists. In past struggles in the West, ideologies nearly always had pragmatic and radical wings. Under some conditions pragmatists were willing to break with radicals and work with adherents of an opposing ideology. But deep, sustained cooperation across ideological lines was always elusive as long as the underlying ideological struggle—the opposing visions for the right ordering of society—endured.

Lesson 3: Foreign Interventions Are Normal

U.S.-led interventions in Afghanistan and especially Iraq have been roundly and often fairly criticized, in both origin and execution. But Western history shows that such forcible interventions are a normal part of transnational ideological struggles. More than two hundred such cases have occurred over the past five hundred years. They occur because, in such ideologically polarized times, people in "target" states are strongly predisposed toward either friendship or enmity with foreign great powers. Outsiders are sorely tempted to interfere in such polarized countries in order to boost their friends and weaken their enemies. We should expect more foreign interventions as long as Muslims contend over the best way to order their societies.

Lesson 4: A State May Be Rational and Ideological at the Same Time

The venerable tradition in international relations called *realism* insists that ideology is a cloak for material interest. Even revolutionary states, which proclaim that they are following God's will, or History, have interests like any other state—security and prosperity—and can be dealt with on that basis. History shows, however, that ideologues who rule such states can so reshape circumstances that it actually becomes rational for them to live up to their own propaganda. States such as Habsburg Spain, Napoleonic France, Maoist China, and Islamist Iran can defy Realpolitik for many years and confound the predictions of experienced diplomats and scholars.

Lesson 5: The Winner May Be "None of the Above"

Like all prolonged, region-wide ideological contests, that between Islamism and secularism will end. History shows that such contests may end in one of three ways: with the *victory* of one (as happened with democratic capitalism in the 1980s); with the *transcending* of the contest, when what were once deep, zero-sum divisions become irrelevant (as happened with the Catholic-Protestant contest in the late seventeenth century); or with the emergence and triumph of a hybrid regime and ideology that combines elements of the contestants in ways that had once seemed impossible (as happened with republicanism and monarchism in the 1860s). In the Middle East, an Islamist-secularist hybrid is showing signs of strength today, and outside powers seem little prepared to deal with it.

Lesson 6 : Watch Turkey and Iran

We cannot know when or how the Islamist-secularist struggle will end. But Western history teaches that the eventual winner triumphs by virtue of the relative successes of *exemplary states*—that is, states that exemplify one ideology (or a hybrid). An exemplar that manifestly outperforms exemplars of competing ideologies inspires imitation throughout a region. Thus the U.S. victory over the Soviet Union in the Cold War meant the transnational defeat of communism and victory of democratic capitalism. Today, Iran exemplifies Islamism, while Turkey exemplifies a new Islamist-secularist hybrid; gauging the relative success of each country can help us predict which regime will eventually come to predominate. Egypt is also an important state, and will likely become an exemplar for whatever regime it settles upon.

A Few Qualifications

Above I noted that most Middle Eastern Muslims are neither extreme Islamists nor extreme secularists, but have moved toward the center; and yet, profound and often violent disagreements remain over how much influence Islam and the clergy ought to have over law and policy. Important, too, is that not all Islamists are of one mind or part of a single unified movement. Islamists disagree sharply with one another as to the content of Sharia, the role of clergy in interpreting it, whether a Sunni or Shia version is correct, and so on. Shia-Islamist Iran is archrival to Sunni-Islamist Saudi Arabia. Iran also is a deadly enemy to the Taliban and welcomed the U.S.-led overthrow of the Taliban regime in Afghanistan in 2001. Sunni and Shia have fought viciously in post-Saddam Iraq.

It is crucial to recognize, too, that most Islamists are not radical or militant. The great majority say that terrorism is not a legitimate means to increasing Islam's influence in society. A 2013 poll by the Pew Research Center showed that a majority across eleven majority-Muslim countries held unfavorable views of al-Qaeda and the Taliban, and pluralities held unfavorable views of Hamas and Hezbollah.[23] These include the countries in Table 1.1, in all of which a majority wants laws to follow the teachings of Islam. The Middle East, then, has millions of what are often called moderate Islamists. Concerning Sunni Islamists it is standard among analysts to distinguish jihadis, who are radical and approve of direct violence, from Ikhwan or Muslim Brothers, who pursue gradual, lawful means.[24]

That said, it is important to recognize that it is their means, not necessarily their ends, that are moderate. Militants and jihadists are Islamists in a hurry. Moderates are Islamists willing to wait and to compromise along the way.

Secularists, too, are a diverse lot. As mentioned above, old-time absolute secularists are nearly gone. Most secularists grant some role to Islam in shaping laws and institutions. Secularists differ over democracy and individual rights, and how far to admit Islamist parties into power. The Egyptian Army has evinced little attachment to democracy and no qualms about extirpating even nonviolent Islamists. Liberal secularists, by contrast, want to try inclusion in hopes that it will induce moderation. Probably the most famous liberal Muslim secularist in recent years has been Wael Ghonim, the former Google executive who played an important role in the overthrow of Hosni Mubarak in 2011.[25] Other prominent liberal secularists are Amr Hamzawy of Egypt and Marwan Muasher of Jordan.[26] These reject authoritarianism and seek ways to include Islamists and their concerns in political institutions.

Two Objections

There are reasons to be skeptical about the arguments so far. One type of skeptic will doubt whether the problems of the Middle East named above—unrest, repression, terrorism, revolution, intervention, international tensions—really are linked in any meaningful or causal sense. Better, they say, to analyze each of these separately and to propose separate solutions. Another type of skeptic will doubt that ideology is an important cause of the difficulties and challenges facing Muslim societies. These skeptics argue that the root cause lies somewhere else—in deprivation, or American imperialism, or in Islam itself. I address these objections in order.

Are the Problems Not Actually Connected?

Some skeptics of the importance of ideology say that there is no single problem, but instead a set of unconnected problems. These critics point out that various non-Muslim societies and regions also feature some combination of terrorism, governmental instability, repression, civil conflict, anti-Americanism, and nuclear and missile proliferation. If you want the most threatening nuclear proliferator, look to North Korea. It was the Tamil Tigers of Sri Lanka—Hindus, not Muslims—who pioneered suicide terrorism. For anti-Americanism, look to Venezuela and Russia. If we conclude that these problems have to do with Muslims, it is because we look only at Muslims. We should rather, say the skeptics, decompose what appears to be a general problem, like an ideology, into smaller problems.

Consider the narrow but significant problem of suicide terrorism, which takes place when the terrorist deliberately kills himself or herself in carrying out the attack. Across history, most terrorism has not been suicidal. But suicide terrorism has proliferated in recent years, and its seeming irrationality—why kill yourself to bring about some change that you will not be around to enjoy, precisely because you will have killed yourself?—makes it particularly terrifying.

Mia Bloom's *Dying to Kill* and Robert Pape's *Dying to Win* are two outstanding recent books that purport to explain suicide terrorism. Both authors show that Islam has no monopoly on this kind of killing. Both gather and analyze data on suicide terrorism in general. Probing as far back as the ancient world for cases, Bloom argues that two conditions are necessary for actors to turn to suicide terrorism: "when other terrorist or military tactics fail, and when they are in competition with other terrorist groups for popular or financial support." Suicide terrorism is a way to attract recruits and money by demonstrating extraordinary dedication to the cause.[27] Pape makes a different argument, based upon twenty-two hundred cases of suicide bombing since 1980: the primary cause of suicide terrorism is foreign occupation. Suicide terrorists do what they do in order to get foreign troops to leave their country (and they are remarkably successful).[28]

Mindful that most foreign occupations never provoke any suicide terrorism[29]—the U.S. occupations of Germany and Japan after the Second World War come to mind—Pape and coauthor James Feldman add in a subsequent book, *Cutting the Fuse*, that two more conditions help cause suicide terrorism: wide religious differences between occupier and occupied (as between the Tamil Tigers, who are Hindu, and the Sinhalese, who are Buddhist), and the failure of other tactics to end the occupation.[30] Pape and Feldman note that the frequency of suicide terrorism skyrocketed after 2003, that 90 percent of it is anti-American, and that the vast majority is by occupied against occupier. They conclude that "Islamic fundamentalism" is not an important cause of suicide terrorism.

True enough. It is not the desire that Muslims live under Sharia (Islamism) that causes suicide terrorism. Instead, it is the clash between that desire (Islamism in its various versions) and its rejection (secularism in its various versions) that helps cause this nightmarish practice. But Bloom, Pape and Feldman, and other analysts downplay the causal role of ideology, and the trouble is that they do so by assuming at the outset what they end up claiming to demonstrate—namely, that suicide terrorism is causally unrelated to many of the other phenomena alongside which it has been occurring.[31] Suicide terrorism in Muslim lands has coincided not only with foreign occupation, but also with governmental instability, corruption, repression of dissent, torture, vehement anti-Americanism, the threat of nuclear proliferation—and of course with the long and severe legitimacy crisis discussed above. In pulling recent cases of suicide terrorism out of their time and place and plugging them into a dataset of cases from very different times and places, scholars may move toward a general explanation of suicide terrorism, but they may move away from a full explanation of the very Middle Eastern cases that we need to explain.

In fact, we have strong reasons to believe that these concurrent problems in the Middle East are all causally related in complex and reciprocal ways. Terrorism is not only caused by U.S. occupations: it helped cause and sustain those occupations to begin with. The Middle East and outsiders who interact with it are caught not in a single problem, or a pair of problems, but in a knot of problems.

Consider that although foreign occupation surely can be a cause of suicide terrorism, the causal arrow seems to run both ways. Why were U.S. troops occupying Iraq and Afghanistan in the 2000s? Because of the catastrophic suicide attacks of September 11, 2001.[32] In turn, the 9/11 attacks were caused at least in part, as Osama bin Laden himself said, by the presence of U.S. troops on the Arabian Peninsula. Those American troops originally were deployed to Arabia in late 1990, in response to Iraq's conquest of Kuwait and threat to invade Saudi Arabia. Iraq had invaded Kuwait in August 1990 because Saddam Hussein's regime needed more oil revenue owing to the costly war against Iran in the 1980s. And the Iran-Iraq War itself, which began in September 1980, was partly caused by the efforts of Iran's then-new Islamist regime to topple Saddam Hussein and vice versa.[33]

We could push the chain of events further back in time, but the point should be clear. A full explanation of suicide terrorism in the Middle East today cannot simply reduce to foreign occupation, or that plus the failure of other tactics and the religious distance between occupier and occupied. Islamist suicide terrorism is embedded in a number of chicken-and-egg relationships. It is caused by and causes rebellions, repressions, civil wars, transnational ideological networks, and foreign interventions and quagmires.[34]

In other words, the Middle East does not just happen to be on an uncanny streak of bad luck. It is not just torn by a coincidental set of separate problems. It has a number of problems that are entangled into one very big problem.

Does any of this matter, in practical terms? Indeed it does. Pape's policy advice follows logically from his explanation. The United States should quit Afghanistan: end the occupations and you end suicide bombing. But if suicide terrorism is one of a number of phenomena that are causally entangled, then quitting Iraq and Afghanistan may not end it. It may even aggravate regime instability in Afghanistan and Pakistan, the probability of nuclear proliferation, or India's fears of Pakistani militancy. Indeed, perhaps the United States stayed in Afghanistan for so many years because U.S. officials suspected that quitting would only create a situation that required returning later. As this book went to press, Barack Obama became the fourth president in a row to use force in Iraq. He found that pulling one loop of string just tightened the knot.

But Is Ideology So Important?

Some skeptics will agree that the Middle East's political problems, including political extremism and terrorism, are related, but will not like the "knot" metaphor. Instead, they will say, there is one true cause of all of the problems; remove that cause, and the problems would disappear or at least shrivel.

One putative master cause is *deprivation*. The story goes something like this: Muslims, like all people, have a familiar set of needs and wants—security, material goods, dignity—and, as with all people, when denied these goods to a sufficient extent over a sufficient period of time, some turn to violence.

One version of the deprivation thesis is that most Muslims are poor and have little prospect of an improved lot in life. From Indonesia, the world's largest Muslim state, the influential scholar Ahmad Syafii Maarif told an APEC summit in 2006 that poverty causes terrorism; the solution, he said, lies in further international economic integration.[35] Management theorist Russell Ackoff and colleagues spoke for many when they asserted that both "fundamentalism" and terrorism are caused by underdevelopment, or the lack of "an increase in the ability and desire to satisfy one's own needs and legitimate desires and those of others."[36] Ackoff and Johan Strümpfer argue that nations that produce terrorism tend to be those with the least economic freedom.[37]

The Arab world in particular has been studied closely since 2002 through an annual *Arab Human Development Report* (*AHDR*), written by a team of Arab scholars and published by the United Nations Development Program. The 2009 report notes that one in five Arabs lives on less than two dollars per diem. Measured by the Human Poverty Index (HPI), which is a function of life expectancy, literacy, and basic services, Arab states scored at 35 percent, as contrasted with "a 12 percent average in high income countries."[38] Muslims living in Western Europe are less likely to be employed and have less wealth than are native Europeans. In a 2009 Gallup poll only 38 percent of British Muslims said they were employed; the figures in France and Germany were hardly better, 53 percent and 45 percent, respectively.[39]

A second version of the deprivation thesis is that Muslims lack personal security. In the Middle East and Southwest Asia, most governments have been authoritarian in one form or another since gaining independence from the Europeans or Turks. Islamist regimes in Saudi Arabia and Iran, and secularist regimes in Egypt and Syria, have suppressed individual liberty. Freedom House, a U.S.-based organization that rates countries by degree of individual liberty and democracy, calls the Middle East "the most repressive region in the world."[40] The *AHDR 2002* notes, "The wave of democracy that transformed governance in most of Latin America and East Asia in the 1980s and Eastern Europe and much of Central Asia in the late 1980s and early 1990s has barely reached the Arab states."[41]

Part of what we mean by authoritarianism is arbitrary rule: the government is not bound by law; a knock on the door by the secret police could come at any time during any night. Millions of ordinary Muslims in the Middle East live in fear of their rulers. The *AHDR* stresses as well the special plight of the Palestinians, who lack a state and whose territories are under perpetual threat of invasion and reoccupation by the powerful Israel Defense Forces.[42] Physically insecure people, so goes the argument, will likely find more acceptable the risks of violence.

A third version of the deprivation thesis is that Muslims have been subject to foreign domination for so many decades that many find it necessary or appealing to strike back with violence. The old formal empires of the British, French, Russians, Turks, and others helped stir up nationalism. In the late nineteenth century the British provoked the Sudanese rebellion of Shaykh Muhammad Ahmad, self-proclaimed Mahdi (savior), whose armies killed the storied British General C. G. Gordon in battle.[43] More recently American hegemony over the Arab monarchies and Egypt, and U.S. sponsorship of Israel— which many take to be the West's latest ploy to keep Muslims from ruling Jerusalem—is, to most Muslims, more of the same. Each *AHDR* stresses the baleful effects of the Israeli occupation of Palestinian lands and U.S. occupation of Iraq—not only on the Palestinians and Iraqis but on all Arabs.

So is relative deprivation the cause of the violence, instability, and militancy we see in the Middle East? Each version of the thesis has some validity, but none can explain the full picture.

The first two versions—that Muslims tend to be poor and insecure—cannot explain why other regions of the world with similar or even worse afflictions are not torn by a similar tangle of problems.[44] Taken as a whole, the poorest region of the world is sub-Saharan Africa. According to the World Bank, in 2005 half of that region's population lived on less than a dollar twenty-five a day. Only 3.6 percent of the population of the Middle East and North Africa did so. (The figure for South Asia, predominantly Hindu, was 40.3 percent; that for East Asia and the Pacific, 16.8 percent.)[45] At the very least, we see that poverty is insufficient to cause violence, and indeed extreme poverty seems to lower it. Another difficulty is that, regarding terrorism specifically, several rigorous studies claim that poor people are not more likely to become terrorists.[46]

What about American foreign policy? It is suggestive that Latin America, whose people have equal grounds for complaint about U.S. imperialism or hegemony, exhibits nothing like the congeries of problems that we see in the Middle East. There is no suicide bombing; terrorism, yes, but limited to the jungles of Colombia; relatively little regime instability; no evident nuclear or missile proliferation. U.S. Special Forces are active in Colombia against the FARC, and the U.S. Navy can easily reach any target in the Americas quickly. But nothing in Latin America has provoked armed interventions on anything like the scale of those in the Middle East. Venezuela has sought to lead a transnational anti-American movement, but it is minor league beside that of al-Qaeda or even the Iranian government.

Or Is the Problem Islam Itself?

On the other hand are those who blame the problems of the Middle East on the religion of Islam itself. The online world is teeming with opinions of this sort.[47] Author Robert Spencer has defended the thesis in several influential books.[48] Ironically, the Netherlands, which may enjoy the strongest reputation for religious and social tolerance, has produced voices (some of which have been silenced) declaiming on Islam's intrinsic viciousness. Here is Geert Wilders, leader of the Dutch Party for Freedom (PVV):

> There might be moderate Muslims, but there is no moderate Islam. Islam will never change, because it is build on two rocks that are forever, two fundamental beliefs that will never change, and will never go away. First, there is Quran, Allah's personal word, uncreated, forever, with orders that need to be fulfilled regardless of place or time. And second, there is al-insal al-kamil, the perfect man, Muhammad the role model, whose deeds are to be imitated by all Muslims. And since Muhammad was a warlord and a conqueror we know what to expect.[49]

Ayaan Hirsi Ali, a Somali Dutch author who was raised a Muslim, says, "Violence is inherent in Islam—it's a destructive, nihilistic cult of death. It legitimates murder."[50]

Some find the charge plausible. Observe the September 11 attacks and the long wave of suicide terrorism in dozens of countries; the multinational rioting and violence among Muslims following the publication of a Danish cartoon depicting the Prophet Muhammad with a bomb in his turban;[51] an Iranian President's open wish that Israel "disappear from the map" and assertions that the Nazi Holocaust is a myth:[52] only the Middle East seems to produce such odious actions and statements in such volume.

In 1996 political scientist Samuel Huntington argued that Islam has "bloody borders," that is, that in the late twentieth century an uncannily high percentage of the world's violent conflicts took place between Muslims and non-Muslims: Turks *versus* Greeks, Russian *versus* Chechens, Bosnian Muslims and Albanians *versus* Serbs, Armenians *versus* Azeris, Uighurs *versus* Han Chinese, Muslim *versus* Hindu Indians, and of course Arabs *versus* Jews. In an era when ethnic conflict is common, Huntington argued, no group is as prone to conflict as Muslims.[53]

Then there is the history of Islam, specifically the way it spread in its early centuries by the sword. The Prophet Muhammad himself was a warrior; after his move to Medina in A.D. 622 (year 2 in the Islamic calendar), he led his followers in fighting and subduing the Meccans, thus establishing his prestige in Arabia. In the generations after Muhammad's death in 632 (year 12), his successors—the caliphs—conquered parts of the Byzantine Empire to the west, including Syria, Palestine, Egypt, and Libya, as well as the Sassanid (Persian) Empire to the east. Islam *was* the caliphate, an empire.[54] Osama bin Laden's 1996 declaration of war on America appealed to Islamic traditions that valorize holy war. Muslim poets have glorified violent jihad. When bin Laden used the word "martyr" (or "witness"—*Shahid* in Arabic), he had in mind not the peaceful witness who clings to the faith at the cost of his life, but rather the active warrior who dies while using the sword against the faith's enemies.[55]

Do these specific violent incidents and this broad history convict Islam the religion? Not necessarily. Most Muslims never commit acts of violence; if Islam is intrinsically violent, then roughly a billion believers either do not understand their own religion, or are too cowardly or unfaithful to follow its precepts. (The latter, of course, is the claim of the radical Islamists.)

But there are more serious problems with the "it's Islam" thesis. In investigating the claim that "Islam has bloody borders," political scientist Jonathan Fox found that, since the end of the Cold War, there has been no increase overall in violence between Islamic and non-Islamic societies. There has indeed been a rise in violence between Islamic and *Western* societies, but that rise has appeared only since 1989.[56] That suggests that Muslim violence is dependent upon other factors.

A broad view of the history of the Middle East suggests that Islam is much like other religions. It is marked by times and places of conquest and brutality, but also by times and places of peace. The early caliphates (Umayyad, Abbasid) were expansive empires, but for some stretches of time did not force Christians and animists to convert. The Ottoman Empire was tolerant for its time, allowing religious and ethnic minorities to flourish.[57] This chapter opened with some episodes from early modern—Christian—Europe, involving violence, unrest, repression, and war. While Catholics and Protestants were doing these things, the Muslim Ottomans were living in relative peace and prosperity.

Indeed, Christendom has had its sustained spasms of violence, both toward outsiders (as in the Crusades) and fellow believers (as in the Counter-Reformation). Christian crusaders from Pierre Dubois in medieval France to Stonewall Jackson in the Confederate States of America have cited the Bible and Christian teaching to justify holy war. As a Christian myself, I would maintain that those who kill in order to expand Christendom are either cynical or terribly mistaken. But many Muslim clergy—even Islamists—lodge a similar charge against radical jihadis who kill in Allah's name. Mohammad Khatami, a former president of Iran and prominent Shia cleric, repeatedly condemned the 9/11 attacks and declared that suicide bombers will not go to heaven.[58]

The point is not that Islam or Christianity is a "religion of peace," nor is it to establish whether jihadists or their critics are more orthodox. Our concern is how actual self-identifying Muslims and Muslim societies act, and clearly they have acted differently in different times and places.

The Ideological Struggle

The root problem, then, is not poverty, insecurity, or American imperialism. It is not Islam itself. We do not really know what the root is. The best way to think about the Middle East's problems is that they are a tangle, in which each problem aggravates the others. The knot of problems is self-tightening. And one of those problems, a crucial and misunderstood one, is that for many decades the Middle East and other places where Muslims live have been going through a legitimacy crisis. This crisis polarizes Muslims, sometimes to an extreme, and is partly responsible for the poverty, insecurity, religious violence, and even some of the American intervention that leads to charges of imperialism. Sometimes the polarization has been severe enough to bring civil war. Even when violence has been absent, the crisis has kept Muslims from agreeing on what a good society or regime looks like. It has made people more loyal to foreigners who share their principles than to their own countrymen who do not.

Deep and abiding disagreement over where law should come from helps keep the problems entangled. If we are to understand the Middle East, we must understand the old but ongoing competition between Islamism and secularism.

Once we see the matter this way, we can begin to use the West's own history—to be precise, its history of prolonged legitimacy crises and bouts of ideological strife—to help us understand what is going on in the Middle East. Plans for ordering public life that call for direct violent action against established rulers and authorities are always out there, being refined in books and tracts, expounded in speeches and sermons, debated in clubs and coffeehouses, dissected in academic seminars. At certain times and in certain places, they have attracted significant followings and have serious domestic and international political consequences.

How do ideologies influence politics? There are two common, and opposite, mistaken views of ideologies. Some people think of them as spirits that possess individuals, or the voices heard by paranoid schizophrenics, and make them do things they otherwise would not ("You will strap this bomb to yourself and blow up everyone at this market!"). Ideologies become like irresistible forces, unseen puppeteers. Others, finding such a view ridiculous, see no alternative but to argue that ideologies are not consequential at all. Spirits do not exist, or if they do we cannot observe them; either way they do not belong in a social-scientific explanation. Rather, say these skeptics, ideologies are stories invented by elites trying to manipulate the gullible into doing their bidding. Ideologies do not matter; what do matter are powerful and clever elites.

In fact, as we shall see time and again in this book, ideologies can be more than simply cover stories, but not because they are spirits or mental illnesses. They are what scholars call social facts, such as norms, mores, or cultures. Take a seemingly unrelated topic: clothing styles. Time was, not too many years ago, that adult men in the Western world in white-collar jobs all wore neckties to work. No doubt some—perhaps not many—liked neckties, while others did not like them but believed that they or their organization or society as a whole would pay a high price if they did not wear a necktie. The wearing of neckties was a norm, a socially accepted behavior; going tieless was frowned upon, and few dared do it. Today, the norm has reversed: the open shirt collar has become de rigueur, the occasional cravat wearer the nonconformist who makes others uncomfortable and threatens established order.

Norms such as "neckties are a sign of status" or "neckties are for the unhip" are not spirits forcing men to obey. And although some actors have an interest in perpetuating the norm—the silk industry, suit makers—it would be silly to suppose that such interests were able to coerce the entire male Western world until the 1990s. It is plausible that some elites had an interest in a conformist or disciplined society and that neckties were once a tool or sign of that discipline. But note that even then, elite men who hated neckties, whose fondest wish was to get a different gift for Father's Day, would still have to wear them. The norm would still be powerful.

Like norms, ideologies are neither spirits nor observable objects. And like norms, ideologies can still constrain people, even people who do not believe in them. The more people talk and act according to an ideology, the more others are constrained to do the same and the more people, even cynical elites, come to believe in them.

Ideologies are especially compelling and consequential when competing with other ideologies. It is then that people tend to polarize over ideology—to think of people with whom they agree as friends (regardless of other differences) and of people with whom they disagree as enemies (regardless of other similarities). Conformity, ideological correctness, becomes an important social asset. Nonconformity becomes disruptive and dangerous.

The West's own history, so scarred with ideological struggles, can help us understand the consequences of the prolonged contest between political Islam and secularism. As I show in the following chapters, sixteenth-century Europeans were not only devout; there were times and places where they were severely polarized over religion. They felt acutely threatened by people who disagreed with them about sacraments or salvation. Indeed, their vision was a negation of what they took to be their enemies' vision. It often has been noted that one cannot be "Protestant" without something against which to protest. But to be a militant Protestant requires more than the existence of Catholicism; after all, Catholicism exists today, but very little iconoclastic, revolutionary Protestantism does. By the same token, the militant Catholicism of some of the Habsburgs or the Guises in France requires more than the simple presence of Protestantism.

From the 1770s through 1870s in Europe and the Americas, monarchists and republicans often experienced the same severe polarization across national boundaries. A French monarchist felt more in common with an Austrian monarchist than with a French republican. An Italian republican felt more in common with an American than with an Italian monarchist. Waves of revolt, repression, revolution, foreign intervention, and war were partly due to this ideological contest.

During the twentieth century, communists, liberals, and fascists went through very similar struggles, with similar consequences. Communists' explicitly internationalist vision gave them a special reason to communicate and move across national boundaries. But fascists and liberals did likewise, and their periodic polarizations produced all manner of entangled political strife within and across countries. In turn, the political strife—the rebellions and revolutions, the fifth columns and fears thereof, the foreign interventions and shuffling of alliances—fed back into the ideological struggles and prolonged them. That is what we mean by a knot of problems.

Common to all of these periods was not just the presence of ideologies, but a deep struggle among them—a competition that sometimes looked zero-sum. The struggle fed the sense of threat on both sides and supported the notions that the other side could not be compromised with and that direct violent action was necessary. Individual leaders play prominent roles in most of these stories. Charles V, a Holy Roman emperor in the sixteenth century; Frederick V, the Count Palatinate in the early seventeenth; Edmund Burke, the late eighteenth-century British statesman; U.S. President Harry Truman; Atatürk, founder of modern Turkey; the Ayatollah Khomeini: these and scores of others were highly consequential, for good or ill. But one way in which they were consequential was in formulating, propagating, or opposing "isms." Some of the leaders found, too, that the ideologies they thought to control took on lives of their own, shaping the thoughts and expectations of others and constraining the leaders.[59]

For these and other reasons, in the following pages I mine the history of these three long Western struggles—Catholic-Protestant, republican-monarchist, and communist-liberal-fascist—for lessons about the current ideological contest in the Middle East. I pay more attention to Islamism than to secularism, both because it is far stranger to Westerners and because, in the contest of ideas, it continues to enjoy momentum.

The book contains no technical material. It is not a work of rigorous social science; it does not formulate a deductive theory or test hypotheses according to strict methodological rules. This book is rather a set of arguments based on some remarkable similarities across time and space. It proposes no ultimate solutions, either for Muslims or for the rest of the world. Western history does not yield a clear algorithm for dealing with Islam's political legitimacy crisis. Indeed, as one of the characters in this book—Burke, founder of modern conservatism—would insist, politics does not admit ultimate solutions, and to assert otherwise is to invite disaster. Even the good resolutions recounted in this book were impermanent and bred new problems. But the history of the West does show that leaders and countries can take steps that make better outcomes—temporary, to be sure, but less violent and more conducive to human flourishing—more likely.

Readers should be mindful, too, of the hazards of using historical lessons for present policy. Political scientist Yuen Foong Khong shows how the administration of Lyndon B. Johnson deepened U.S. involvement in Vietnam by employing faulty analogies from the past.[60] Political scientist Richard Neustadt and historian Ernest May wrote about how to use history for policy, precisely because policy makers so often misuse the past.[61] One lesson of history is to be careful about extracting lessons from history—in particular, not to lurch toward historical analogies that support conclusions we have reached for other reasons. In the following pages I take care to let history speak for itself, but I invite readers to scrutinize the results critically.

People in the West are sometimes perplexed at the sound and fury they see in the Middle East. They forget, if they ever knew, that the West itself, at various times in history, has been loud and furious. And then, as now, the sound and fury did signify something.

Lesson 1
Don't Sell Islamism Short

I know I am leaving the winning side for the losing side.
—*Whittaker Chambers, explaining to his wife his decision to quit the American Communist Party, 1938*

"The Islamists Are Not Coming." This reassuring title headed an article in early 2010 in the influential U.S. magazine *Foreign Policy*. The authors, experts on Islamist movements, reported that religious parties usually do not perform very well in elections in Muslim countries: in campaigns over the past forty years, 80 percent of these parties received less than 20 percent support, and most receive less then 10 percent. And when Islamist parties do manage to get elected, they soften their policies, sometimes dropping their core program of imposing Sharia on society.[1]

"Islamism seems to be fading as a revolutionary force," pronounced the *Economist* at roughly the same time. Yes, young Egyptians are more pious or observant of the religion than was the case a generation previous. But, the magazine reassured readers, "[t]he symbols of commitment among today's radical youth are no longer guns and beards but pious conduct and knowledge of scripture. The religious wave has certainly not passed and may still carry a lot in its wake. But in Egypt, at least, it no longer looks like a revolutionary force."[2]

Just over a year later, as the first buds of the Arab Spring were appearing, pundits calmly predicted that the incipient revolutions would usher in secular democratic governments. "Look at those involved in the uprisings, and it is clear we are dealing with a post-Islamist generation," wrote Olivier Roy.[3] "Egyptians have seen Mubarak and the mullahs and want neither," wrote Fareed Zakaria.[4]

By the end of 2011, however, a sober *Economist* was openly acknowledging that the real winner of the Arab Spring might be the Islamists—and that their victory might come at the ballot box. Islamist parties were winning post-revolution elections. Islamism, or at least politicians espousing it, was popular. "Indeed," ventured the magazine, "political Islam now has more clout in the region than at any time since the Ottoman empire collapsed almost a century ago, and perhaps since Napoleon brought a modernising message to the Arab world when he invaded Egypt in 1798."[5]

Since those days Islamists have had setbacks across the Arab world, most pointedly in Egypt, where the government of Mohamed Morsi was ousted by the secularist Egyptian Army in July 2013. The point is not that Islamists have won or are going to win in the end. It is rather that Westerners, time and time again, have underestimated their popularity and power. As Middle East expert Shadi Hamid notes, "Analysts always seem to be finding signs of Islamist decline," yet real decline is not evident. Take the March 2010 parliamentary elections in Iraq, well before the Arab Spring began. A coalition of parties headed by Ayad Allawi won, and Western pundits hailed this victory for secularism in the new Iraq. But in fact, Allawi's coalition included an overtly Islamist party. Adding all the seats that other Islamist parties won yields 159, just shy of the 163 needed to form a government.[6]

Underreporting of this kind often happens when a Muslim country holds elections: analysts note that Islamists are divided, ignoring the overall strength of Muslim sentiment that "Islam is the solution." "In short," concludes Hamid, "it would be a mistake to assume that when Islamist parties lose, that this reflects a broader shift away from religious politics or from religion, and towards 'secularism'—the kind of thing we like to believe is happening in the Middle East but, for both better and worse, rarely does and most likely won't."[7]

Analyses and predictions that short-sell Islamism disclose a deep conviction, prominent among many Western observers, that *political Islam cannot last*, that it is simply an unsustainable, impractical set of ideas in the modern world. We Westerners come by this conviction honestly. For at least two hundred years, we have tended to believe in historical progress. Much of our discourse and the way we think about social and technical problems suggest that we believe that the human race is moving in the direction of rationality and morality (as we define those things). History, we believe, is a story not of decline, nor of stagnation, nor of cycles of progress and regress; it is a story of forward or upward movement. Indeed, it seems self-evident to us that society has steadily improved over the past several centuries.[8]

Our unprecedented and growing power over nature, owing to the spectacular successes of modern science, is probably the most important source of that belief. But we also are less violent and superstitious, and more tolerant, fair, and productive, than the forebears we read about on Wikipedia or see in movies.[9] Even our parents and grandparents, who likewise believed in progress, were backward, we agree—greedy, violent, sexually repressed, lacking environmental consciousness—and we congratulate ourselves for being more enlightened. Thus the critically acclaimed television show *Mad Men* depicts America in the early 1960s as experiencing a kind of collective mental illness. Perhaps people back then dressed better than we do, but they smoked, drank too much, littered, repressed their feelings, and were sexist.

We do not know what America will be like in 2060, but we can be fairly certain that Americans will consider us backward, exotic, morally suspect, and embarrassing. This Western narrative of progress is old and probably invincible. The Enlightenment philosopher Immanuel Kant famously proposed that human history was a story of unsteady but real progress.[10] A generation later G. W. F. Hegel wrote a philosophy of history depicting the emergence of universal rationality that influenced thinkers as diverse as Karl Marx and John Stuart Mill.[11] Progressive or teleological histories have long had their severe critics. In the 1930s the British historian Herbert Butterfield chastised the members of his guild for assuming that developments in Britain's past had led ineluctably to the best of all possible worlds, parliamentary democracy.[12]

Butterfield's complaint was that this "Whig interpretation of history" distorted our understanding of the past. But there are other objections to it. What would constitute progress, anyway? More consumer goods? Less suffering? Better art (whatever that might mean)? More individual autonomy? More social solidarity? More mastery of nature? Or perhaps more deference to nature? If we cannot agree on what progress looks like, then we cannot know whether it is happening.

Lesson 1 from the West's own past is about caution: *simply because we find Islamism irrational and inconsistent with what we take to be the movement of history does not mean it is disappearing any time soon.* Particularly when an ideology is exemplified and sponsored by one or more countries, it may enjoy a much longer life than its opponents and observers imagine. The history of the West's own prolonged ideological struggles bears this out.

The Longevity of Europe's Catholic-Protestant Struggle

At many points, the legitimacy crisis in early modern Europe seemed to have ended but had not. The end of 1559 was one such time. The Catholic and Lutheran estates of the Holy Roman Empire (roughly today's Germany) had recently fought two wars: the Schmalkaldic War of 1546–47, which ended in an overwhelming victory for the Catholics (particularly the Habsburg emperor);

and, when the emperor overreached after his victory, a follow-up war in 1552 that turned the tables. In 1555 the estates and Habsburgs agreed to the Religious Peace of Augsburg. At Augsburg Lutherans and Catholics agreed that the ruler of an estate has the sole right to determine the established religion in that estate. Using force to try to alter a neighboring estate's religion was illegal.[13] The formula was later to be restated as *Cujus regio, ejus religio*: "Whose the realm, his the religion."[14] Europeans continued to be devout Catholics and Lutherans, and each group regarded the other as heretical, but their differences were depoliticized. The heresy of one prince or realm was no concern of another prince. The empire could return to normal politics, with its mundane jealousies and rivalries and its periodic diets (congresses) to sort things out.

But that was only in Germany. To the northwest of the empire, England was going through a violent re-Catholicization under Mary I. The first daughter of Henry VIII was raised a Catholic by her Spanish mother and married Philip II of Spain. She undid the Protestantization of her half brother Edward VI, the sickly king who had died at age fifteen in 1553. Mary burned hundreds of Protestant clergy and bishops; hundreds of others fled into exile. But upon her own death in 1558, her half sister Elizabeth, raised as a Protestant, became queen and wrenched England back into the Protestant camp using similar means.

The Elizabethan Settlement of 1559, Protestant yet sensitive to the persistent Catholic convictions of many of Elizabeth's subjects, seemed another sign that Europe's decades-long religious strife had ended in a sort of stalemate. It was not to be, however. The trouble was that Lutherans and Anglicans were not the only Protestants. Most consequential of all in political terms was the movement begun by the Frenchman John Calvin. Calvinism was, in the telling of its own adherents, simply the logical completion of Lutheranism: if man could not voluntarily move toward God, if saving faith was solely God's to grant, then it follows that God preordains who is to be saved and who damned. In practice, whereas Lutherans tended toward political quietism, Calvinists stressed the active building of a righteous society in the here and now.[15] The movement was disciplined, fervent, and revolutionary, validating commerce more than its rivals and tending toward republicanism and social equality.[16] And it spread rapidly from the city of Geneva, Calvin's headquarters and model polity from 1541, gaining converts among the nobility and commoners in France, England, Scotland, the Netherlands, Germany, Bohemia, Poland, Hungary, Transylvania, and elsewhere.[17]

As noted in this book's introduction, in the late 1550s a Calvinist rebellion broke out in Scotland and spread to other countries. These explosions, detonated by wealthy and middle-class people with political as well as religious discontents, were related. A Calvinist revolt in one place would encourage

Calvinists and frighten Catholics in another, making repression and rebellion more likely there. The Calvinist revolts also attracted foreign intervention by Catholics (especially Spain) and Protestants (especially England and the Palatinate in Germany), thus aggravating the situation.

The larger point is this: just when a religious settlement emerged in one time and place, and it seemed that Western Europe had returned to more normal, less ideological times, religious polarization would happen elsewhere and make clear that normal times were still a long way off. The Protestant Reformation was not finished, and hence neither was the Catholic Counter-Reformation.

A few violent decades later, at the end of the sixteenth century, it again appeared that the so-called wars of religion were over. Within the countries in question, the religious questions had been settled by force of arms and truces. The Catholic-Protestant ideological warfare that had shaken Northwestern Europe for so many years was history. Swiss cantons and Scotland were firmly in Calvinist hands, as was the new Dutch Republic. England's Elizabeth had made her peace with the Puritans. In France, Henry IV, who converted to Catholicism to ease his path to rule, issued the Edict of Nantes in 1598, granting wide toleration to Huguenots within certain territories.[18] In the Holy Roman Empire, Emperor Rudolf II was in practice relatively indulgent of all religious minorities. Pockets of religious conflict remained—the occasional German city would heave with the old sectarian strife—but on the whole princes, nobles, city councils, and their subjects seemed to have settled upon a practical peace. A Machiavellian political rationality appeared regnant, in which states looked after their interests and religious zeal was put toward other purposes.[19]

Yet Europe was not finished with ideological strife and violence. Within two decades, Central Europe fell hard into what became its worst war until 1914: the Thirty Years' War (1618–48), in which an estimated 15 to 20 percent of Germany's population (three to four million persons) died.[20] This ferocious conflict was not only about religious ideology, any more than any political conflict is only about ideology; dynastic ambition, resistance to political centralization, technological change, greed, and sheer bloody-mindedness all played a role.[21] But those things are always with us. What triggered the war was a revolt in Bohemia in 1618, in the far east of the empire, by Calvinists fearful of increasing Catholic persecution under the heir apparent to the imperial throne.

Catholics and Calvinists had begun to repolarize in the empire two decades earlier. Calvinism was spreading in Germany, and in 1598, the same year that France gained religious toleration, Emperor Rudolf sent troops to suppress Calvinism around the town of Aachen. Calvinists and Lutherans alike began to boycott imperial diets (periodic congresses), and in 1609 a new

Protestant Union formed, led by the Elector Palatinate. A Catholic league quickly formed in response. The two tussled over Cleves-Jülich in 1609–10 and again in 1613. In 1612 the Protestant Union formed an alliance with James I of England.

In that same year Matthias, a moderate, succeeded Rudolf as emperor and tried to conciliate his Protestant subjects. But in 1617 his cousin Ferdinand, a militant Catholic, was elected next in line to the imperial throne, and that aggravated religious tensions still further. Ferdinand was determined to restore all Habsburg-ruled lands to the Catholic fold. When Protestants in Bohemia revolted the following year, he took matters into his own hands, overthrowing Matthias and seizing the throne. But the blame for the horrific war to come did not all lie with Ferdinand. To the west, in the imperial estate of the Palatinate, the Elector Frederick, a zealous Calvinist, had ambitions of his own. He accepted the rebels' offer to crown him king of Bohemia, and Habsburg armies marched to put down the revolt.

The lines of conflict in the Thirty Years' War, then, had been laid down gradually in the two preceding decades. And those lines, in turn, had been laid down a half century earlier. The conclusion is clear: an ideological struggle can appear dead, even to smart people for whom the stakes are high; yet if the questions that gave rise to it remain unresolved, the struggle can later reignite in a new place. The trouble in 1618 was that the fundamental questions that had emerged in Germany a century earlier were still unsettled. Those questions—concerning which church should be the established one, the Roman Catholic or some Protestant alternative—remained because most Europeans continued to believe that permanent political stability required religious uniformity. Thus Catholic and Protestant rulers and aspiring rulers could live in peace, but the peace was uneasy. They continued to fear one another and the growth in one another's branch of Christianity. So long as that fear persisted, a spark could ignite conflict by repolarizing people into radically opposed ideological groups. The threat of ideological-religious war could not disappear until rulers became indifferent toward the relative growth rates and encroachments of the various branches of Christianity. As we shall see in Lesson 5, that indifference was not to take hold for yet another century.

The Nineteenth Century: Liberalism's Resiliency

A century and a half after the Thirty Years' War ended, Europe began another multidecade, multicountry struggle over, among other things, the best way to order society. At issue was not which religion was to be established, but who or what was sovereign in society: king, people, or law. The wars of the French

Revolution (1792–99) and Napoleon (1799–1815) were efforts by France's rulers to extend French power by not only conquering the rest of Europe militarily but also setting up republican or Bonapartist institutions—often run by one of Napoleon's relatives—in place of the old monarchical ones.

In the spring of 1814, following a string of military defeats, Bonaparte abdicated and was exiled to the Mediterranean island of Elba; a year later he escaped, gathered his old army, and tried to conquer Europe one last time. His final defeat at Waterloo (in present-day Belgium) was decisive. He was exiled again, this time to Saint Helena in the South Atlantic. France was occupied by allied troops. At the Congress of Vienna the allies—Britain, Austria, Prussia, Russia, and smaller powers—set about making sure that the vicious ideological strife of the preceding quarter century would not erupt again. They thought and planned carefully.

The allies' general strategy was to restore the old regimes that the French armies had overthrown, and to make sure that those regimes stayed in place. In France itself, source of the problem, they restored the old Bourbon monarchy. In Spain, Switzerland, the Netherlands, and what are now Belgium, Germany, and Italy, the allies tried to root out all traces of revolution. On Switzerland they imposed a new constitution, essentially the old pre-Napoleonic one. On the other lands they allowed monarchies to be restored—"legitimist" regimes, ruled by the old families, as distinguished from the illegitimate monarchies imposed by Napoleon.[22]

The great powers agreed to meet periodically to cooperate against any new threats to stability. This so-called Metternich System—named for the influential Austrian minister of state, Prince Clemens von Metternich—was supposed to maintain domestic and international peace and order. Metternich himself saw the system as a safeguard against the root of the problem: the presumptuous middle-class intellectuals who had taken it upon themselves to overturn centuries of traditions and rights and remake society according to their own abstract principles.[23] These principles were, to Metternich and other conservatives, an alien presence in Europe, a foreign body that had been rejected and must never return.

The trouble for Metternich and his fellow conservatives was that the revolutionary principles had not been rejected after all. Notwithstanding the restoration of legitimate rulers throughout post-Napoleonic Europe, the ideas of the French Revolution remained, kept alive by various networks of students, Freemasons, and others. As early as 1819 student groups in Germany (*Burschenschaften*) began agitating against the system. Metternich responded by persuading the German Confederation to agree to dissolve the *Burschenschaften* and censor university activity. This bit of repression did not cure the problem. Within a year the nephew of France's King Louis XVIII was assassinated in Paris; an antigovernment conspiracy in London came to light; revolts broke out in Italy and Spain.[24]

Metternich knew that these events were connected, that agitation in one country or city could trigger the same in another. His spies told him that republicans and other radicals, united by a conviction that the events in France in 1789–93 could be repeated—inevitably *would* be repeated—continued to communicate across political boundaries. As historian Frederick Artz writes, "the mere introduction of democratic or nationalist ideas anywhere in Europe could easily stir up disruptive movements in [Austria]. Hence, revolutionary ideas in speeches, books, or newspapers frightened Metternich, even if they appeared as far away as Spain, Sweden, or Sicily."[25] Another historian, Eric Hobsbawm, writes,

> It was now known that revolution in a single country could be a European phenomenon; that its doctrines could spread across the frontiers and, what was worse, its crusading armies could blow away the political systems of a continent. . . . No country was immune from it. . . . And the doctrines and institutions [the French armies] carried with them, even under Napoleon, from Spain to Illyria, were universal doctrines, as the governments knew, and as the peoples themselves were soon to know also.[26]

So long as enough Europeans continued to believe in the principles of 1789, political life could not permanently revert to the old "normality."

The great powers—with the significant exception of Britain, the most liberal and constitutional of the great powers—followed through with their grand strategy and coordinated their forces to overturn these revolutions. The revolutions in Italy (Piedmont and Naples) were overturned by Austrian troops; that in Spain, by French troops. But this cooperation among Europe's most powerful was not to lay liberalism to rest. In 1830 France itself had another revolution, and a wave of rebellion passed through Belgium, Switzerland, Germany, Italy, and Poland. Again, great-power troops intervened in most of these to reverse the revolutions. The French Revolution was saved only by the establishment of a new constitutional under Louis-Philippe, the "citizen-king," who assured the conservative rulers of Europe that his regime would not export revolution. Nearly two decades of relative calm followed. But in 1848 yet another revolutionary wave—the most serious since the 1790s—rolled through Europe, engulfing Austria and Prussia themselves.

Between 1790 and 1848, then, we find periods of calm in which reasonable people assumed that the ideological struggles were over and politics, domestic and international, might finally return to normal. But these periods of calm were deceptive: all the while networks of liberal activists carried on, communicating, encouraging one another, planning and eventually carrying out agitations and revolts. All of the spies and suppressions of Metternich and his fellow absolutists could not change that.

When Democracy Appeared Doomed: The 1930s

To see just how dreadfully wrong knowledgeable and clever people can be regarding the outcome of an ideological contest, let us consider the 1930s.

It remains an acute embarrassment to intellectuals with long memories that in the 1930s, during the depths of the Great Depression, many Western intellectuals stopped betting on liberal democracy and free-market capitalism. Unemployment in industrial societies had skyrocketed, deflation had set in, and confidence that times would improve was collapsing. Many of the best and brightest held that the old institutions of the Western democracies were poorly equipped to handle the stresses of modern life; democracy was too susceptible to wild boom-bust cycles and to capture by moneyed interests. The British historian E. H. Carr argued that the failures of laissez-faire economics were even more profound than most imagined: they meant the failure of the liberal vision of international peace and through free trade and law.[27] Democratic capitalism was no longer seen as *progressive*, as moving with history.

The general solution that gained traction in the 1930s was statism, or the increasing centralization of economic and political power in the state. Most industrial democracies moved in a statist direction. In the United States Franklin Delano Roosevelt's New Deal was, by trial and error, expanding public works and federal regulation of the economy. The publication in 1936 of John Maynard Keynes's *General Theory of Employment, Interest, and Money* gave a theoretical underpinning to states' efforts to regulate demand for good and services.[28] The contrast to the response of wealthy countries to the Great Recession of 2008–10 is striking. In the latter, voters in Europe, North America, and Japan were at best ambivalent about whether the state was competent to manage the economy back into good health. In the 1930s, far less ambivalence was evident. In America Roosevelt built up the state, attacked the "fat cats" of Wall Street, and won four presidential terms.

Roosevelt was not trying to replace the American regime of democratic capitalism. He saw himself as "saving capitalism from itself,"[29] and many in Britain's Labour Party had a similar plan for their country. Others in the European Left did set out to eliminate capitalism—they regarded Roosevelt's New Deal as being incoherent and retrograde—but were committed to electoral democracy.[30]

But for many elites, even social democracy was not enough. Democracy appeared ineluctably captive to capital, and so democracy had to go. Yet, the antidemocratic statists were divided as to the right form of statism. Some laid their bets on fascism; others, on communism. The division was deep; communists and fascists regarded on another as mortal enemies.

Capitalism Was Regressive: Communism and the Fellow Travelers

On the one hand were those intellectuals and public figures who saw in democracy a colossal failure to deliver the goods it promised across society. Democratic capitalism often generated impressive amounts of wealth. But it distributed that wealth in an increasingly skewed manner. Furthermore, the poor—especially the millions of factory and farm workers—were vulnerable to the cycles of growth and shrinkage endemic to capitalism. Because democracy placed power in the hands of the wealthy (or "plutocracy"), it could not and would not do anything serious to relieve the condition of the poor majority. These intellectuals tended to cotton to the developing Soviet model of communism, which wrested power from the owning classes and, it was claimed, placed it in the hands of the workers or proletariat—a system its advocates called democratic centralism. Communism promised full employment and rational management of the economy.

Marxism-Leninism may need little introduction to today's readers, but it is important to see it as it was seen in the 1930s. V. I. Lenin and the Bolsheviks had shocked the world in November 1917 by seizing power in Russia from the provisional government that had replaced the tsarist regime nine months earlier. The Bolsheviks proclaimed a dictatorship of the proletariat, working through the soviets or workers' councils in various cities. Over the next few years they seized the property of the aristocracy and church, and triumphed in the civil war against the "whites" or partisans of the old regime (who were aided by troops from several Western capitalist countries). Socialism had been an international movement for more than a half century; communist parties already existed across many countries and had great influence in labor unions. Bolshevism had a devoted and growing following among labor leaders and intellectuals throughout the industrial world.

Over the coming years many Westerners became "fellow travelers," not outright communists but sympathizers who saw communism as the wave of the future. In 1921 the American muckraking journalist Lincoln Steffens helped blaze the trail from the West to Moscow, and announced, "I have been over into the future and it works."[31] Steffens was an early adopter. It took the Crash of 1929 and the Great Depression to convince the weight of left-wing opinion in the West of the obsolescence of democratic capitalism and the superiority of the Soviet model. Leftists from Europe and the Americas—Fabians from Britain, Socialists from France, labor activists from the United States—began to visit the Soviet Union to see for themselves. They saw only what the Soviet Communist Party wanted them to see. In an ironic twist to the old tsarist Potemkin villages, the Bolsheviks took Western visitors on whitewashed tours of factories and collective farms. The Westerners badly needed to believe that communism worked, and so were satisfied to trust their hosts and not to investigate matters for themselves.

The fellow travelers included some of the great intellectuals of the age: from Britain, George Bernard Shaw, Sidney and Beatrice Webb, Harold Laski, Sir John Maynard, Sir Bernard Pares, and Hewlett Johnson, Dean of Canterbury; from France, André Gide, Henri Barbusse, and Romain Rolland; among German exiles, Lion Feuchtwanger, Heinrich Mann, and Arnold Zweig; and from the United States, Steffens, Theodore Dreiser, Anna Louise Strong, Corliss Lamont, and Upton Sinclair. Each of these was alienated from democratic capitalism and defended the Soviet system and Stalin's rule, including the catastrophic collectivization of agriculture and the purges and show trials.

Consider Sidney and Beatrice Webb, fixtures in English polite society, prolific social scientists, and cofounders of the London School of Economics. Leading members of the Fabian Society, the democratic socialist organization that helped form the Labour Party in the late nineteenth century, the Webbs were utilitarian socialists who believed that the "greatest happiness for the greatest number" of people entailed public ownership and state planning of the economy. They were not revolutionaries; the Fabians were named for Quintus Fabius Maximus, the ancient Roman general famous for his cautious tactics.[32]

Lenin, the revolutionary, did not much care for the Fabians. At first, the Fabians did not think much of the Bolsheviks either. In 1923 the Webbs published *The Decay of Capitalist Civilisation*, whose thesis was this:

> [T]here was a moment, roughly placeable at the middle of the nineteenth century, when [the capitalist system] could claim that, in a hundred years, it had produced, on balance, a surprising advance in material civilisation for greatly increased populations. But we must add that from that moment to the present it has been receding from defeat to defeat, beaten ever more and more hopelessly by the social problems created by the very civilisation it has built up and the very fecundity it has encouraged. In short, that it began to decay before it reached maturity, and that history will regard capitalism, not as an epoch but as an episode, or Dark Age, between two epochs.[33]

But *Decay* was critical of the Bolsheviks for their violence and apparent anarchism, and the Webbs abhorred revolution through the 1920s.

In 1929 Beatrice Webb began to read Soviet documents carefully, and within a year was entertaining the notion that Russian socialism was in fact superior to British. At the time Sidney was a member of Ramsay MacDonald's embattled Labour government. In August 1930 the Soviet ambassador to Britain, Ivan Maisky, began cultivating Beatrice by telling her that, now that the Soviet Union had achieved equality, Soviet workers were willing to accept low wages for the sake of society. She was deeply impressed at the contrast with British workers, who were rather less willing to accept reductions in pay. When the Labour government fell in May 1932, the suddenly underemployed Webbs set sail for Leningrad.[34]

Their timing was unfortunate. In 1932 the forced collectivization of agriculture—the Soviet state's seizure of the remaining privately held farmland—was under way. Stalin focused particularly on the Ukraine with its fertile black soil and large peasant class. As Robert Conquest writes, the peasantry was a sort of ideological obstacle to Marxism-Leninism, which saw the urban proletariat as the progressive class; peasants were naturally conservative and attached to private property. To eliminate the peasantry, Stalin invented the concept of the *kulaks*, wealthy capitalist landowning peasants, allegedly hated by the poor peasantry. The goal of good socialists became to "liquidate the kulaks as a class." The dreary story of what followed has been told many times. "Kulaks" were arrested and deported; Soviet agricultural output plummeted; in response the party invented statistics showing huge crop yields, seized the alleged surplus, and left the peasantry to starve. In the Holodomor, the terror-famine of 1932–33, an estimated four to five million died in the Ukraine and another two to three million perished in the North Caucasus and Lower Volga region. Documents show that the Soviet government knew precisely what it was doing.[35]

Sidney and Beatrice Webb might also have known, but did not allow themselves to. Already convinced of the progressiveness of Stalin's Soviet Union, and the need to rationalize agriculture by bringing it under state control, they explained away the internal exile of the "kulaks": "It must be recognised that this liquidation of the individual capitalist in agriculture had necessarily to be faced if the required increase of output was to be obtained." The Webbs went on to claim that the prosperous Russian and Ukrainian peasant class had always been hated, and that if brutality had been used against some kulaks, it was partly because they had left crops rotting out of sheer obstinacy.[36]

The Webbs were not communists. Like most fellow travelers, they did not wish to live under the dictatorship of a party or a man; not for them were the political strictures of Stalinism. Steffens wrote in 1926, "I am for them to the last drop, I am a patriot for Russia; the future is there. . . . But I don't want to live there. It is too much like serving in an army at war with no mercy for the weak. . . . My service to it has to be outside, here." "Here" being, in his case, the Italian Riviera.[37] The Ukrainian kulaks had to settle for doing their service in Siberia.

There were exceptions to this depressing rule. A few journalists, who set out to evade their Soviet handlers, pierced the fable. One was the Welshman Gareth Jones, who sent dispatches from the famine-wracked Ukraine in 1932– 33. Another was Malcolm Muggeridge, husband of Beatrice Webb's niece, who went to the Soviet Union in 1932 convinced that capitalism had failed and desperate to find some workable model of society. Muggeridge took the trouble to visit the Ukraine himself, without minders. What he saw turned him decisively against communism. He witnessed famine "planned and deliberate; not due to any natural catastrophe like failure of rain or cyclone or flooding. An administrative famine brought about by the forced collectivization of agriculture . . . abandoned villages, the absence of livestock, neglected fields: everywhere, famished, frightened people." The *Manchester Guardian* published a smuggled three-part article by Muggeridge on the Soviet famines, concluding that the Soviet Union was a dictatorship. Muggeridge was condemned as a liar and a reactionary by his Fabian former comrades.[38]

Democracy Was Too Decadent: Fascism and the Appeasers

It is hard to decide which story is more shameful and depressing: that of communism's fellow travelers, or that of fascism's. The 1930s featured plenty of the latter as well, although they were less likely to be academics and more likely to be businessmen and artists. These perceived the basic problem with democracy as decay and a loss of virtue. Fascism's fellow travelers tended to be deeply impressed with the centralized authoritarianism pioneered by Benito Mussolini in Italy and imitated and modified by Adolf Hitler in Germany. Today a label from which everyone runs, fascism was in the 1930s one that many openly embraced.

Then as now, fascism was difficult to define precisely. It is often seen in essentially negative terms, as an effort to "turn the clock back" to some mythical pristine past. And it was a negative movement in the sense that it was partly defined by its repulsion from international socialism. Socialism was offensive for its claim that the "workingman has no country"—that the proletariat across countries form a class whose political significance outweighed that of the nation. For fascists, the nation was the most important social unit, a mystical thing. The central task of the state—embodied in the visionary, heroic leader— was to bind the nation into an organic whole.

Fascists rejected democracy because they believed it was inadequate to the demands of the twentieth century. Political scientist Juan Linz puts it this way: "The obvious distortion of the idea of democracy in the reality of the early twentieth century and the incapacity of the democratic leadership to institutionalize mechanisms for conflict resolution provided the ground for the appeal of fascism."[39] Fascism was a modern movement that combined Romantic and Enlightenment elements in an odd mixture. Fascists were idealists: they rejected materialism, insisting that ideas move the world. They called for a return to nature. Perhaps most strikingly, fascists held a strong view of the human will as embodied in the nation. The nation must liberate itself from all constraint and let the chips fall where they may. Wrote the British fascist Oswald Mosley, "No man goes very far who knows exactly where he is going." And here is the Belgian fascist Léon Degrelle—"You must get going, you must let yourself be swept away by the torrent . . . you must act. The rest comes by itself."[40] The "you" ended up meaning the state, which under fascism sought power recklessly, both domestically and externally via expansion, imperialism, and war. Fascists were unabashed social Darwinists: nations were in a struggle and it was natural for the strong to conquer the weak. They also were rhetorically anticapitalist and anticlerical, but in practice reached accommodation with merchants and bishops alike.

Mussolini, once a socialist newspaper editor, launched the first fascist movement in Italy in 1919 and formed a government in 1922. Imitators soon emerged in Germany, Austria, Hungary, Romania, Britain, Spain, France, Finland, South Africa, and Brazil. In 1923 Hitler and his circle, inspired by Mussolini, launched a putsch in Bavaria that failed miserably.[41] With the Great Depression that began in 1929, and the catastrophic losses of wealth and jobs that followed throughout the industrial world, fascist parties gained support in many countries. In 1932 a fascist government took power in Hungary; in 1933 fascists took power in Austria and Portugal; and, most significantly, Hitler's Nazis did so in Germany. And fascist parties formed in many other countries: the Dutch National Socialist Party in 1931; the Falange in Spain in 1933; Norway's National Union Movement in 1934; the Rexist Movement in Belgium in 1935; the French Popular Party in 1936. In December 1934 Mussolini attempted to organize a Fascist International at Montreux, Switzerland. The effort failed because Hitler refused to participate; the two dictators were in a serious territorial dispute at the time. But the movement had impressive momentum across industrial societies.

Mosley of Great Britain began as a Labour politician. Frustrated at his government's refusal to put the state in charge of the national economy, he broke away in 1931 to form the British Union of Fascists. The author H. G. Wells had been an antifascist, but he too changed his attitude once the Depression set in.

In "Liberal Fascism," a notorious speech to the Young Liberals in Oxford in July 1932, Wells called for an entity—a "competent receiver," in his words—that would replace outmoded parliamentary democracy and "guide and rule the new scale human community." Wells also renounced private property and individualism, and cited the Italian *fascisti* as exemplifying what he had in mind. As historian Philip Coupland summarizes, "Thus, in order to seek this 'prosperous and progressive' utopia, liberals had to 'move with the times', discard the 'sentimental casualness of nineteenth-century Liberalism' and transform themselves into a 'Liberal Fascisti.' In doing so, liberalism would become an organization to '*replace* the dilatory indecisiveness of parliamentary politics.'"[42]

Nor was the United States immune to fascism's appeal. The poet Ezra Pound embraced it. The most infamous fellow traveler was the heroic pilot Charles Lindbergh. Lucky Lindy, the Lone Eagle, who had captured the world's imagination in 1927 as the first human being to fly across the Atlantic, became a leader of the America First Council in 1940, arguing vigorously and very publicly against American involvement in the European war. But Lindbergh was not only an isolationist: he was also an open admirer of Nazi Germany and had deep disdain for Great Britain and his native United States. As an aviator who believed in air power, he was taken with Hermann Göring's Luftwaffe and tirelessly warned the Americans and British that German air power would conquer Europe. Charles and his wife Anne Morrow Lindbergh visited Germany several times and in 1940 contemplated settling in Berlin. Upon his first visit in 1936 Lindbergh wrote to a friend, "I think Germany is in many ways the most interesting nation in the world today, and that she is attempting to *find a solution for some of our most fundamental problems*."[43] Following another visit in 1937—at the invitation of Göring—Lindbergh wrote another friend that Germany and Italy were the "two most virile countries in Europe today," with a "sense of decency and values which in many ways is far ahead of our own." Living in Britain at the time, Lindbergh contrasted German order with the "headlines of murder, rape, and divorce on the billboards of London."[44] In 1939 he expressed concern that England was no longer able to defend "our civilization," and stated that the task had been passed on to the New Germany.[45]

Susan Hertog, biographer of his wife Anne Morrow Lindbergh, explains Lindbergh's views:

> Clearly, Charles saw the Third Reich as the embodiment of his values: science and technology harnessed for the preservation of a superior race, physically able and morally pure. . . . Social and political equality, together with an ungoverned press, had produced a quality of moral degeneracy. . . . He did not disdain democracy so much as he did the common man—the uneducated and enfeebled masses. . . . To

Charles, Germany under Hitler was a nation of true manhood—virility and purpose. The strong central leadership of a fascist state was the only hope of restoring a moral world order.[46]

Morrow Lindbergh, a noted writer, was torn over her husband's fascist sympathies. After a long silence she ended up publishing in 1940 *The Wave of the Future: A Confession of Faith*, a confused, lyrical statement of her conviction that democracy was finished and Germany was a prototype of the future society. Like Charles, Anne expressed concern at the cruelty of some Nazi practices, particularly toward the Jews. But the movements of history, she reminded her readers, can be cruel. Morrow Lindbergh concluded, "We, unhappily, are living in the hiatus between two dreams. We have waked from one and not yet started the other. We still have our eyes, our minds, our hearts, on the dream that is dying—How beautiful it was, tinting the whole sky crimson as it fades into the west! But there is another on its way in the gray dawn."[47]

Charles Lindbergh became the leading spokesman for the America First Committee, organized in 1940 to keep the United States out of the European war at all costs. The movement began as a core of patriotic isolationists, but attracted a grotesque assortment of fascists, anti-Semites, and German sympathizers.[48] By no means did most Americans—even isolationists—agree with the Lindberghs that democracy had become a bad bet. Both Lindberghs were met with condemnation from many quarters. But they were by no means alone in their sense that fascism was better equipped to "find a solution for some of our most important problems."

They were wrong, of course. The German Luftwaffe proved unable to best Britain's Royal Air Force in 1940. More generally, while fascist states were able to mobilize resources to an impressive degree during the Depression, they were doing so by putting their societies on a war footing in peacetime. The fascist drive for autarky—economic self-sufficiency—moved them to expand aggressively, and attempt to swallow other major powers so as to build massive empires, to the point that they provoked their communist and democratic enemies to fight them. And those enemies proved at least as adept at mobilizing resources when it came to real war. War and conquest, a goal of the fascist state, proved its undoing in the 1940s. But a shamefully high number of influential people in the democracies themselves did not foresee this in the 1930s.

※ ※ ※

What do we take from all of these misbegotten and confused analyses, romantic and naïve justifications, risible predictions, and staggering attempts to justify the most gruesome regimes of the twentieth century? Some may conclude that it is never smart to bet against liberal democracy. Perhaps the mistake of the fellow travelers of the 1930s was not to realize that free-market capitalism, individual liberty, and popular sovereignty together compose the most successful regime ever invented. The Great Depression was bad, but the institutions of liberal democracy proved superior at pulling societies out of it with minimal damage. That interpretation would come naturally to Americans, for reasons I gave earlier in this chapter. It may be correct, in the long run, and indeed I suspect that it will be. But the problem with the long run is that we do not know how long a run it is.

A safer, if more modest, conclusion from this dreary and embarrassing history is that even people of high achievement—writers, academics, titans of industry, adventurers, clerics—can be tragically wrong about how an ideological competition is progressing. They can be utterly convinced that side A is moving with history while side B is not, and begin to invest in A—and eventually find that their investment in A has ruined them.

Today, the narrative of progress remains powerful for us, and Westerners do tend to agree that, whatever we mean by progress, Islamism is not progressive. Look no further than the common Western reaction to the al-Qaeda attacks of September 11, 2001. People who perpetrate such acts or embrace the ideas supporting them, we said, are "medieval," in need of a "Reformation" or "Enlightenment" such as the West itself went through centuries ago. (Never mind that medieval Europe saw no wars as destructive as those of the Renaissance's own Thirty Years' War, to say nothing of the Enlightenment-infused Napoleonic wars and the world wars of the twentieth century.) And furthermore, we tend to believe that somehow, some way, the Middle East must someday go through such a transformation. Pressure from technology, the need to compete in the global economy, or some mysterious inexorable historical process is bound to do its work in the Muslim societies as it did in Christian ones (and, so goes the narrative, in much of East and South Asia).[49]

Those assertions, sometimes made in haste, have been directed at the terrorism of radical Islamism. But deeper analyses by serious scholars of the Middle East come to similar conclusions about Islamism more generally—moderate and radical alike.

One of the most profound writers on Islamism is the French scholar Gilles Kepel. Known particularly for his "revenge of God" thesis, which put paid to Western social-scientific pronouncements of inexorable global secularization,[50] Kepel nonetheless predicted after the 9/11 attacks that Islamism's days were numbered. Islamism appealed to Muslims in the early and middle twentieth century because its enemy, authoritarian secularism, was so obviously brutal and repressive. Now that many Islamists themselves are themselves using violence—especially against innocent civilians—they are losing the support of the

Muslim middle classes. Thus 9/11, far from being a sign of Islamist strength, "was a desperate symbol of the isolation, fragmentation, and decline of the Islamist movement." Al-Qaeda, writes, Kepel, thought 9/11 would topple America and spark revolution throughout the Muslim world, but it did neither. He concludes, "[T]he Islamist movement will have much difficulty reversing its trail of decline as it confronts twenty-first century civilization."[51]

Olivier Roy is another accomplished French scholar of Islamism, a sociologist who has studied actual Islamists up close in many Muslim countries. Roy's arguments are complex, but his general thesis is that Islamism is so lacerated with contradictions that it cannot work in practice; it must become more moderate to survive. In *The Failure of Political Islam* (1994) Roy argues that the original Islamists of the middle decades of the twentieth century (Hassan al-Banna and Abul Ala Maududi) sought a completely Islamicized polity, but those Islamists who actually attain power, faced with the demands of modern society, back down from many of their extreme demands.[52] More recently, Roy argues that most Islamists have abandoned their universalist vision for more familiar, decidedly ordinary nationalism.[53] Roy is doubtless correct that holding real political power presses Islamists into moderating some of their goals, a trend I examine in Lesson 5. But, as he acknowledges, they retain their core goal of establishing Sharia. Furthermore, as the history covered in this book shows, sometimes when some ideologues moderate their program, others break with them, maintain their radicalism, and form a new group. For secular Muslims, those are no trivial facts.

Roy and Kepel are brilliant and learned analysts of Islamism. They may be correct that radical jihadism, of the al-Qaeda type, cannot be sustained for long among particular people in particular places. But we should be careful before betting on their claims about Islamism in *general*, because one powerful lesson of history is that ideologies are typically underestimated by their enemies and by outsiders.

This tendency to sell a foreign ideology short may come from our need to reduce cognitive dissonance. If I subscribe to ideology A, and hence reject its opposite B, then I make things simpler for myself if I think that B is not only unjust and wrong, but impractical. We want good things to go together: what is morally bad is also destined to fail. Prophecies of Islamism's doom are as old as the movement itself. Early Muslim secularists such as Atatürk believed that traditional Islamic society, with its religiously shaped institutions, was collapsing under the assault of modernity. That belief helped justify—and perhaps cause—their adoption of secularism. The Muslim secularists of the twentieth century set out to prove their case by eradicating traditional institutions and trying to show that a secular Muslim state—Turkey, Iran, Pakistan, Egypt, Syria, Iraq, others—can thrive in the modern world, like Western states.

Atatürk's project of modernizing Turkish society, called Kemalism, included urbanization, and so the young Turkish state neglected rural Anatolia, where traditional Islamic institutions and practices were strongest. In the countryside, under the noses of the Kemalists, traditional Islamic orders, outside the control of the state, continued to flourish. These orders, and general antisecularist sentiment, began to enter the political arena in 1946 with the coming of multiparty democracy.[54] Today's Justice and Development Party, a moderate Islamist entity, exists because the Kemalists underestimated the power of traditional Islam to endure through private networks and to modify itself into a modern movement.

The case of Iran is far more dramatic. As mentioned in this book's introduction, Reza Shah sought to replicate Atatürk's modernizing and secularizing project in Iran. He and his son Mohammed Reza Shah took power from the *ulema* or clergy, and the ulema acquiesced. The shahs and their fellow modernizers were convinced that Islam as it existed traditionally—as a strong, institutionalized influence in society—was dying away. But all the while the ulema quietly regrouped and developed their thinking on how to maintain Islam and cultivate pious Muslims in a modern, technological, Western-influenced society. Even as Ali Shariati, Ruhollah Khomeini, and others leading ulema declared their loyalty to the shah (and particularly his anticommunism), their vision for Iran deviated more and more widely from his.[55]

Neither the shah nor his Western admirers took seriously the notion that Islam might actually rebound as a social and political force. The November 4, 1974, edition of *Time* magazine featured several stories on Iran, including "Iran: Oil, Grandeur and a Challenge to the West." Five years before Iran's Islamist revolution, America's leading newsmagazine mentioned no Islamic threat to the so-called Peacock Throne.[56] Political scientist Robert Jervis studied why the CIA did not foresee the fall of the shah of Iran in 1978–79 and concluded, among other things, that American intelligence analysts found it hard to take seriously that a religiously based opposition could be so consequential in a society where secularization was evidently so successful. "Although modernization theory had taken a battering by the late 1970s, it still seemed inconceivable that anything as retrograde as religion, especially fundamentalist religion, could be crucial."[57]

It is clear, then, that the secularist dismissal of Islamism runs deeply in Western minds. As Jervis notes, it is connected to an old, now discredited, social-scientific consensus that traditional religion is incompatible with the modern world. For many years scholars took for granted that modernization was tied up with secularization—they caused each other, or perhaps they were simply the same thing. The narrative was entrenched in the Western academy: societies, at different times and paces to be sure, undergo a related set of changes:

technology replaces manual labor, people move from country to city, they belong to more and more overlapping social groups, institutions become more efficient, science replaces revealed religion as source of understanding of the world. As the sociologist Peter Berger—himself once a leading theorist of secularization—points out, this narrative applies particularly well to the Western academics who thought it up, and perhaps it applies to Western Europe and certain areas on the coasts of North America. But as most of the world has become more technologically sophisticated, urbanized, and socially complex, it has remained as religious as it ever was. Indeed, as Kepel himself has argued elsewhere, modernization has generated religious reactions that attempt to reestablish and reconfigure traditional belief.[58]

We must grapple with the following unsettling fact: secularism has been tried in the Middle East, and in many places it has not worked. Islamism is in fact a reaction to secularism, imposed many decades ago by Europeans and by Muslim secularists. Those who say that the Middle East simply must go through what the early modern West went through must recognize that that has already happened. What is more, far from killing off traditional Islam, secularization transformed it into a potent, variegated modern ideology. All over the Muslim world, Islamist groups and parties—some extreme, some moderate, all determined to weaken or eliminate secular government—draw support. Nowhere is the irony more striking than in the lands where secularism was tried with the most determination. Islamists rule Iran, and have influence in Pakistan. Even Turkey itself is governed by a party "with Islamist roots." In Egypt following the Arab Spring, free elections put in office an Islamist president and parliamentary majority; it took a military takeover in the summer of 2013 to restore secular rule.

It could be that what seems to be political Islam's kinetic energy is instead its death rattle. It could be, too, that secularism will regain its lost momentum at some point. Secularist governments in the Middle East have been authoritarian, and liberal-democratic secularism may yet have its day. But that day seems remote at present. This is no time to short-sell Islamism.

Lesson 2
Ideologies Are (Usually) Not Monolithic

To borrow a computer term, if Ayatollah Khomeini, Osama bin Laden,
and Nidal Hasan represent Islamism 1.0, Recep Tayyip Erdoğan
(the prime minister of Turkey), Tariq Ramadan (a Swiss intellectual),
and Keith Ellison (a U.S. congressman) represent Islamism 2.0.
The former kill more people but the latter pose
a greater threat to Western civilization.
—*Daniel Pipes, 2009*

A multitude of states and organizations with extremely divergent ob-
jectives and methods are grouped together as a part of this monolithic
threat. Hezbollah in Lebanon, the government of Iran, al-Qaeda, the
Taliban, Hamas in Gaza and the Somali al-Shabaab are but a
few of the many faces of the same worldwide monster
in the eyes of many American leaders.
—*Brendan O'Reilly, 2011*

A monolith is, literally, a monument carved from a single block of stone. History shows that whenever an ideological movement exists, outsiders who oppose it debate whether it is like a monolith: undifferentiated, of a single piece,
indivisible. In the 1790s the British argued over whether the young American
and French republics were of a piece. All through the Cold War of the twentieth

century, Western governments puzzled over whether communists around the world formed a tight bloc.

Is Islamism monolithic? Islamists do share the general goal of making Sharia the actual positive law of their societies. But Islamists come in many different varieties. Some are Arab, others Persian or Pashtun or Bengali. Some are Sunni, others Shia. Some practice terrorism, others work through peaceful means. Some are nationalists, others internationalists or imperialists. Cutting across all of these groups are deep disagreements as to who has the right version of Sharia, and who gets to say so.

And some Islamists regard other Islamists as enemies. Enmity between the Taliban and Iran's ruling regime is long-standing and deep. One of the Saudi dynasty's most lethal enemies is al-Qaeda. Both of these regard Iran as an enemy.

So is Islamism better seen as a *polylith*—a structure made of multiple stones that can potentially separate? Islamists seek the same general thing—Sharia—but clearly they are not acting in concert. In fact, some Islamists are enemies with others. Should we outsiders recognize their differences and act accordingly, perhaps seeking to cooperate with some of them? Might we play the ancient Roman game of *divide et impera* (divide and rule), using some Islamists—say, moderate ones, or democratic ones, or pro-Western ones—against others?

Some commentators call for a monolithic strategy. Daniel Pipes's writings make clear that he regards Islamism, the ideology not the religion, as a monolith. "Islamism is a scourge," he writes, "a global affliction whose victims include peoples of all religions, [but] Muslims are the main casualties."[1] In broad agreement is the neoconservative *éminence grise* Norman Podhoretz, who coined the term "Islamofascists": "Like the Nazis and the Communists before them, they are dedicated to the destruction of the freedoms we cherish and for which America stands."[2] The view of Podhoretz and Pipes is common among analysts: the problem is the ideology, not the religion, but the ideology is a monolith that must be opposed wherever it is found. (Logically, it is possible to see Islamism as monolithic yet counsel accommodation, yet it seems that few if any "monolithists" are accommodationists.)

On the other hand, plenty of analysts take the opposing view that Islamism is polylithic. These insist that Islamists come in various types, and not all are dangerous. Charles Kurzman, a sociologist, notes that very few Islamists are militant—even most of those who profess admiration for Osama bin Laden never carry out violent jihad—and in fact moderate Islamists are siphoning away potential militants from groups such as al-Qaeda.[3]

Whether Islamism is monolithic or polylithic matters for American foreign policy. Youssef Aboul-Enein, a U.S. Army officer, distinguishes Muslims,

Islamists, and Militant Islamists. Militant Islamists use violent means to achieve Sharia, whereas ordinary Islamists generally use peaceful, constitutional means, and often view the militants as enemies. Aboul-Enein counsels working with the first two against the third.[4] In similar fashion, journalist Brendan O'Reilly writes, "The motivations for Iraqi and Afghan insurgents are primarily personal and nationalistic. To conflate these disparate groups with the terrorists of al-Qaeda is not only unfair, it is a basis for self-defeating policy."[5]

In fact, the United States and many other non-Muslim countries already do make or recognize distinctions among Islamists. Washington has had close relations with the Saudi dynasty—whose Wahhabi Islamism is among the strictest in today's world—since the 1940s, and with other, milder Islamist Gulf monarchies as well. But some critics, such as Pipes and Robert Baer, call for a rethinking of the Saudi-U.S. relationship.[6]

So: to treat Islamism as a monolith, or a polylith? To lump Islamists together, or split them?[7] It is a most difficult question to answer, because our predispositions are so powerful.

Some people are prone to see similarities wherever they look, others to see differences. The ancient Greek poet Archilochus wrote that "the fox knows many things; the hedgehog, one big thing." The political theorist Isaiah Berlin argued that writers could be categorized either as hedgehogs, who relate all events, statements, and objects to a single master principle; or as foxes, who hold many ideas, some contradictory to others.[8] (Berlin was a hedgehog, at least in that essay.) Hedgehogs like to create broad categories. Foxes delight in showing the crudeness of broad categories and the ignorance of hedgehogs.

Even being aware if you are fox or hedgehog does not eliminate the problems. Political correctness, of the Right or of the Left, heavily influences how we answer the "monolith or polylith" question. A sure way to invite ridicule on American talk radio is to suggest that not all Islamists are the same—that, for example, the Egyptian Muslim Brotherhood might really want democracy—for that amounts to the deadly sin of appeasement. A sure way to invite outrage on most American college campuses is to suggest that all Islamists *are* the same—that, for example, even moderate Muslim Brothers have an illiberal agenda—for that amounts to the deadly sins of stereotyping and intolerance.

Fortunately, we can look to Western history for clues. The West's own past teaches that transnational ideological movements always present outsiders with this dilemma; that outsiders respond differently; that sometimes monoliths are actually easier to handle than polyliths; and, most vexing of all, that there is no master universal strategy for outsiders. Whether one plays fox or hedgehog, one takes on risk.

Before we delve back into that history, we must note one more thing that makes the monolith-polylith question especially perplexing. The right answer depends in part on one's values—how much one opposes the ideology, for moral or prudential reasons. Even most foxes would agree with hedgehogs that some ideological groups are beyond the moral pale and ought to be treated as monolithic. National Socialism is the most obvious case. The factionalism and betrayal among Nazis is not only fodder for jokes in the 1960s television series *Hogan's Heroes*: it is a matter of historical fact. And there were Nazis who wanted to cut a deal with the West against the Soviet Union. Rudolf Hess, a deputy to Hitler, flew to Scotland in 1941 to offer the British such a deal. Few would criticize Winston Churchill for rebuffing Hess and clapping him in prison.

Is Islamism like Nazism, in that sense? Is the very notion of state-enforced Sharia so morally offensive that its advocates—even nonviolent, democratic ones—must never be accommodated? Some will say yes, and no appeal to strategy and tactics will move them. Theirs is a serious argument, particularly because even moderate Islamists such as the Egyptian Yusuf al-Qaradawi, who repudiates terrorism and favors democracy, have made vile anti-Semitic statements and agree that apostates—who leave Islam for Christianity or other religions—should be killed.[9] Still, I do not adopt this categorical rejection of Islamism here, because it is not clear that Islamism in all of its forms entails such extreme religious bigotry. Many Islamists, such as the Saudi regime, have proven pragmatic in dealing with Israel.[10] That does not mean they are liberal. It does not even mean that outsiders should always cooperate with moderate Islamists. It simply means that it is legitimate to distinguish forms of Islamism and to posit that opposing all Islamists—moderate and extreme—all the time may bring other heavy costs. In other words, we shall be on guard against letting the best be the enemy of the good.

Lesson 2, then, is complicated. Ideological groups sometimes are monoliths, and sometimes polyliths. Determining which is the case requires careful monitoring and judgment. As if the matter were not bewildering enough, outsiders can affect how monolithic an ideological group is: treating it as one can be a self-fulfilling prophecy. But too much can be made of that insight. Sometimes whether an ideology is monolithic is beyond the control of outsiders.

We begin with the Europe of two centuries ago, just after the final defeat of Napoleon.

The Nineteenth Century: Metternich Lumps Together the Liberals

In the Europe of the early nineteenth century, "conservative" did not mean exactly what it means today in America. Conservatism was born as a reaction to the French Revolution that began in 1789. Its chief concern over the next sixty years was to preserve Europe's hierarchical social order from revolution. Today free-market capitalism is a hallmark of American conservatism, but in the Europe of two hundred years ago free markets, which redistributed power from the landed nobility to the merchants and bankers, were actually one of the changes that conservatives feared.

In 1814 and for the three and a half decades following, Europe's leading conservative statesman was Prince Clemens Wenzel von Metternich, Austria's minister of state. As a young man Metternich had been affected by Edmund Burke's famous broadside, *Reflections on the Revolution in France*, and even had been a guest at Burke's home in 1794.[11] But whereas Burke, as a British Whig, was a *constitutional* monarchist—insisting that the king be constrained by law as made by parliament—Metternich was an *absolute* monarchist, who steadfastly held that the king—in his case, the Habsburg emperor—must be unconstrained except by the God by whose decree he ruled.

Late in his life Metternich wrote that all of the decades of revolt, upheaval, and war in Europe resulted from the migration of British ideas about the "rule of law" to the Continent: "Among the causes of the tremendous confusion characterizing present-day Europe is the transplantation of British institutions to the Continent where they are in complete contradiction to existing conditions, so that their application becomes either illusory of distorted. The so-called 'British school' has been the cause of the French Revolution, and the consequences of this revolution, so anti-British in tendency, devastate Europe today."[12] For Metternich and other Continental conservatives in post-Napoleonic Europe—Friedrich von Gentz and Adam Müller in Prussia, Joseph de Maistre and François-René de Chateaubriand in France, and others—this British notion of the "rule of law" was the chief enemy of social order. And conservatives knew that even though the French Revolution was long over, the threat of revolution still hung in the air. Liberal networks continued to thread across Europe (and European colonies in the New World), humming with ideas and plots. In Masonic lodges and secret societies, revolutionaries kept the dream alive and schemed to reenact 1789.[13]

But liberals came in two basic types. Some were constitutional monarchists, others republicans. Republicans would not be satisfied with parliamentary constraints on monarchs. The only good society, for republicans, was one that had no monarch at all—like France had had for a few years in the 1790s, and like the young United States had had since 1776.

For European conservatives, the divide between republicanism and constitutional monarchism was a distinction without a difference. Both "isms" were illegitimate because monarchs must never be constrained except by God's law.[14] Besides, constitutional monarchies usually degenerated into republics. In 1792, the third year of the French Revolution, the Assembly had forced

Louis XVI to submit to laws it made. Many observers thought that the Assembly would be satisfied with a constitutional monarchy. But a year later, the same body overthrew Louis altogether and declared a republic. A few months after that the radicals beheaded Louis.[15]

Metternich and the conservatives, then, were hedgehogs: a constitutional monarchist was a republican was a liberal was a radical.

The first major test of this hedgehog strategy came in the early 1820s. The trouble began in Spain. On January 1, 1820, liberal Spanish army officers revolted and declared the country's Constitution of 1812 in effect. Drafted eight years earlier, during the war against Napoleon, the 1812 Constitution was moderate by today's standards. But the very notion of a written constitution scandalized many conservatives. What was worse, this written constitution explicitly placed legal constraints on the monarch, King Ferdinand VII. The Spanish Revolution of 1820 sparked similar insurrections in Portugal, Naples, Piedmont, and Greece—and in Latin America, the young states of Gran Colómbia, Venezuela, Argentina, Uruguay, Peru, and Mexico. All of these adopted some version of the 1812 Spanish Constitution.

This eruption of liberalism in so many lands sent shock waves through the conservative courts of Europe. The rulers of Austria, Russia, and Prussia declared that they—the so-called Holy Alliance—reserved the right to overturn these revolutions so as to restore peace and order in Europe. At the time France was a constitutional monarchy governed by absolutists who wanted to make their king, Louis XVIII, into an absolute monarch. So France joined the Holy Alliance.

In March 1821 Austrian troops invaded Naples to restore absolute monarchy. Other invasions of small constitutional monarchies followed. The biggest came in 1823, when a hundred thousand French troops invaded Spain itself, shredded the Constitution of 1812, and restored the absolute rule of Ferdinand.[16] Never mind that these hapless rebels were all monarchists: they were *constitutional* monarchists, no better than republicans, and the absolutists of Europe had rallied to put them down.

A similar wave of liberal revolution broke in the 1830s, beginning with France itself and spreading to Belgium, Italy, Poland, and Germany. Only in the German case did rebels demand a republic; the rest simply wanted their kings constrained by a constitution. Again, however, the conservative powers used troops to roll back the revolutions—except in France itself, too powerful to conquer without a massive invasion.

The final wave of liberal revolution, the biggest, swelled and broke over most of Europe in 1848. In France the monarchy fell and a Second Republic was established. To the east, in Vienna, the aged Metternich finally fell as well, as did the government of Prussia. But the absolute monarchies of Austria,

Russia, and Prussia struck back in 1849, invading and restoring absolute monarchy in small state after small state in what are now Germany and Italy.

In making no distinctions among liberals—in lumping republicans and constitutional monarchists together as a single enemy—nineteenth-century conservatives were true to their principles. Seen from their perspective, they also may be said to have pursued the prudent course. They did succeed in rolling back liberalism abroad. Had they played divide-and-rule, befriending moderates (constitutional monarchists) in order to defeat the extremists (republicans), they might have encouraged liberals in their own lands. Instead, Europe entered the 1850s with absolutism still predominant and liberals scattered and in hiding or exile.

The conservatives paid a price, however. They alienated another great power, Britain. The British openly disapproved of their overturning of constitutional monarchy in Spain, Italy, Germany, and elsewhere. Indeed, Britain counter-intervened in Portugal in 1826 to restore the constitutional rule of Pedro IV.[17]

Then too, as we shall see in Lesson 5, the conservatives' victory of 1849 was far from final. By the 1870s all European great powers, with the exception of Russia, had evolved into constitutional regimes, with responsible parliaments. The absolutists' hedgehog strategy bought time, but could not eliminate the problem.

The Habsburgs and the Protestants—Europe, Early Seventeenth Century

Three centuries earlier, the House of Habsburg was Europe's superpower, ruling most of Central Europe, all of Spain, and what are now the Netherlands and Belgium. The Habsburg monarchs had foreign enemies—kings of France, Ottoman sultans, sometimes even popes—but for nearly a century had faced a serious threat of a different sort. Protestantism continued a lethal peril, turning princes and peoples both within and without Habsburg lands into enemies of Europe's most powerful dynasty.

From the start Protestants had been divided against each other—in the 1520s, it was Lutherans against Anabaptists against Zwinglians—and the Habsburg monarchs recognized those divisions. Indeed, for Catholics, divisions among Protestants confirmed that they were heretics. The fundamental doctrinal error of the Protestants, they maintained, was to deny the authority of the Catholic Church and to put in its place the authority of the individual conscience. No surprise to them that opening the door to individual interpretation of the Bible or God's will would lead to all manner of strife.

To popes and most bishops, however, intra-Protestant strife was beside the point. All Protestants must be opposed at all times; the movement must be seen as a monolith.

The Habsburgs, however, were princes, not priests. They had to worry not simply about eradicating heresy, but also holding their sprawling empire together and keeping external enemies—the French and the Turks—at bay. Thus the Habsburgs faced a perpetual question: since Protestantism seemed to be polylithic, should they try to exploit divisions among the Protestants? Or was that too risky? They answered the question in various ways. One particularly unsetting story is from the early seventeenth century.

Rudolf II and the Calvinists

By the 1550s the main division among Protestants was that between Lutherans and Calvinists. John Calvin (1509–64) was a French scholar who admired Luther and saw himself as pushing the German monk's insights to their logical conclusions. Calvin wrote a massive treatise, *Institutes of the Christian Religion*—first edition published when he was only twenty-seven—that stated his doctrines in systematic form.

The two Protestant giants, Luther and Calvin, differed on some matters. For our purposes, the chief differences had to do with church and earthly society. Calvin emphasized not only that God alone decided who shall be saved or "justified"—Luther agreed—but also that he makes the saved (or "elect") holy or sanctified. Where Luther was pessimistic about how far earthly life could be improved, Calvin pressed for the establishment of a godly society. Calvin also leveled church governance, getting rid of bishops and putting elders and deacons in charge of local congregations. In 1536 Calvin began putting his ideas into practice, building Geneva into a model city in which the reformed church was integral to public order.

Calvinism began to spread rapidly through Central and Northwestern Europe. Its appeal owed in part to its vision of a purified, disciplined, righteous society flourishing under God's decrees. For half a century the Habsburgs tried to exploit the Lutheran-Calvinist divide by playing the fox, pursuing a divide-and-rule strategy among the Protestants. In 1555 they agreed to the Peace of Augsburg, recognizing the right of Lutheran princes and city councils to establish their version of Christianity in their realms without outside interference. Calvinism was not included in the Augsburg Peace. In effect, it was illegal in the Holy Roman Empire.

But far from dying out, Calvinism flourished under its ban. It grew in part because the Habsburgs not only helped divide Lutherans from Calvinists—they also indirectly helped cause a split among Lutherans. Following the death of Luther himself in 1546, there were those Lutherans who held that Luther's original teachings must never be altered or amended—the Gnesio-Lutherans ("genuine" Lutherans). There were those, following Luther's disciple Philip Melanchthon, who believed that Luther's teaching could in fact be supplemented. The Gnesio-Lutherans eventually prevailed, and Melanchthonians began to separate from them and identify as Calvinists. Among these were leading princes of the empire: Elector Frederick III of the Palatinate, Count John of Nassau, Landgrave Maurice of Hesse-Cassel, Elector Christian I of Saxony, and Elector John Sigismund of Brandenburg.

"Small wonder," write Geoffrey Parker and Simon Adams, "that the Lutheran clergy cordially detested the Calvinists even more than they loathed the Catholics." A leading Lutheran, Matthias Hoë von Hoënegg, published tracts with titles such as *A Solid, Just, and Orthodox Detestation of Calvinists and Papists* (1601) and *A Weighty (and in These Dangerous Times Very Necessary) Discussion of Whether and Why It Is Better to Have Conformity with the Catholics . . . Than with the Calvinists* (1610).[18]

The result was that, within the empire, the Habsburgs aligned with the moderates (Lutherans) against the extremists (Calvinists). The polylithic strategy worked in the sense that Catholic-Lutheran peace held, for the most part, for a number of decades. Lutheranism did not disappear, but stabilized and Lutherans gained a stake in the imperial establishment.

In another sense, however, treating Protestantism as polylithic—playing the fox—failed. The Habsburg strategy did not count on the growth in Calvinism from the defection of the Melanchthonians out of the Lutheran ranks. Excluded and persecuted by Catholics in Germany and the Netherlands, as well as in France, Calvinists became all the more militantly anti-Catholic, engaging in periodic bouts of icon smashing. Followers of Calvin pointed to their militancy as a sign that they had gone further in purging Christianity from the superstitions of the Roman Church. Calvinism gained converts by accusing Lutherans of selling out to the Catholics through the Peace of Augsburg.

Calvinism benefited from having a web of tightly disciplined networks across much of Europe. By the 1570s the "Calvinist International," centered in Geneva, stretched from southern France through the Netherlands, England, and Scotland to the Palatinate and other German states eastward to Bohemia and Moravia. Calvinists mobilized and engineered revolts in Scotland (1559), France (1562), the Spanish-ruled Netherlands (1567), and Bohemia (1618). They had influence in England and pressed Queen Elizabeth into an anti-Habsburg policy. Blessed with a strong sense of transnational solidarity, Calvinists in one realm drew encouragement from their brethren's progress in other realms.[19]

The Habsburg strategy of playing the fox, luring the Lutherans away from the Calvinists, failed in a second way. The Lutherans eventually started to coalesce with the Calvinists in a monolithic Protestant front. What is worse, it happened because of events outside the Habsburgs' control.

The Habsburg Rudolf II, Holy Roman emperor from 1575 to 1612, was not a particularly devout Catholic. A patron of the arts and sciences—including the occult—Rudolf tolerated Protestants out of conviction, it seems, not simply prudence. Unlike some of his relatives and predecessors, he was far from wanting a war over religion.[20] But events ran ahead of Rudolf. In 1581 Calvinists took over the city of Aachen, in northwestern Germany, and suppressed Catholicism. Rudolf tolerated the situation for seventeen years. Eventually, bound to safeguard the Peace of Augsburg, in 1598 he sent Spanish troops to Aachen to restore Catholic rule.

In that same year, some of the empire's Catholic princes tried to pass a measure in the Imperial Diet restoring to the Catholic Church all lands that had been seized by Protestant rulers—Lutheran and Calvinist alike—for the previous forty-six years. The proposal failed. But, coupled with the Catholic invasion of Aachen, it was enough to change the way Lutherans thought about their situation. They began to sense a Catholic threat to all Protestants, not just Calvinists. Lutherans began to boycott imperial meetings out of protest.

Protestant-Catholic polarization continued in 1607 when Lutherans, in violation of the Augsburg Peace, attempted to prevent a Catholic procession in the southern city of Donauwörth. With Rudolf's approval, Bavarian (Catholic) troops invaded the city and threw out its Lutheran rulers.

Two years later Lutheran and Calvinist princes and cities coalesced into a Protestant Union. In the following year, 1610, a Catholic League was formed in response.[21] (It may be that the Lutheran von Hoënegg's strident anti-Calvinist tracts were partly in response to these moves.) The situation the Habsburgs had worked so hard to avoid—a monolithic, hostile Protestantism—was now taking shape.

Rudolf died in 1612, and his successor Matthias tried to conciliate the Protestants. But Matthias was old, and his cousin Ferdinand, a much more militant Catholic, was elected his successor while Matthias was still alive. In 1618 Calvinists in Bohemia revolted against Habsburg rule, intending to set up a separate Protestant kingdom. Catholic troops invaded to put down the rebellion. The Protestant Union counter-intervened. The rest, sad to say, is history: the conflict spread and the miserable Thirty Years' War, already recalled in Lesson 1, was the result.

What is the lesson of this history? Starting in 1555 the Habsburgs treated Protestantism as a polylith, and for more than four decades they nurtured enmity between Lutherans and Calvinists. But in the longer term the vulpine divide-and-rule strategy failed and may even have backfired.

So far, we have seen that playing the hedgehog (lumping all adherents of an ideology together) can work for a time, as can playing the fox (splitting ideologues). Both approaches also bring risks. Indeed, both ultimately failed. The larger lesson is that there is often no ultimate solution to the problems presented by an ideology that one opposes. Not, at least, until that ideology fades away, a possibility we address in Lessons 5 and 6. For now, let us move forward several centuries to see how one great power played the fox-hedgehog game more subtly and managed to succeed.

Communists and Socialists

During most of the twentieth century the United States confronted what we can broadly call the modern political Left. By "Left" we mean, roughly, an ideology hostile to free-market capitalism, the economic system exemplified and propagated by the United States, and that called for complete or significant state control of the means of production. American leaders faced the question: should the Left be treated as monolith or polylith? If polylith, where precisely did one stone in the monument end, so to speak, and another begin? What were the fault lines separating communists and socialists, and could some be used against others?

The modern Left had been divided ever since the collapse in 1876 of the International Workingmen's Association or "First International." The International, founded by Marx and Engels themselves, was destroyed by theoretical disagreements between anarchists and socialists over whether the state—a central coercive authority—was necessary to bring about common ownership of resources (socialists said yes, anarchists no). The Second International, organized in 1889, settled that dispute by excluding anarchists. But its members likewise did not take long to split over strategy: Was it better to take over the state through parliamentary institutions, as the French and many Germans wanted, or through revolution, as the Russian and other German socialists wanted?

The reform-versus-revolution divide became a wide fissure as the First World War began in August 1914. In Germany, then in France, socialist parties in national legislatures voted overwhelmingly to extend war credits to the governments of their countries. Marxism taught that "the worker has no country," but August 1914 proved that actual workers and their political parties did not see it that way. Radical socialists from various countries saw these parliamentary socialists as sellouts. The hard-liners met in Zimmerwald, Switzerland, a year later but found that even they were divided over whether to call for a general strike across Europe.

These amoeba-like divisions on the Left convinced one charismatic, driven hard-liner, V. I. Lenin, that what was needed to bring about true socialism was a disciplined, hierarchical, centralized party to resist the seductions of bourgeois nationalism. Thus was born the Bolshevik movement in Russia. The Bolsheviks seized power in November 1917, during the Russian Revolution, established the Soviet Union, and created the Third International (or Communist International).

Bolsheviks or communists loathed socialists, as seen by the exquisite insults they routinely hurled at them: right-deviationist, revisionist, opportunist, social-fascist, running dog, lickspittle, and so on.[22] The official Leninist line was that democratic socialists were fooling themselves. In working within "bourgeois" (liberal-democratic) regimes, socialists were co-opted by the capitalists and were only delaying the arrival of true socialism. Democratic socialists, meanwhile, were divided over the proper attitude toward the Bolsheviks and revolution. In 1935 the British social scientists Sidney and Beatrice Webb published *Soviet Communism: A New Civilisation?*, which embraced the general Bolshevik model while criticizing its more blatant coercion. Others in the British Labour Party shunned communists and wanted something more like Franklin Roosevelt's New Deal, which saw itself as taming capitalism rather than replacing it.[23]

Further fissures were to emerge within communism itself. Joseph Stalin became dictator of the Soviet Union and purged most of the old Bolsheviks, including Leon Trotsky, who established the Fourth International. In 1948 Josip Broz Tito, communist strongman in Yugoslavia, broke with Stalin. In the late 1950s Maoist China and the Soviet Union began to fall out. In Lesson 4, which concerns whether ideological states behave rationally, we analyze the division between Maoism and Soviet communism, which proved to be highly consequential indeed.

Now, however, we look back at a somewhat different Cold War quandary that faced the United States: how to respond to, and perhaps exploit, relations between communists and social democrats in Europe following the Second World War. To Americans adamantly opposed to any deviation from a laissez-faire economy, all of the Left was unacceptable. But America had its own Left, galvanized in support of Franklin Roosevelt's New Deal. The American Left was to the right even of the most moderate European socialists, but many American Leftists—labor unionists, academics, clergy, journalists, and others—had contact with their counterparts across the sea. To them, the divisions in the European Left—between democratic socialists and communists, and among communists themselves—were meaningful, even crucial. They treated the Europeans in various ways, sometimes lumping, sometimes splitting.

How to Treat the Socialists? The Late 1940s

In the immediate aftermath of the war, communism in Europe was effectively monolithic. The vast majority of communists were doctrinaire and obedient Stalinists. Many communist leaders—such as Maurice Thorez of France and Palmiro Togliatti of Italy—had spent the war in the Soviet Union. The communist movement enjoyed broad public prestige. Communists had been among the most dedicated antifascists during the war—starting in June 1941, when Germany invaded the Soviet Union. The Soviet Union itself was riding high. It had broken the back of Nazi Germany at Stalingrad in 1943 and repulsed the largest military invasion in history. From VE Day onward, in Germany, Italy, France, Belgium, and across Eastern Europe, communists were prominent in labor unions and promised relief and equity for the masses.

There were at the same time popular Marxist and other Leftist parties that were not communist. European socialists were a mixed group. All were affiliated with the Second International, from which Lenin and the communists had defected back in 1916. All were generally hostile to capitalism and wanted the state to own the means of industrial production and (for some) finance as well. But in 1945 socialists took varying attitudes toward communism. Some, such as the Socialist Party of Italy (PSI), were in lockstep with communist parties. Others, such as the British Labour Party, were led by anticommunists such as Clement Atlee and Ernest Bevin.

The Truman administration recognized these intricate divisions and was remarkably nimble in dealing with Western European socialists. Harry Truman was a Democrat, and with his Fair Deal was determined to go beyond the New Deal of his predecessor Franklin Roosevelt. But even Fair Deal Democrats were to the political right of European socialists, and the Democratic Party was not affiliated with the Socialist International. Even so, Truman Democrats not only did not regard the larger Left as a monolith: they did not regard the socialists (the noncommunists) as monolithic. Instead, they paid close attention to how closely aligned various socialists were with communists (and hence the Kremlin). Let us look briefly at three cases: Italy, France, and Germany.

Italy: No Daylight between Socialists and Communists

Among European socialist parties, that of Italy (the PSI) sat at the extreme Left. Although the PSI and the Italian Communist Party (PCI) were institutionally separate, in the late 1940s both were pro-Stalin and anti-American. Pietro Nenni, head of the PSI, aligned his party with the PCI at the end of the war because the latter had abandoned its commitment to a Bolshevik-style revolution and committed to achieving socialism through democratic institutions. Palmiro Togliatti, the communist leader, had made this historic change of strategy because U.S. and British troops occupied Italy and presumably would not tolerate revolution.

The PCI-PSI Popular Front that formed in 1946 was a significant threat to U.S. goals for the postwar order in Italy and Europe. Togliatti and Nenni pledged to cooperate in building a "workers' state." They opposed Italy's receiving the millions of dollars of aid the Americans were offering—the Marshall Plan—and any tilt toward the Anglo-American bloc of states that was already forming. Some anti-Stalinist Italian socialists, led by Giuseppe Saragat, split off and formed the Italian Socialist Workers' Party in 1947; their departure cemented the PSI-PCI bloc.[24]

Both the PSI and PCI had large followings, especially in Italy's industrial north. In the nationwide election of June 1946 to select a constituent assembly to write a new constitution, the Popular Front received 40 percent of the vote (roughly 20 percent apiece for the PSI and PCI), while the nearest competitor, the Christian Democrats, received 35 percent.[25]

The result was trouble for the United States: the pro-Soviet Popular Front had beaten the pro-American Christian Democrats. At this point the Truman administration might have tried the polylithic strategy of hiving the PSI off from the PCI. But American officials judged that impossible. Instead, recognizing the Italian Left as a monolith, Washington focused on preventing the Popular Front from winning the crucial elections of April 1948, which would elect the new Italian Republic's first government. The U.S. Congress approved six hundred million dollars in aid to Italy and France (which also had a strong communist party). The CIA received ten million in funds, which it used to help local organizations to make sure conservative voters turned out on election day.[26]

In the end, the Christian Democrats prevailed over the Popular Front in a landslide.[27] Crucial to the Italian Left's defeat in 1948 were the communist seizure of power in Czechoslovakia two months before the election and the refusal by Nenni and Togliatti alike to condemn it. The Czechoslovak communist party had been part of a democratically elected coalition government, but in February it had engineered a coup d'état. Italian voters asked: if communists did that in Prague, why would they not do the same in Rome? The silence of the PCI and PSI was answer enough for a majority of Italy's voters.[28]

Truman treated the Italian Left as a monolith beholden to Moscow. It was the right policy because the Italian Left was in fact monolithic at the time. And Italy's socialists paid the price.[29] The PSI was shut out of the Italian governments until the 1960s.

France: America Works with the Socialists

The story was different in France. In the early years after the war three French parties dominated elections. In legislative elections in October 1945, the communists (PCF) gained a plurality with 26 percent. In second place was the Center-Right Popular Republican Movement (MRP) with 24 percent, and then the Socialist Party (PS) with 23 percent. Just over a year later, the communists held their numbers, while the MRP raised its percentage to 28 percent and the PS fell slightly to 21 percent.[30]

Like their Italian comrades, the French communists were Stalinist, wanted to align France with the Soviet Union, and intended to take power through France's reconstituted republican institutions rather than through revolution or coup d'état. In Washington, the Truman administration was determined to keep communists out of France's government as far as possible.

But here the similarity with Italy ended. In France, the Center-Right was not reading from the American page. Truman's general European strategy included rebuilding Germany into a bulwark against Soviet communism. With memories of two world wars still vivid, the MRP categorically repudiated any plan to rearm Germany. General Charles de Gaulle, who had led the Free French during the war, was outside the MRP and had a political following of his own. But he too was adamant about Germany. U.S. officials worried as well that de Gaulle tended toward fascism; and besides, de Gaulle had been an impetuous, unreliable ally to the Americans during the war.[31] The French Center-Right, unlike its Italian counterpart, was not interested in signing up to American hegemony in Europe.

What was the United States to do about France? As it happened, the French socialist party—the SFIO or, literally, the French Section of the Worker's International—was not in lockstep with the communists. The party did have a history of cooperating with the PCF. Under the leadership of Léon Blum, it had joined the communists in 1936 to form a Popular Front government. But that government had dissolved quickly when Blum refused to help another such Popular Front, that of Spain, in that country's horrific civil war. Later imprisoned by the Germans in Dachau during the war, Blum emerged after France's liberation as the socialists' elder statesman. Still dedicated to bringing about public ownership of the means of production,[32] Blum now distanced his SFIO party from communism and sought to prevent France from veering to the far left or far right.

Blum decided to throw his party's lot in with the Americans. In 1946 the old socialist spent nearly two months in the United States. The State Department warmed to him, noting that he was more "flexible" regarding the rebuilding of Germany than either the communists or the Gaullists.

Blum's relatively pro-American stance created space for Americans to distinguish him from France's communists. As one American journalist put it at the time, "A Wall Street banker might feel that France is too far to the left for his liking and might resent the French nationalization program. But he would agree that there are different brands of Socialism and that if France went bankrupt she would be likely to opt for the Russian brand."[33] In other words: Americans do not like socialism, but Blum is a socialist we can work with; and if we do not, we will drive the French socialists into the arms of the communists.

More recently, a historian has written, "[S]o powerful did the United States view her communist opponents that she never tried to isolate the entire French left or the entire French working class as she might be wont to do in other situations. Instead the Americans decided to rely most heavily on the socialists and non-communist union leaders rather than on elements more to the right. Their only hope was to use the left to fight the left, ultimately to split the left."[34] The Truman administration recognized a genuine split on the French Left and, with skill and patience, made the most of it.

Germany's SPD: A Plague on Both Superpowers

The West German case was something yet again. The Social Democratic Party of Germany (SPD) was Europe's oldest socialist party. Kurt Schumacher, the SPD's leader until his death in 1952, was equal parts anticommunist (and anti-Soviet) and anticapitalist (and anti-American). A man of undoubted courage, veteran of twelve years in Nazi concentration camps, Schumacher saw himself and his party as the true representatives of the German workers. As a socialist, Schumacher believed those interests sharply opposed to those of the owning classes who, as he saw the matter, ruled the United States. Schumacher thus sought a united, neutral, socialist, democratic Germany, neither penetrated by Anglo-American financial and commercial interests nor allied with the United States, but at the same time neither in thrall to the Communist International (Comintern) nor allied with the Soviet Union.[35]

Officials in the Truman administration worried that Schumacher was an authoritarian socialist and maintained an aloofness from him. They threw U.S. support behind his Christian Democratic rival, Konrad Adenauer, who—like the Italian Christian Democrats—was pro-American. But American elites do not appear to have lumped Schumacher's SPD with the German communists.[36] They knew that Schumacher was anti-Stalinist. The Truman administration simply found the man impossible to work with, similar to the Center-Right de Gaulle of France.[37]

In sum, in the aftermath of the Second World War the Americans did not treat the European Left as a monolith. They recognized differences between communists (uniformly anti-American) and socialists (heterogeneous). Truman administration officials paid attention to whether European socialists co-alesced with communists, and also to their respective attitudes toward the United States and the Soviet Union. In the Italian case, there was no question of working with socialists. In the German case, but for different reasons, the same was true. But in France, the socialists turned out to be anticommunist and open to accepting American leadership.

Foxes, Hedgehogs, and Islamists

What are the lessons of all of this Western history for the United States in deal-ing with Islamists today? Ought outsiders to treat Islamism as monolith or polylith, to play hedgehog or fox?

Let us distinguish moderate from radical Islamists, in a descriptive sense. Moderates we define as Islamists who are publicly committed to using peace-ful, legal means to bring about Sharia. Examples are the AK Party in Turkey and the Ennahda Party in Tunisia. These are parties that compete to win fair elections, who serve in legislatures alongside secularist Muslims and non-Muslims, and who disavow terrorism. A leading Arab moderate Islamist, Yusuf al-Qaradawi, has written, "[W]hoever contemplates the essence of de-mocracy finds that it accords with the essence of Islam." Qaradawi, the leading intellectual in Egypt's Muslim Brotherhood, harshly condemned the al-Qaeda attacks of September 11, 2001.[38]

Radicals we define as Islamists who are committed to violence and other-wise coercive means to effect Sharia. Examples are al-Qaeda, the Taliban, and the ruling regime in Iran. Radicals and moderates are typically at daggers drawn. The rivalry and mutual condemnation between the Egyptian Muslim Brotherhood and its offshoot al-Qaeda is legendary among Arabs.[39]

Note that, defined in this way, *moderate Islamists are not liberals*—liberals, after all, must oppose Sharia—but may be democrats and may favor the rule of law. Note also that we can be certain neither that moderates will forever main-tain their commitments to peaceful, legal means, nor that they will be pro-American in the future. "Moderate" does not mean "good" or "like us" (who-ever "we" may be). It simply means Islamists who have made a strategic choice against violence. Dealing with moderates entails some risk. Of course, so does refusing to deal with them.

Hedgehogs

The United States could follow the script of Europe's absolute monarchies of the first half of the nineteenth century and play the hedgehog. Two centuries ago the absolutists treated moderates (constitutional monarchists) and radicals (republicans) as virtually the same—dangerous enemies of social order. Constitutionalists, they said, were a Trojan horse who would usher in republicanism, revolution, chaos, and general war.

Following a hedgehog strategy with Islamists would mean lumping moderate and radical Islamists together and opposing both wherever they appeared. It is, essentially, the policy called for by Daniel Pipes. For Pipes and others, the end (Sharia) is much more consequential than the means (law *versus* violence). A consistent application of this policy would entail not cooperating, ever, with the Muslim Brothers in Egypt, or Syria, or Tunisia, or Libya, or anywhere else. Indeed, it would mean more distance from moderate Islamists in Iraq and Afghanistan. A monolithic policy would be ideologically consistent and clear, and true to America's liberal principles.

When used by conservatives against liberals nearly two centuries ago, this kind of monolithic strategy worked for several decades. It worked in the sense that the absolutists were able to quash the various waves of liberal rebellion that broke over Europe from 1820 through 1848. But that was because the absolutists could invade and conquer the unstable states of Europe at little cost. Toppling a republic in Rome or even a constitutional monarchy in Spain was not difficult for the massive armies of Austria or France. Had these regimes lacked the muscle to enforce their wishes, lumping all liberals together would have been much harder. Conservatives might well have been forced to make distinctions among liberals, and reach out to at least some moderate constitutionalists.

The United States has learned just how costly it is to effect full regime change in Muslim countries today. It has the capability to conquer the military of Turkey and oust the regime in Ankara, but would find it horribly costly to set up a new, sustainable secular regime. Of course, that is one reason why the very idea of America's invading Turkey is absurd. Yet, the very absurdity of forcible regime change in a large, moderate Islamist country suggests that treating all Islamists as enemies is a bad bet. If we must live with these regimes and we have undeniable enemies—al-Qaeda, for example—history teaches that it makes more sense to seek cooperation with some of the moderates.

Crazy Like a Fox

How to be a fox, but a prudent one, is not straightforward, however. Academics are fond of the idea of finding and working with moderates. But history teaches that distinguishing moderates from radicals is not always easy and sometimes proves self-defeating in the long run. In the Europe of four hundred fifty years ago the Catholic Habsburgs played the fox, cooperating with moderates (Lutherans) and excluding radicals (Calvinists). This polylithic strategy worked for several decades but, as recounted above, ultimately failed.

Calvinism continued to thrive even under Catholic persecution and Lutheran exclusion. And some of the Habsburgs' fellow Catholics, outside of their control, essentially pushed the Lutherans into the embrace of the Calvinists. The two Protestant rivals began to coalesce, and in 1618 the Habsburgs ended up facing a larger and more united Protestant enemy than had ever existed.

The United States has been dealing with moderate Islamists, assuming—or hoping—that they would not coalesce with radicals and could be cultivated into a more pro-Western stance. As noted earlier in this chapter, since 2002 Turkey has been governed by the Justice and Development (AK) Party. The AK Party has Islamist roots and is clearly moving Turkey at least somewhat off of its historic secularist path. Thus far Turkey remains a U.S. ally as a full member of NATO. It continues close military cooperation with the United States by, for example, joining in the annual Eager Lion exercises.[40] Playing the fox—continuing to treat Turkey as a moderate Islamist state, with little in common with radical Islamists—seems the prudent policy.

Western history, however, teaches that America should be cautious. Turkish foreign policy has defied U.S. wishes in several arenas in recent years—most obviously in the Iraq War that began in 2003, and also in encouraging private actors to break the multinational embargo against Hamas-ruled Gaza. Turkey's foreign minister, Ahmet Davutoğlu, has laid out a new vision for Turkey, saying that it is no longer "a 'wing country' under NATO's strategic framework," but is going to be flying on its own more. Davutoğlu envisages a Turkey with "zero problems" with its neighbors, equally friendly to Russia, Arab states, and Iran as with the European Union and United States.[41]

The United States faced an even more perplexing situation during the brief Islamist government in Egypt in 2012–13. Since Egypt flipped from being a Soviet client to being an American one in the 1970s under Anwar Sadat, Washington had counted on its secular-authoritarian regime to maintain the peace with Israel and generally support U.S. policy in the Middle East. Egypt's president in 2012–13, Mohamed Morsi, hailed from the Muslim Brotherhood, a moderate Islamist group (indeed, the world's first Islamist movement, founded in 1928). For years the Muslim Brothers or Ikhwan have been committed to working through nonviolent means, and are adversaries of the radical jihadists of al-Qaeda. Political scientist Marc Lynch argues that al-Qaeda and the Muslim Brothers differ not only regarding means, but also ends. Al-Qaeda repudiates the notion of separate nation-states and works for a reunited Islamic empire that will rule the world. The Muslim Brothers would be content with separate nation-states.[42]

The Obama administration labored not to spoil relations with the short-lived Islamist Egypt. It was surely significant that Egypt, like Turkey, participated in Eager Lion 2012.[43] But Morsi made clear that Egyptian foreign policy would change. He made conciliatory gestures toward Iran. Under Hosni Mubarak Egypt had supported the secularist Palestinian Authority, which has a peace treaty with Israel, and undermined Hamas, which remains committed to Israel's destruction. Hamas, which rules the Gaza Strip, developed out of the Palestinian Muslim Brotherhood, and there were signs that under Morsi Egypt was going to realign and support Hamas. Like the Catholic Habsburgs dealing with moderate and radical Protestants 450 years ago, the United States feared it could find itself facing an Ikhwan Union in the Middle East.

Be Like Truman

Such a Union is conceivable, but far from inevitable. Whether moderate Islamists coalesce with radicals and form a monolith depends in part on how outsiders, especially the United States, treat them. The most useful historical lesson is probably the most recent: that of America's own post–World War II dealings with the Left in Europe. The Truman administration was willing to work with European socialists, even though they were to the left of even its own New Deal–oriented Democratic Party. But Truman officials paid close attention to how anti- or pro-American various West European socialist parties were. When they encountered pro-Soviet socialists, as in Italy, they would not work with them. When they encountered (sufficiently) pro-American socialists, as in France, they worked with them. When they encountered determinedly neutral socialists, as in Germany, they were cordial but aloof and worked with more cooperative parties.

As in other questions of U.S. foreign policy, when it comes to Islamists, America's leaders could do much worse than to be like Truman. A Truman-esque policy would be a version of a polylithic strategy, but a subtle version: recognize that some Islamists are moderate, and be open to cultivating and working with them; but pay close attention to whether the moderates' vision for regional order is compatible with that of the United States. Of course, Truman may have been lucky in that he always found a viable pro-U.S. party: in Italy and West Germany the Christian Democrats, in France the Socialists. Perhaps in some Muslim countries no such politically viable parties are available. As regards Israel in particular, one principle common to moderate and extreme Islamists alike is hostility to Zionism or the very idea of a Jewish state.

The importance of the question is seen in the contradictory reports about a "Grand Bargain" that some allege Iran offered to the United States in 2003. Hillary and Flynt Leverett, Trita Parsi, and other Iran specialists claim that, following the toppling of Saddam Hussein in neighboring Iraq, Iranian President Mohammad Khatami approached the George W. Bush administration via the Swiss ambassador with an offer to resolve all outstanding issues between Iran and America, including Iran's nuclear program, its support for Hezbollah and Hamas, and the Palestinian problem. Parsi writes that Secretary of State Colin Powell was interested, but others, including Vice President Richard Cheney, dismissed the approach.[44] Other officials at the time, however—American and Iranian—have heaped scorn on the seriousness and even the authenticity of the offer.[45] In the Bush administration some were hedgehogs, but even the foxes were not sure whether there really was daylight between the moderate Khatami and Iran's hard-liners.

It is striking, however, that in the late 1940s, somehow or other, the United States always found leaders and parties willing to work with it—and correspondingly skeptical of or hostile to the Soviet Union. It took careful cultivation over time—the French socialist Léon Blum spent two months in the United States—which does show that, up to a point, how one treats leaders of an ideological group can affect how monolithic that group is.

This raises the interesting case of Saudi Arabia, the world's strictest Islamist regime—and an absolute monarchy—yet a longtime economic and security partner of the United States. The Saudis are far from being pro-Israel, but their jihadist enemies are correct: in practice the royals of Riyadh have never lifted a finger against Israel and, with the significant exception of the 1973 oil embargo, have been one of the chief supporters of U.S. hegemony in the Persian Gulf. If rigid Islamists can be, in effect, pro-American, it stands to reason that moderate Islamists can be as well.

We close, however, by repeating a caution. Marc Lynch points out that even moderate Islamists are Islamists, not liberals. Across Arab countries, the Muslim Brotherhood really does aim to make Sharia the law of the land. Such a regime can never sit comfortably alongside modern Western notions of human rights. And hence, even if AK Party–governed Turkey maintains stable good relations with the United States, and even if America and the Islamic Republic of Iran were to enter a period of détente, relations will not be perfectly harmonious. History teaches that neither side should expect them to be.

Lesson 3
Foreign Interventions Are Normal

We have a chance to support a real new beginning in the Muslim
world—a new beginning of accountable governments that can provide
services and opportunities for their citizens in ways that could dramatically decrease support for terrorist groups and violent extremism.
—Anne-Marie Slaughter, March 2011

Iran must instill its Islamic system among Arab nations with
the concept of religious democracy.
—Ayatollah Ali Khamenei, September 2011

"Libya's none of our business," Ron Paul, Republican candidate for president
and longtime congressman, told a journalist in June 2011. Paul was referring
to the bombing campaign by the United States, France, and Great Britain that
began the previous March to protect rebels against the dictatorship of Muam-
mar Qaddafi.

Representative Paul was not alone: as the bombing began, 70 percent of
Americans opposed the introduction of ground troops into Libya.[1] Comedian
Jon Stewart, oracle for an entire generation of Americans, questioned the wisdom of attacking Qaddafi while U.S. forces already were fighting in Afghanistan and Iraq: "You know, wars aren't kids," Stewart shouted to his appreciative
audience, "where you don't have to pay attention to the youngest one because
the older two will take care of it."[2]

But the bombing campaign—Operations Odyssey Dawn and Unified Protector—proceeded, and ultimately helped the rebels oust Qaddafi from power. The three NATO allies, in other words, militarily intervened and were instrumental to regime change in Libya. Jon Stewart was at least right that this was the third such intervention involving American forces. Why does the United States engage in these sorts of interventions so often?

The American people certainly were interested in the Arab Spring, especially in early 2011. In late January and early February, as the Egyptian revolution reached a climax, U.S. ratings of most network and cable news shows decreased slightly, while the number of American viewers of the Al Jazeera website increased fivefold.[3] For hundreds of thousands of Americans, it was as if the Arab Spring blossoming in Tunisia, Egypt, Libya, Syria, and elsewhere was not just about citizens of those countries, or Arabs, or even Muslims, but all of us. No doubt many Americans felt they had some kind of moral stake in what was happening in the Middle East. These were oppressed people risking their lives to overthrow repressive regimes. Americans tend to identify foreigners' struggles against oppression with their own country's founders' fight against British colonialism and despotism. In 1989 their attention was riveted to television screens showing the fall of communist regimes in Eastern Europe. In the 1810s and 1820s they thrilled to news of Spanish colonies in Latin America freeing themselves from Spain and Portugal and setting up new republics.

The call by Anne-Marie Slaughter, former head of policy planning in the U.S. State Department, for intervention in Libya may sound like pure idealism—"We have a chance to support a real new beginning in the Muslim world—a new beginning of accountable governments that can provide services and opportunities for their citizens." Here, say many critics, is where the cause of American foreign policy activism lies. Some analysts have claimed that the United States is peculiarly likely to do these sorts of interventions because of its broad liberal tradition. Political scientist Michael Desch argues that American Liberalism—an ideology of "individual freedom, equality of opportunity, free markets, and political representativeness"—drives the country toward crusading when, as in recent years, no foreign power is capable of constraining the United States.[4] Others argue that U.S. foreign policy has lately been captured by ideological crusaders. Tony Smith, another political scientist, warns, "There are liberal extremists afoot in the land, liberal jihadists we might say. In the war on terrorism they are calling for liberalism to become a form of fundamentalism . . . a faith militant, a holy war."[5]

The inference is that America is peculiarly likely to concern itself with the domestic affairs of other countries. It is curious, then, that Iran's supreme leader evinces the same kind of concern: "Iran must instill its Islamic system among Arab nations with the concept of religious democracy." Evidently the impulse to help foreigners attain what you have is not confined to Americans.

Indeed, America is far from being the only country that uses force to change other countries' domestic regimes or leaders. More than two hundred such interventions have been attempted by great powers over the past five hundred years—one every two and a half years. Other liberal democracies have done it (France and Britain included, and not just in Libya in 2011). Communist and fascist states have done it, as have monarchies, Catholic and Protestant states, and Islamist ones. And the vast majority of those interventions took place during region-wide legitimacy crises and ideological struggles, like the one the Middle East is experiencing.[6]

Furthermore, interveners usually have not only idealistic motives but self-interested ones. Put simply, when one or more countries is undergoing civil unrest that could produce a regime change, outside countries often have a *strategic* or *material* stake in the outcome. Slaughter does not stop with the selfless desire to help Libyans gain self-government: democracy, she claims, "could dramatically decrease support for terrorism and violent extremism." She is voicing a bipartisan conviction that the United States is better off—more secure—the more foreign countries have democratic governments.

Iran's case is parallel. Ayatollah Khamenei's call for "religious democracy" sounds entirely principled, but it was clear that the regime in Tehran was hoping that the Arab Spring would produce Iranian-style regimes that would increase Iran's influence in the Arab world. Iran's regime had long-standing ties with various national chapters of the Muslim Brotherhood, a Sunni Islamist group founded in Egypt in 1928. Back in 1979 the Egyptian Muslim Brothers loudly welcomed Iran's Islamist revolution.[7]

Iran also saw the Arab Spring in terms of its long-standing strategy to empower Shia Muslims in other countries, a strategy that derives from the notion that Shias will be more open to Iranian influence. Thus did Arab monarchies accuse Iran of stirring up the Shia revolt in tiny Bahrain, a monarchy just across the Gulf from Iran, ruled by a Sunni dynasty but a majority of whose population is Shia. Tehran denied any involvement, but clearly Iran, which officially considers Bahrain a "lost province," had an interest in that country's switching from a Sunni to a Shia-Islamist regime.[8] The Shia uprising in Bahrain drew a Saudi-led invasion by the Gulf Cooperation Council, an organization of Sunni monarchies of varying flavors of Islamism.

A mirror-image case was Syria, where Bashar al-Assad's regime fell into civil war against various factions of the country's Sunni Muslim majority. The Assad regime is secular but ethnically Alawite. The Alawites are an offshoot of Shia Islam, and Iran backed Assad against the rebellion by training Syrian forces in suppression techniques and pressing Lebanese Hezbollah to fight for the Alawite regime.[9] Meanwhile Syria's regime was roundly opposed by the Saudis and the other Sunni-Islamist states, which no doubt made it easier for the Arab League to condemn Assad's savage repression of the rebellion.[10]

In both Bahrain and Syria, Iran's rulers supported whichever party was Shia. As political scientist Vali Nasr noted, the Arab Spring was entangled in the cold war between Iran and Saudi Arabia, its longtime rival for the status of leading Islamist exemplar.[11] The United States has strategic interests that line up fairly closely with those of its client Saudi Arabia—the U.S. Navy's Fifth Fleet is headquartered in Bahrain—but the Obama administration was publicly unhappy with the Saudi-led suppression of the Bahraini uprising.

Little surprise, then, that although the United States has not intervened directly in Syria, there have been strong arguments from some leaders that it should do so, and that many of those arguments had to do with the opportunity to remove a key Iranian ally. In the U.S. Senate, John McCain, Lindsey Graham, and Joseph Lieberman were the most vocal supporters of intervention. They cited the human cost of Assad's brutal war, but also the material stake for the United States: "Assad is the number one ally in the Arab world of Iran," said Lieberman, "and Iran is the greatest threat to stability in the region and beyond the region at this point."[12]

Political Islam did not cause the Arab Spring. The chain of revolts and revolutions that began in Tunisia in December 2010 and spread over North Africa and into Southwest Asia were the products of deep discontent across Arab societies with failed authoritarian regimes. But as history shows, the causes of revolutions are not necessarily good predictors of their outcomes. Revolutions are typically propelled by coalitions of people who have in common only the conviction that the status quo regime is irredeemably bad and that the probability of toppling it unusually high. Only after a regime is ousted do ideological cleavages reappear.[13]

That leads us to Lesson 3: When a region is torn by ideological strife, expect foreign interventions. By "intervention" I mean any policy designed to affect the internal affairs of another state. Joseph Nye offers a spectrum of foreign interventions, ranging from the most benign (public speeches) to the most lethal (military invasion). In between are policies such as economic aid, support of opposition, and blockades.[14] All of these types of action—including military invasion—are to be expected in regions that are crisscrossed by a contest among ideologies. Although foreign interventions also can happen when such contests are absent, when they are present outsiders often find intervention irresistible.

Such interventions may be badly done, adorned with crusading rhetoric, and even truly motivated by idealism. But they may still be, in a sense, rational. Sometimes they may even work to the intervening country's advantage. Foreigners often perceive material stakes in the outcome of the struggle in various countries. They perceive these stakes, in the end, because the struggles are transnational—that is, taking place in more than one country at once. The competition between secularists and Islamists has existed across Muslim countries for many decades, and the competition in one country has not been sealed off from that in other countries. Instead, participants have seen the triumph of Islamism in one country as affecting its prospects in other countries. The Iranian Revolution of 1979 encouraged Islamists and alarmed secularists all over the region. Their respective national struggles are interdependent.

The same was true of ideological struggles in the history of the West: they have been transnational in this strong sense, and they have triggered many foreign interventions. Western history suggests that these foreign interventions take place for one of two reasons—or sometimes both.

First, the future of the intervening states' own regimes may hang in the balance. In 1789 a liberal revolution broke out in France; in 1791 a similar one erupted in Poland, and the Polish rebels proclaimed that they had been inspired by the French. The following year Catherine the Great of Russia sent troops to put down the Polish revolution. A year later Frederick William of Prussia sent troops to join the Russians. Both monarchs feared that the revolution was infecting their own lands and must be halted.

Second, when a country has a revolution its foreign policies and alignments can change, sometimes radically. The year after the Polish revolution, the young French Republic declared war on Austria and Prussia. Frederick William of Prussia feared not only that revolution would spread from Poland to his lands, but also that a new Polish Republic would join France in warring against him. Prussian security and the balance of power in Europe were implicated in the Polish revolution.

Just so, Lebanese journalist Rami Khouri has noted that the Arab Spring was bound to affect the balance of power between the two Islamist exemplars, Saudi Arabia (Sunni) and Iran (Shia); the cold war between the two states that glower at each other across the Persian Gulf was aggravated by the rebellions and repressions across the region precisely because each of them had sympathizers in some of the states.[15] This dynamic affected the interests of faraway countries as well, including in the West. The Obama administration was acutely aware that the fall of the Mubarak regime in Egypt or the al Khalifa monarchy in Bahrain might well move those countries out of the "American ally" column, precisely because the Islamists who stood to gain in both of those countries looked less kindly upon American power and influence.[16]

Sometimes both of these problems—revolutionary contagion and the balance of power—are present. Governments typically understand the stakes well, and often try to influence the outcomes of insurrections and revolutions.

They use economic sanctions, covert action, and, sometimes, outright military intervention to try to overturn (or preserve) a revolution. The clash of ideas in the Middle East is not only a contest for power cloaked in ideological language. But make no mistake: power is at stake in the prolonged struggle among Muslims over the best regime—the power of various Muslim elites, but also of outsiders, including the United States.

In what follows, we shall see that in all three of our historic cases—the early European Catholic-Protestant struggle, the later monarchical-republican struggle, and the twentieth-century communism-fascism-democracy contest—these same dynamics were at work. The cases show that although ideology and crusading impulses were often evident, foreign interventions were sometimes rational under the circumstances.[17] We begin with the middle case, focusing on the French Revolution of 1789 and its effects on the international balance of power, especially as regarded France's archrival Great Britain.

Edmund Burke, Britain, and France's "Armed Doctrine," 1790–99

For most of his political career, Edmund Burke (1729–97) seemed one of the least likely British politicians to oppose a revolution defending the "rights of man" such as the one that erupted in France in 1789. The Anglo-Irish man of letters, legendary in the British House of Commons for his rhetorical power, was a Whig—a member of the party dedicated to limiting the power of the monarch. In the 1770s Burke sided with Britain's restive North American colonists, defending their right to be taxed only by their own colonial assemblies and not by the Parliament in Westminster. "Seek Peace, and ensue it," Burke declared to the House of Commons in 1774. "Leave America, if she has taxable matter in her, to tax herself."[18] In 1776 Burke labeled capital punishment "the Butchery which we call justice."[19] In the 1780s he defended South Asians from the unrestrained rule of Britain's representative: "Arbitrary power," Burke averred, "is a thing which neither any man can hold nor any man can give. No man can lawfully govern himself according to his own will; much less can one person be governed by the will of another." Most significantly, Burke argued that the rule of law is a universal right: "all dominion of man over man . . . is bound by the eternal laws of Him that give it, with which no human authority can dispense."[20]

But then came July 1789, the outbreak of the French Revolution. The revolution excited liberals all over Europe and the Americas. For these politicians, publicists, and clergy, what was happening in France was very much their business. They wanted the revolution in France to succeed because they wanted a similar upheaval in their own country. On November 4, 1789, the Unitarian Rev. Dr. Richard Price exhorted his congregation, "Be encouraged, all ye friends of freedom. . . . Behold, the light you have struck out, after setting America free, reflected to France, and there kindled into a blaze that lays despotism into ashes, and warms and illuminates Europe!"[21] A breathless Thomas Paine, the masterful pamphleteer of the American Revolution, wrote Burke, his political ally, "The revolution in France is certainly a Forerunner to other Revolutions in Europe.—Politically considered it is a new Mode of forming Alliances affirmatively with Countries and negatively with Courts."[22]

To the astonishment of his friends, Burke did not even remotely see it that way. From the start he hated the French Revolution because it was a *revolution*, a violent overturning of the institutions of society. And precisely because it excited such fervor in Britain and elsewhere, the revolution in France genuinely alarmed him. He devoted the remainder of his life to warning against the revolution and its debasing and violent effects.

For Price and Paine on the Left, and Burke (now) on the Right, then, the revolution in France was not just about France. It was about Britain: its institutions, its way of life, its stability, and its national security and power. When the French Republic declared war on Britain in early 1793, so-called Radicals—Paine, Price, and others—began to press the government of William Pitt the Younger to negotiate peace. Burke, meanwhile, urged Pitt not only to prosecute the war but also to state publicly that it sought to reverse the revolution and restore France's monarchy.

Burke had two worries. The first is evident in his very language: it was not the "French Revolution" but the "revolution in France."[23] The revolution was not only French: *potential* revolutions were all over Europe. There were signs that Britain's time was coming. Burke loved British life and institutions as they were; that political upheaval would cross the English Channel was a repulsive thought. "Formerly," he writes to his French correspondent, "your affairs were your own concern only. We felt for them as men; but we kept aloof from them, because we were not citizens of France. But when we see the model held up to ourselves, we must feel as Englishmen, and feeling, we must provide as Englishmen. Your affairs, in spite of us, are made a part of our interest; so far at least as to keep at a distance your panacea, or your plague."[24]

Burke's second fear was that the revolution posed a threat to Britain's global position and national security. British security could be compromised in at least two ways. First, Britain depended on the independence and stability of the German states as a buffer against the eastern powers of Austria and Prussia. (No united Germany existed at the time.) Revolutionary principles were infecting the German states and sowing chaos; that infection might lure Austria and Prussia into an alliance that would partition German-speaking Europe among the two of them and form a terrible combination that could invade England. The second threat was more direct: the revolution was increasing France's national power by energizing and mobilizing its once inert population. As the late Christopher Hitchens has pointed out, Burke even predicted—correctly—that France would degenerate into a military dictatorship (as it did nine years later with the infamous coup d'état of Napoleon Bonaparte).[25] By the end of 1791 Burke declared, "The Revolution was made, not to make France free, but to make her formidable."[26] France already was annexing some old territories, and was poised to try to exploit its influence in various European lands to become an empire.[27]

Edmund Burke did not speak for every Englishman. Liberals and radicals—those who found France's system most appealing—wanted peace and wanted to leave the decision about the French regime to the French.[28] But Burke won the debate: the official British war aims did include regime change in France, although British cabinets were hazy as to what they wanted to replace the republic with.

The years following the French Revolution saw a great deal of foreign intervention *both* by Britain *and* by France. Interventions happened in part because public opinion was so heavily polarized across Europe concerning the revolution. Most people were either very much in favor of revolution, or vehemently opposed to it; there was little middle ground. This polarization gave both the French and their foes, including the British, Fifth Columns—sympathizers eager to rise up and fight with them—in a number of countries. Starting in 1795 France's armies exploited these Fifth Columns by invading various smaller states—the Netherlands, Switzerland, and various Italian states—and setting up republics that in turn were so loyal to France that they became virtual satellite states. The infectiousness of the revolution enabled France to build a European empire and to gain extra resources that fed its war machine. The British did the same with their own less extensive but very real Fifth Columns. In 1794 they invaded Corsica and, in cooperation with Pasquale Paoli, set up a constitutional monarchy that became their ally.[29]

Twenty years later, after Burke had died and Napoleon had risen, nearly conquered all of Europe, then finally been defeated by a multinational coalition, the British and their allies finally did as Burke had wanted and reestablished the old Bourbon monarchy in France. Indeed, in smaller European states where French armies had imposed republican regimes in the 1790s or Bonapartist (bureaucratic-authoritarian) regimes in the 1800s, the allies also favored the restoration of old royalty. As we saw in Lesson 1, the policy of the victors was to rout not simply France's armies, but the very ideology that had inspired those armies and that they had spread and sustained. The Republican Spring of the 1790s and the Napoleonic Winter that followed it were far from being only about France. They were about the power and interests of most other European states and rulers. What happened within France and other countries—their revolts, revolutions, and restorations—was very much their business, and that is why they intervened so often.

Democracy Promotion in Europe and Soviet-American Rivalry, 1945–49

If the liberal Edmund Burke seemed an unlikely enemy of the French Revolution, a U.S. Army general may seem an unlikely person to steer the democratization of West Germany more than a century and a half later. But General Lucius Clay of Georgia was just that man.

General Clay, deputy governor of the U.S. occupation zone in Germany following the defeat of the Nazi regime, wanted a democratic, free-market Germany not only because he believed in democracy and free markets and liked Germans. He also became convinced that America had a concrete security interest in the democratization of Germany. Indeed, he only began pressing his superiors for democratization when he became convinced that it was a useful tool in helping America compete with the Soviet Union.

The American stake in a democratic-capitalist Germany sprang from two related facts: a Soviet-American rivalry was emerging, and deep ideological divisions ran through most of the countries of Europe. U.S., British, and Canadian forces had invaded and occupied Germany from the West. The Soviet Red Army had done so from the east. By the spring of 1945 the Soviets occupied the nations of Central Europe and a large zone in eastern Germany. Across all of these countries people were highly polarized according to ideology. Ever since the Russian Revolution of 1917 much of the world, including Europe, had been in what political scientist Carl Friedrich called a "revolutionary situation" in which communism, fascism, and democratic capitalism vied for supremacy.[30] The devastation of the war meant that governments were weak, stakes were high, and trust among ideological groups was low. Some people felt stronger ties to foreigners with whom they shared an ideology—say, Italian and French communists—than to countrymen with whom they did not.

Lucius Clay understood that this ideological polarization meant that the ideological winner in Germany would decide Germany's foreign alignments and hence the balance of power in Europe. A communist Germany would be a

Soviet ally. A democratic Germany would lean toward the United States and the West.

Not all U.S. policy makers saw things as Clay did, at least not at first. Up to his death in April 1945, President Franklin D. Roosevelt hoped that the United States and Soviet Union would not be rivals. FDR also was hazy regarding the postwar fate of Germany. At the close of the second world war in twenty-five years, the most urgent problem to the president was how to make sure Germany never started another war. At the Tehran Conference of 1943 Roosevelt had agreed with Winston Churchill and Joseph Stalin that Germany would permanently be divided. FDR's treasury secretary, Henry Morgenthau, pressed for a "Carthaginian" peace, the destruction of all German industrial capacity and the imposition of a permanently agrarian society. A Joint Chiefs of Staff memorandum from April 1945 stated, "Germany will not be occupied for the purpose of liberation but as a defeated enemy nation. . . . The principal Allied objective is to prevent Germany from ever again becoming a threat to the peace of the world."[31] FDR and his advisors did understand that the Soviet Union was newly powerful and a potential future problem for America. But they wanted to reassure the Soviets that the United States did not threaten them.[32]

Other leaders, however—Winston Churchill and U.S. diplomat George Kennan among them—were already focused on Soviet power as the West's biggest problem. They saw that defeated Germany still had its strategic assets: a large, educated population, huge industrial capacity, and strategic location. Germany, they thought, could be a bulwark against the Red Army and Soviet power. But they disagreed as to what to do with Germany. Kennan had in mind a kind of soft authoritarian regime, something like the rule of Antonio Salazar in Portugal. Hull, the secretary of state, wanted to rehabilitate Germany as a liberal, market-oriented democracy.[33] Hull and his group eventually won the debate when General Clay convinced enough players in Washington that making Germany a democracy would make it a strong and faithful ally.

The Soviets had their own plan for Germany, much like the Morgenthau Plan: keep it divided and weak permanently. At the same time, the Kremlin was working to promote communism in Western Europe by infiltrating labor unions. Stalin hoped the unions would control the parties of the political Left in France, Italy, and elsewhere, which in turn would exploit the devastated condition of Europe to take power and establish communist regimes under Soviet influence or control.

In May 1946 the Soviet strategy suffered a setback as the French Communist Party lost a referendum on France's new constitution. Vyacheslav Molotov, the Soviet foreign minister, decided that the plan to make France communist had failed and that the Soviets should focus on Germany. The Kremlin decided to try to make Germany into a united, communist-dominated country obedient to the Soviet Union. But with most of Germany occupied by the Western powers, the Soviets knew that they could not simply take over the country. They decided to wage a charm offensive. In June Molotov announced that the Kremlin had reversed its harsh German policy: now the Soviets favored a reunited, reindustrialized Germany.[34]

Clay, who had quietly been promoting democracy in the American zone, quickly understood what Molotov was doing. The Soviets were making a bid for the hearts and minds of Germans, with the ultimate goal of folding all of Germany into an emerging communist bloc. The threat was serious, because the German Left—consisting of the communist and socialist parties—was powerful. Before Hitler took power in 1933, the two parties together had routinely drawn between 40 and 50 percent of the vote. Now within their occupation zone the Soviets merged those two parties into the Socialist Unity Party, in hopes that the communists and socialists in the Western zones would follow suit and form one German-wide pro-Soviet party.[35]

Seeing the Soviet pincers closing, Clay urged James Byrnes, now U.S. secretary of state, to make a countermove: America should declare, Clay said, that its goal is a united *democratic* Germany. As his biographer writes, Clay "was convinced that a united Germany could be attained and that liberal, democratic values would ultimately prevail. The result would be to extend Western influence to the Soviet zone and bring Poland and Czechoslovakia into direct contact with democratic ideas."[36]

Some high officials in the State and War Departments opposed Clay's plan, and in August he came close to resigning. But he finally persuaded Byrnes. In a speech in September Byrnes declared an American reversal: from now on America was going to reconstruct a self-governing, democratic Germany.[37] The United States was doing the right thing, but for reasons that were decidedly strategic.

Because most of Europe was ideologically polarized just as Germany was, the Soviets and the Americans had similar incentives to interfere in other countries. Each superpower knew that if its system prevailed in a given country, that country would likely be its ally. Hence a chain reaction of foreign regime promotions and impositions was set off in Europe and East Asia after the war. Soviet impositions of communism in Poland, East Germany, Hungary, Czechoslovakia, Romania, and Bulgaria amounted to expansions of Soviet power and influence. Americans in turn felt compelled to make sure that democratic capitalism triumphed in Italy and France, so that those countries would be U.S. allies. These dueling regime promotions fed off one another and helped to intensify Soviet-American rivalry and to bring about the Cold War.

Stalin, who understood the connection between ideology and power as few have before or since, saw the future of Europe before most. It was in April

1945 that he declaimed to Tito, the communist leader in Yugoslavia, "This war is not as in the past; whoever occupies a territory also imposes on it his own social system. Everyone imposes his own system as far as his army can reach. It cannot be otherwise."[38]

Table 3.1 makes the point clear: Soviet and American promotions of communism and democracy yielded geopolitical dividends. Europe in the late 1940s was in at least one respect just as it had been in the time of the French Revolution: in the throes of an ideological contest, in which people across many nations were highly polarized as to the best system of government. And which system of government one favored was a good predictor of which foreign power one wanted to align with. Each European country was an ideological battleground with geopolitical stakes. But in the 1940s the European struggle was not only about Europe: the two new superpowers, the Soviet Union and United States, one on either side of Europe, had significant stakes in which ideology won. Where communism triumphed, the Soviets would have more influence and power. Where democratic capitalism triumphed, the Americans would enjoy hegemony. That is why Europe after the war was such a laboratory for foreign intervention.

The promotions of democracy in West Germany, as well as Japan and Italy, are often cited as some of America's greatest successes, both moral and practical. Rightly so: since 1945 average Japanese, German, and Italian citizens all have been better off economically and politically than at any time in history. But they also have been some of America's most crucial and loyal security (and

Table 3.1.
Foreign interventions and realignments in Europe, 1945–50

Dates	State	Winning intervener	Realignment toward intervener?
1944–47	Italy	United States	Yes
1944–46	Bulgaria	Soviet Union	Yes
1945	Poland	Soviet Union	Yes
1945	Yugoslavia	Soviet Union	Yes/no[a]
1945–47	Hungary	Soviet Union	Yes
1945–48	Romania	Soviet Union	Yes
1945–49	East Germany	Soviet Union	Yes
1945–49	West Germany	United States	Yes
1948	Czechoslovakia	Soviet Union	Yes

Source: *Encyclopædia Britannica* (1997).
a. Yugoslavia and the Soviet Union broke with each other in 1948.

economic) partners. The outcome was stated nicely by Italy's ambassador to France in June 1948: "The reality is that, like all the other countries of Europe, we have ceased to be independent. . . . We are as free to approach Russia as Poland is to approach the United States."[39] Precisely: it was crucial to American security that Italy and Germany be capitalist democracies, because then they would recoil from the very idea of aligning with Soviet Russia. When a region is torn by ideology, expect foreign interventions.

A True Outsider: A Muslim Superpower and Europe's Warring Christians, Sixteenth and Seventeenth Centuries

Neither the 1790s nor the 1940s captures a crucial feature of the Islamist-secularist struggle today, and in particular the stake that outsiders have in that struggle. In those historic cases, the geopolitical powers that intervened so often in other countries' domestic ideological battles were very much ideological insiders. France exemplified the republicanism that it sought to spread. The Soviet Union exemplified communism, and the United States, democratic capitalism.

But when it comes to the Middle East today, the United States—as well as the rest of the West, India, Russia, China, and other outside powers—are truly *outsiders*, in the cultural and ideological sense. The ongoing legitimacy crisis in Muslim societies is about *Muslim societies*—societies whose majority practice Islam. Radical Islamist terrorism remains a threat to American life and property, but Islamism is no threat to the American constitutional order. The U.S. population is only roughly 1 percent Muslim. That figure will likely rise to 1.7 percent by 2030, but even 1.7 percent is a tiny minority.[40] Notwithstanding the fears of some, Sharia is not coming to America.[41]

Furthermore, notwithstanding the insistence of others, conservative Christians are not joined with Islamists in some kind of "religious international." For years Americans have been debating the proper relation of church to state, with a "religious right" pitted against a "secular left."[42] But neither side seeks to change the American regime in any fundamental sense. All sides accept the U.S. Constitution's First Amendment prohibition of the establishment of religion and guarantee of the free exercise thereof. The American Religious Right and Middle Eastern Islamists may share complaints about secularism and decadence, but "Christianists" and Islamists do not form a global political movement; indeed, conservative Christians are among the most anti-Islamic of Americans. A victory for Islamism (or secularism) in the Middle East would not affect the culture wars in the United States.[43]

History does kindly offer us at least one example of a region undergoing ideological strife and a genuinely outside power with material stakes in the outcome of that strife. The example is ironic.

In the Europe of five hundred years ago, it was the Christian world that was torn by ideological strife and the Muslim world that had a stable ruling regime—the Ottoman Empire. Based in Europe's periphery, in what is now Turkey, the Ottoman Empire was generally acknowledged to be the caliphate or universal Islamic empire. And just as the United States today has serious material interests in parts of the Middle East, particularly the oil-rich Middle East, the Muslim superpower five centuries ago had serious security and economic stakes in the Mediterranean Sea and Southeastern Europe.

The Ottoman emperors or sultans regarded themselves as successors to the caesars and destined to reunite the Roman Empire.[44] Their ambition was not delusional. In 1453 Sultan Mehmed II conquered Constantinople, capital of the Byzantine or Eastern Roman Empire for more than a millennium.[45] With a strategic foothold in Europe, Mehmed's armies went on to conquer Serbia, Greece, and Wallachia over the next decade. Ottoman forces made frequent attacks on Hungary as well, and the Ottoman navy vied with Venice for supremacy in the eastern Mediterranean.[46] The greatest sultan of all was Suleyman the Magnificent (1494–1566). Change a few words, and Suleyman's proclamations might make a suitable prologue to the autobiography of Donald Trump: "I, who am the Sultan of Sultans, the King of Kings, the Distributor of crowns to the princes of this world, the Shadow of God upon earth, the Supreme Sovereign of the White Sea and Black Sea, of Roumelia, Anatolia, and of the countries subjugated by my own triumphant sword."[47]

Suleyman conquered Belgrade in 1521 and Rhodes in 1522. Venice, Europe's leading commercial power of the time, decided to stop fighting the Turks and signed a treaty with the sultan. The Ottomans were to dominate the eastern Mediterranean until 1571. Over the following century and a half Ottoman armies were to conquer what are now Romania and Hungary and to besiege Vienna twice.

The Turks were deeply interested in the progress and outcome of the Catholic-Protestant contest in Europe that began in 1517. Because the Reformation scrambled political authority in Europe, it presented threats and opportunities to the Ottoman sultans. The Ottomans thus had strong incentives to shape the outcome of the intra-Christian struggle. For their part, European Christians were torn about accepting Turkish help. They regarded the Muslim infidels as a grave long-term threat. It also was politically and theologically incorrect for them to be seen cooperating with the Turks.

So the Ottomans never directly intervened in the Reformation-Counter-Reformation struggle by force. They did, however, put their thumb on the scales in various indirect ways. They opened diplomatic relations with various Protestant princes and entertained thoughts of treaties. In using force against the Catholic Habsburgs they gave the Reformation breathing space at crucial points and became partly responsible for the survival and flourishing of Protestantism.

The Ottomans' Incentives to Intervene

The Ottomans' stake in Europe's Catholic-Protestant strife arose from their intense rivalry with another claimant to be successor to the Roman emperors: the House of Habsburg, which ruled the Holy Roman Empire (roughly modern Germany), Spain, and vast portions of the New World. At various times in the sixteenth and seventeenth centuries the Habsburgs bid for supremacy on the Italian Peninsula and farther east in Europe. The two early modern empires, Habsburg and Ottoman, pressed against each other in Southeastern Europe and in the Mediterranean. Their enduring rivalry gave the Ottomans an interest in the success of the Protestant reformers. The Protestants, after all, had the potential to drive a stake into the heart of Habsburg power by dividing and perhaps dissolving the Holy Roman Empire. In that interest, the Ottoman sultans were like the kings of France, the Habsburgs' other chief rivals. Indeed, the French and Turks signed a treaty in 1526 and coordinated attacks on the Habsburgs two years later—the French from the west, the Ottomans from the east.[48] Sultans also cooperated with other Catholic rulers, including those of the Republic of Venice and the princes of Hungary.

Ottoman sultans reached out to German Lutherans and Dutch Calvinists at various points, proposing cooperation against the common Habsburg foe. Interest sometimes ran in the opposite direction as well. William of Orange, leader of the Calvinist Dutch Revolt against Catholic Spain, sent an envoy in 1569 to Selim, heir apparent to the Ottoman throne, proposing an alliance against the Habsburgs.[49] The Ottomans did not respond right away, but at some point in the 1570s sent a letter from Suleyman I to the "Lutheran" sect in Flanders—he almost certainly meant the Calvinists—praising their religion and proposing making common cause against the Spanish "papists."[50]

No Ottoman-Dutch treaty was ever signed, but the Turks provided indirect help to the Dutch Calvinists. In 1572 a Mediterranean naval battle between the Ottomans and Philip of Spain drew the Spanish navy away from the Netherlands, allowing the "Sea Beggars," Calvinist privateers, to capture the key port of Brill; from Brill they were able to capture more towns and territory.[51] Little wonder that the Sea Beggars had as their slogan "Liever Turks dan Paaps" ("rather a Turk than a Papist"). Their banners were red—the Turkish color—and even featured a crescent, symbol of Islam.[52]

In similar fashion, the Protestant realm of England sought aid from the Ottomans against Spain. The Ottomans did not grant it, but there is evidence that rumors of an Ottoman-English alliance kept in the Mediterranean some of Philip's ships that otherwise might have been part of the Armada whose failed attempt to invade England in 1588 lives in infamy.[53]

Bad Optics

Although the Dutch and English Protestants sought Turkish aid, dealing with the Muslim superpower was a sensitive matter for early modern Christians. That brings us to another striking similarity between then and now. Muslims today are loath to cooperate openly with outsiders, particularly the United States, because many are convinced that America is waging war on Islam. Just so, early modern Protestants were loath to be seen cooperating with the "unspeakable Turk," who was generally believed by Christians to be bent on eliminating Christianity.

All Europeans understood that working with the infidel Turk involved both high risk and bad optics. At least since Muslim rulers had expelled Christians from Jerusalem in 1009, triggering the infamous wave of Crusades, Islam had been the "Other" for Christians, the enemy against which Christendom was defined. Islamic doctrine taught that the religion of Muhammad had superseded Christianity, which it regarded as a flawed and corrupted religion. Muslims denied the divinity of Christ and the doctrine of the Trinity (that God exists in three persons, Father, Son, and Holy Spirit). Islam's champion, the Ottoman sultan, had begun to conquer parts of Christendom. Europeans knew that the Ottomans permitted Christians in lands they conquered to continue to practice their religion. But they regarded this toleration as a sham because of the Ottoman practice of removing young boys from their families and indoctrinating them into Islam in order to make them into dedicated soldiers of the sultan. The Turkish siege of Vienna in 1529 convinced Germans in particular that the Ottomans were bent on wiping out Christianity and imposing Islam everywhere.[54]

That Christians were not to cooperate with Muslims helps explain the ambivalence of Europe's Protestants regarding cooperation with the Ottomans. From the early 1520s Lutheran princes feared—prophetically, as it turned out—that some day the Habsburgs would make war on them to force them back into the Catholic fold.[55] In the early years, when struggling to achieve toleration from Holy Roman Emperor Charles V, the Lutherans knew that the Ottoman threat gave them leverage. The Habsburgs—particularly Charles's brother Ferdinand, responsible for the family's Eastern European lands—sometimes needed Lutheran help to defend their southeastern flank against the Turks. The most acute threat came in 1532, when Turkish armies were outside the gates of Vienna itself. In refusing to help their Catholic lords, the Lutheran princes risked accusations of aiding the Muslim infidel against Christendom.

They also wrestled with their own consciences. Lutheran pamphlets from the time disclose a belief that the sultan and the pope were equally bad, both tools of Satan against the faithful Christians. Islam, they made clear, was a false religion. They regarded Francis of France as a traitor to Christendom for treating with the sultan.[56] But Lutheran views of the Ottomans were softer than those of many Catholic Europeans. The Lutherans regarded the sultan as the "scourge of God," commissioned by him to punish Christendom for its apostasy, rather like pagan kings were used by God, according to the Bible, to chastise ancient Israel for its sins. Luther himself, in his 1529 pamphlet *On the War against the Turks*, called on the Lutheran princes to join Charles in war to repulse the Muslim armies. But he decried the notion of a crusade—as if human armies could defend Christ—and called instead for a "just war" of defense; that is, Luther did not want German armies to drive the Turks out of Eastern Europe and reclaim those lands for Christendom.[57]

The Outsider's Indirect Effects

The Lutheran princes never signed a treaty with the sultan. But they did exploit the Ottoman threat to gain concessions from the Habsburgs. Their chief short-term goal was toleration of Lutheran teaching, practice, and evangelism within Germany. That meant an official imperial declaration of toleration of Lutheran teaching, practice, and evangelism. In the long term, they sought a council of the Church, Lutheran and Catholic alike, to be held (they hoped) in Germany. The Lutherans were confident that such a general council would favor their position and result in a Lutheran-inflected reform of the Catholic Church.

The periodic Ottoman invasions and rumored invasions provided the Lutherans with a stout lever to use against the Catholics. In the summer of 1526, with Turkish armies threatening Hungary—a buffer between the Ottoman and Holy Roman Empires—the Lutherans refused to help the Habsburgs save Hungary unless they were granted immediate toleration and the pledge of an ecumenical Church council. The Habsburgs gave in, and the German princes sent twenty-four thousand troops to Hungary to help repulse the Turks. (It was too little too late, as the Turks triumphed at the Battle of Mohacs.) Nearly three years later, in February 1529, Lutheran troops help lift the Ottoman siege of Vienna.

The following year the Habsburgs, feeling more confident, once again outlawed Lutheranism. The year after, in 1531, with Charles and his brother Ferdinand fearing another Turkish invasion, the Lutherans again refused to help the Habsburgs defend Hungary or Vienna unless their terms were granted. Charles and Ferdinand once again gave in, and the religious peace of Nuremberg (July 1531) guaranteed the Lutherans toleration and their long-sought general Church council.[58] Charles was able to make war on the German Lutherans only when he finally signed a treaty to the Turks in 1545.[59]

The Ottoman superpower, then, had no religious or ideological stake in the Catholic-Protestant strife of the sixteenth century. It intervened, in the minimal sense, nonetheless because it had material stakes. For religious reasons the Protestants were ambivalent about whether to accept Muslim help. In the end, what limited intervening the Turks did was significant enough to help ensure the survival of Protestantism.

Back to the Present:
Islamism, Secularism, and Foreign Intervention

In today's world, the tables are turned: it is the Muslim is world divided by ideology and outside powers that have found it tempting to intervene. That is because the situation is similar in many ways to that in the Western world in the mid-sixteenth, late eighteenth, and mid-twentieth centuries. In regions where people are deeply divided as to the best way or order society, governments have strategic interests in which people and ideologies rule various states. Thus outsiders have incentives to intervene in other states' internal affairs by covert action or by overt force. Ideological contenders in a potential target also have an incentive to invite foreign intervention, but sometimes—as when the foreigner is from a different culture or religion—they are ambivalent and make it harder for the outsider to intervene directly.

Some of the foreign intervention in the Middle East has been by other Muslim governments. In the 1950s and 1960s the secular Arab socialism of Gamal Abdel Nasser spread via military and other elite networks from Egypt to other Arab countries. Nasserists tried to overthrow the Saudi monarchy in 1955 and the allied Ba'athist movement succeeded in overthrowing the Iraqi monarchy in 1958. That same year Ba'athist Syria merged with Egypt to form the United Arab Republic. In 1962 Nasserists began a civil war in North Yemen to bring down the new king. Egyptian troops invaded to help the Yemeni Nasserists; by 1964 Egyptian troops numbered forty thousand. The Saudis and British counter-intervened on behalf of the Yemeni monarchy.[60] Sometimes called "Nasser's Vietnam," the Yemeni civil dragged on until 1970.[61]

The destructive Iran-Iraq War of the 1980s is another example. The revolution in Iran that toppled the shah in 1979 and set up the Ayatollah Khomeini's Islamic Republic agitated Shia Muslims in Iraq, where Khomeini himself had lived in exile for many years. Saddam Hussein, the secular Ba'athist dictator of Iraq, decided to roll back the Iranian revolution, and in response the Khomeinists in Iran determined to overthrow him. In September 1980 fifty thousand Iraqi troops invaded Iran. In the ensuing decade-long war neither government overthrew the other, but as many as a million and a half people died.[62] And of course non-Muslim powers have intervened in the intra-Muslim contests as well. The Soviet invasion and occupation of Afghanistan that began in 1979 was intended to buttress a secular (communist) regime against an Islamist insurgency. In turn, the United States, Saudi Arabia, and Pakistan joined forces to help the Islamist mujahedin against the Soviets. The Soviet failure and withdrawal, and American loss of interest, enabled the radical Islamist Taliban to take control of most of Afghanistan in the 1990s. Within a few years, following the al-Qaeda terrorist attacks on America, the U.S. government overthrew the Taliban by force. Then there are the plentiful covert interventions by Americans, British, Soviets, Israelis, French, and others in Muslim lands over many decades.

The other post-9/11 case, the Iraq War, is more complex. Saddam Hussein's Ba'athist regime had no role in 9/11 and remained the archenemy of Islamist Iran. The causes of the Iraq War, like those of any war, are complex, but it is clear that the Bush administration had as one of its war aims the establishment of liberal democracy in Iraq and, as it hoped, the subsequent domino-like fall of Islamist and authoritarian regimes throughout the Muslim Middle East.[63] Various political scientists regard as a significant motivation the Bush administration's wish to affect the ongoing ideological struggle in the region.[64] In both of these cases, the Americans (and to an extent their allies) cared a great deal about the regime type of the target state, enough to spend a great deal of blood and treasure to change it.

All of these foreign interventions in Muslims' struggles are controversial. Many may well have detracted from the national interest of the interveners. But it is wrong to assert, as realists typically do, that foreign interventions in the ideological squabbles of other countries or cultures are always irrational—simple bursts of crusading hysteria rather than clear-eyed statecraft. Outbreaks of revolt and waves of revolution and repression rejigger the ideas and interests of the countries going through them. They create new opportunities and threats for outsiders to make new friends or avoid the emergence of new enemies. The history of the long bouts of ideological strife in the West makes abundantly clear that outsiders have powerful incentives to intervene and that, unless those incentives are overridden by other interests, they will do so. External intervention is not a separate, foolish, and avoidable addition to the Islamism-secularism struggle. It is part and parcel of that struggle.

Lesson 4
A State May Be Rational and Ideological at the Same Time

A better comparison for Iran than the Soviet Union might be Japan of World War II—another martyrdom-obsessed, non-Western culture with global ambitions. It should call into question the view that Iran operates according to a pragmatic estimate of its own interests.
—*Bret Stephens, July 2010*

We are of the opinion that the Iranian regime is a rational actor.
—*General Martin Dempsey, chairman, U.S. Joint Chiefs of Staff, February 2012*

No doubt that the Iranian regime is maybe not exactly rational based on what I call Western thinking, but no doubt they are considering all the implications of their actions.
—*Meir Dagan, former Mossad chief, March 2012*

Islamism is an ideology of more than just turbaned clerics and chanting mobs of angry young men. Neither is it only an exotic glue that holds together terrorist cells and transnational networks of jihadists. It is, in fact, the ruling ideology of several countries. Saudi Arabia and Iran—rivals for leadership of the movement—are the two most prominent. Sudan is another. Still other countries are governed by Islamist parties striving to implement Sharia, at least in certain areas of law and by legal means. Of these, Turkey is most prominent.

In non-Muslim countries, including the United States, the question often arises: *Are Islamist states, or their governments, rational?* Should any post–Arab Spring countries become dominated by Muslim Brotherhood parties, will those countries follow traditional Realpolitik, maintain peace with Israel, and undermine Islamist militants in Palestinian territories? Or will they instead become ideological, like those Palestinian militants, break the treaty with Israel, renew the specter of war, and work for a radical new order in the region?

What about Turkey under the Justice and Development Party? Is America's NATO ally, once exemplar of secularism in the Middle East, casting aside its Realpolitik tradition in pursuit of fanaticism? Do Ankara's recent policy shifts in favor of Hamas in the Gaza Strip, and Islamist movements in the Arab world more generally, presage an ideological foreign policy? Does the grand vision of Turkey's policy mandarins include some kind of reconstituted caliphate, with Turkey again in the lead?

Or what of Pakistan? Founded in 1947 as a secular Muslim state, Pakistan officially moved in an Islamist direction in the 1970s. Parts of its territory are virtually governed by strict Salafists. Its military intelligence bureau, the ISI (Inter-Services Intelligence), is shot through with Islamists. Opinion polls show the vast majority of Pakistanis believe that their laws should derive directly from Islam. Should Islamists take over the country, what would they do with the country's nuclear arsenal, which outside experts say numbers between 90 and 110 warheads?[1]

And can the Islamic Republic of Iran ever become a moderate country, a good international citizen, as long as it retains its Islamist regime and its religiously minded leaders? Is a country with a domestic order based upon rigid, otherworldly dogma always recklessly going to pursue revolutionary goals and endanger peace? Is Iran so fanatical that it would attack Israel with nuclear weapons, even though it knows that Israel itself probably has at least a hundred nuclear warheads of its own that it could fire back?[2]

As with so many questions about political Islam, the debate over whether Islamist states are rational or fanatical is confused and confusing. One source of the confusion has afflicted statesmen in past times trying to deal with Western countries that professed a particular ideology, be it political Calvinism, republicanism, or communism. Statesmen facing such states often have failed to distinguish ideological states' *means* from their *ends*. The result is that they often miss an important possibility: a state may appear irrational to outsiders, but may be rationally pursuing goals shaped by its ideology.

Take Iran since the revolution of 1979. To say the least, the Islamic Republic has behaved in ways that baffle and offend many of its neighbors, to say nothing of Western countries including the United States. It seized fifty-two American hostages at the U.S. embassy in Tehran in 1979 and held them for 444 days. It fought a futile, destructive war for a decade with neighboring Iraq. It funds terrorists and at various times has refused to cooperate with the United Nations' International Atomic Energy Agency (IAEA), feeding suspicions that it is developing nuclear weapons and daring Israel and the United States to bomb it.

Why has Iran acted in this way? Some will say that its leaders, and perhaps many of its ordinary people, are irrational, fanatical, gripped and directed by a religious ideology. As the German magazine *Der Spiegel* noted, "during [President Mahmoud Ahmadinejad's] speech before the United Nations in September [2005], in which he raged against what he called America's policy of 'nuclear apartheid' and demanded that his country be entitled to its own full-fledged nuclear program, he even laid claim to enlightenment. Ahmadinejad said he was surrounded by a light while speaking at the UN and the world leaders stared at him 'as if paralyzed.'"[3] Iran's politicians and their mullah masters, on this reading, are living on another planet.

The trouble with the Iran-is-crazy explanation is that, as General Dempsey and Meir Dagan seem to agree, the Iranians clearly have paid attention to their situation. They have monitored how others react to their actions and adjusted their own reactions accordingly. They have displayed what social scientists call instrumental or means-rationality—what the great German sociologist Max Weber termed *Zweckrationalität*.

Some analysts have rolled headlong from the observation that Iran is *instrumentally* rational to assertions that the United States and the rest of the world could, if they were likewise rational, deal with Iran as with any other country. This argument comes in two basic versions.

First, if Iran has acted disagreeably, it is because we act disagreeably toward it. America, as the world's only superpower, has the wherewithal to change the relationship. Stephen Walt writes,

> Right now, the United States and Israel are actively engaged in a variety of covert actions directed against Iran, and the United States still have military forces and bases all around that country. Top U.S. officials, Senators and Congressmen have openly called for "regime change" in Iran. And then we wonder why, oh why, Iran might be wary of us, and why some Iranians might think that having an effective deterrent to counter our vast military superiority might be a good idea.[4]

Flynt and Hillary Leverett present the Islamic Republic as rational, concerned to defend itself from attack and protect its hard-won autonomy from a hostile, meddling, greedy America, yet always prepared to engage with that same America. Indeed, for the Leveretts it is the United States that is ideological, captive to myths about mad mullahs bent on destroying Israel even if they set the region or the world on fire in the process.[5]

Or, second, its actions have been obnoxious to us simply because Iran lives in a dangerous neighborhood and must take extra precautions to protect itself. In the early twentieth century Germans feared *Einkreisung*, encirclement, by hostile powers and in response increased its military strength and propensity to bully. Iran may be in a still more difficult situation. As an unnamed Iranian official put the matter to Fareed Zakaria in 2012,

> But if we were to pursue a nuclear weapons program, would it be so irrational? Look at our neighborhood. Russia has nukes. India has nukes. Pakistan has nukes. China has nukes. And Israel has nukes. Then on one side of our border the United States has 100,000 troops in Iraq. On the other side of our border, the United States has 100,000 troops in Afghanistan. . . . Now, if you were in our position, wouldn't that make you nervous and wouldn't you want to buy some kind of insurance?[6]

The Iranian official could have added that Iran possesses vast oil reserves of great interest to an energy-hungry world; it sits across the Persian Gulf from its archrival Saudi Arabia and, stationed in tiny Bahrain, the U.S. Navy's Fifth Fleet; and, for good measure, to its north is the Caspian Sea, home to a Russian naval fleet.[7] Perhaps it would be irrational of Iran *not* to seek nuclear weapons?[8]

But if the entire problem were that Iran lives in a dangerous neighborhood, then its neighbors should have been acting in similar fashion—defying the IAEA, sponsoring terrorism, directly threatening Israel. But most of them have not. And if all Iran really wants is to be treated well by the United States, then it has been acting *irrationally*. It could have had that place at the table had it ceased defying the United States, threatening Israel, building a nuclear program, and setting itself against the Gulf Arab states. Indeed, it did the first two of these—aligning with America and treating with Israel—under Shah Reza Pahlavi from 1953 until the revolution of 1979. Why have the mullahs not returned to that policy?

Zakaria puts his finger on the most plausible reason why Iran acts as it does: "[Iran's] goals are not ours, of course, but that is a very different point." It is indeed a different point, but one to which we must attend.

Some scholars of international relations argue that analysis must start with states' fundamental goals—in the language of social science, their preferences, or the outcomes they would most like to have.[9] Scholars sometimes distinguish two types of state: *status quo* states, which are content enough with the international system and their place in it not to try to change either; and *revisionist* states, which are not content and want to undermine or overturn the international system and build a new one.[10]

Revisionist states are sometimes seen as irrational because they act so as to violate other states' preferences, which the latter take to be self-evidently reasonable and universal. It is often the case, however, that those revisionist states are rationally—efficiently and prudently—pursuing ends that contradict those of the other states. As we saw in Lesson 3, those ends include safeguarding their own regimes from foreign contagion and Fifth Columns, and making other countries friendlier to their ideology and interests. In other words, it is entirely possible for a state to be at once ideological and rational: ideological in its goals, rational in its means. It also is possible for a state to pursue ideological goals irrationally—that is, in a self-defeating manner, by not monitoring how others respond to it or not adjusting its actions accordingly.

Which of these has been true of Iran? How about other Islamist states? The history of the Western world is replete with ideological revisionist states that bewildered other countries. Some of these states were indeed irrational and self-defeating, at least for a time. Others, however, only seemed irrational to others, when in fact they were rationally pursuing goals that made no sense to those others. Here we consider three: the Palatinate, a German estate in the old Holy Roman Empire; the Soviet Union; and, for good measure, the United States.

A Mouse That Roared: The Palatinate, 1556–1621

Four hundred years ago, Europe had a state that seemed irrational to many, even to some of its friends. The Electoral Palatinate (*Pfalz* in German), a state within the Holy Roman Empire, enjoyed unmatched prestige. Its ruler, the Count Palatine (*Pfalzgraf*), with his majestic Heidelberg Castle, was second-highest ranking secular (nonclerical) prince in the empire, surpassed only by the emperor himself. By tradition dating to the Middle Ages, the count had been one of the more independent princes in the empire, determined to prevent the emperor from amassing too much power. Like so many principalities of the time, the Palatinate was divided into two noncontiguous regions, the Rhenish Palatinate, comprising lands in today's German states of Rhineland-Palatinate and Baden-Württemberg, and the Upper Palatinate, in the eastern part of today's state of Bavaria.

But the Palatinate was, to put it mildly, deeply discontented with the international order of its time and place. It was not an early adopter of Protestantism—only in 1544 did the Pfalzgraf declare Lutheranism the official religion—but when it did convert it displayed the zeal of the late convert, leading its religious brethren in anti-Catholic militancy.[11] In 1559 Frederick III—"the Pious"—became Pfalzgraf. Frederick was a devoted Calvinist, and three of his next four successors became the most determined champions of the Calvinism in all of Europe.[12] Over the next several generations the Palatinate punched well above its weight in European politics.

In 1555, after two major wars, Catholic and Lutheran princes in the Holy Roman Empire agreed to the Religious Peace of Augsburg. Each prince, be he Catholic or Lutheran, had the sole right to determine the religion of his subjects; attempts to change another principality's religion from one to the other became illegal. The trouble was that, as we mentioned in Lesson 3, a newer branch of Protestantism, Calvinism, was not included in the Peace of Augsburg. The treaty gave Lutheran princes a stake in the status quo, but the Palatinate, being Calvinist, had no such stake. Its leaders felt excluded from and threatened by the Augsburg Peace, and set themselves the task of eradicating Catholicism from the Holy Roman Empire and ultimately all of Europe.

As historian Claus-Peter Clasen writes, "From about 1556 up to 1618 Heidelberg Castle remained the centre of militant Protestantism." Frederick III and his successors cared less for maintaining peace in Germany than about spreading the Protestant faith and extirpating Catholicism. "They demanded complete religious liberty for the Protestants in Catholic territories without, however, granting the same rights to Catholic subjects of Protestant Princes. In other words the Palatinate sought to do away with the compromise of 1555. . . . More importantly, they were prepared to use any method including armed force to realize these aims."[13]

In the decades that followed, Lutherans and Catholics did not achieve perfect harmony, but they did work out their differences. When residents of various "ecclesiastical territories"—lands directly ruled by a Catholic bishop—converted to Protestantism, the Lutheran princes at first connived to overthrow those Catholic bishops. But the Catholic princes of the empire steadfastly opposed them, insisting that the Peace of Augsburg be followed. Determined to keep the religious peace, most of the Lutheran princes acquiesced.[14]

The Palatinate's Calvinist rulers responded very differently. In 1583 John Casimir, the regent for Frederick IV, tried to turn Cologne from Catholic to Protestant; no Protestant prince supported him. And the Pfalzgrafen used many other tools against the Catholics. In 1557, 1576, 1582, 1594, and 1597 they tried to persuade the Lutheran princes not to help the Habsburg emperor repulse threats from their common enemy, the Turks. The Lutherans refused. The Pfalzgrafen beseeched the Lutherans to vote against Habsburgs standing for election to the emperor's seat (the emperor was elected, and the Count

Palatinate was one of the seven electors). The Lutheran electors refused. The Pfalzgrafen rejected the jurisdiction of the imperial law courts that were enforcing the 1555 Augsburg Peace. In 1591 Frederick IV himself tried to form an empire-wide Protestant alliance, with no success.[15]

Nor did the Palatinate's rulers limit their anti-Catholic militancy to Germany. Their status as champions of Calvinism gave the Pfalzgrafen admirers and allies among their Calvinist brethren in neighboring states, and they often intervened to help them. In 1568, 1576, and 1587 Palatinate armies crossed into France to help the Huguenots in their war against the Catholics. In 1578 Palatinate troops fought with Dutch Calvinists against the Spanish. In 1568 they midwifed an alliance between German Protestants and England; in 1572, a similar alliance France. Whenever any militant policy was proposed or attempted, it seemed, it came from Heidelberg. "In almost all cases," writes Clasen, "the majority of the German Protestants strongly condemned the Palatine radicalism." The Calvinist-Lutheran differences even extended to the way they wrote about international politics. The Palatines typically wrote of "the advancement of the glory of God and the establishment of his church," while the Lutherans wrote in a secular idiom of "steadfast preservation and propagation of the beloved peace, calm, and unity in our beloved Fatherland of the German nation."[16]

Was the Palatinate irrational, in the grip of religious fanaticism? Many Europeans at the time doubtless thought so. The counts Palatine were unquestionably more militant than the other German Protestants, and one source of that militancy was their Calvinism. Not only was Calvinism at the time more determinedly anti-Catholic in doctrine and teaching; its exclusion from the 1555 Augsburg Peace naturally made the Palatines fearful.[17]

But the Pfalzgrafen were not blind fanatics. For several decades, when they encountered resistance from Catholics or indifference from fellow Protestants, they adjusted their behavior. They probed and prodded only until they met firm resistance. They then would maintain their larger goals, but would resort to different strategies and tactics. The counts Palatine were rational ideologues, pursuing the triumph of Protestantism and elimination of Catholicism in Europe, but doing so through careful calibration of means with ends.

And they had some triumphs. They successfully brokered international Protestant alliances. Their help enabled the Dutch finally to drive out the Spanish and win an independent Calvinist republic. In 1608 the Palatinate managed to persuade other German Protestants to withhold aid to the emperor against the Turks. In the following year the Palatinate finally cobbled together a Protestant Union in the empire.[18] What is more, the Pfalzgrafen enjoyed enormous influence in European politics, particularly among the Calvinists they championed across the Continent. In 1612 Frederick V's daughter married King James I of England. Until 1618 they did all of this without triggering a war.

Descent into Irrationality: Frederick V and Christian of Anhalt

Eventually, however, Palatinate leaders forgot when to stop pushing and prob-ing. It was a lower prince, Christian of Anhalt-Bernburg, and his liege, Pfalzgraf Frederick V (r. 1610–23), who brought on disaster. Christian and his circle of friends were convinced that the Habsburgs were on the verge of destroying Protestantism and establishing a universal Catholic empire. It was Christian who was the main forger of the Protestant Union in 1608. In 1612 he achieved an alliance between the Union and England.

In 1618 Christian finally overreached. The Upper Palatinate, the eastern portion of the state, bordered Bohemia, directly ruled by the Habsburgs and regarded as the heart of their vast empire. In May, when some of his Protestant friends in Bohemia rebelled against the Habsburgs, Christian tried to rally Protestant Europe and France to the rebels' cause. But, afraid to challenge the Habsburgs in such a sensitive spot, even most Calvinists declined to answer the call. The Palatinate was nearly isolated, but Christian charged ahead, engi-neering the election of Frederick V as King of Bohemia. Most of Frederick's advisers, understanding the danger, cautioned him not to accept the Bohe-mian crown without the support of his father-in-law James of England. But Frederick did not consult James and in October 1619 agreed to become king.[19]

The Catholics of the empire, realizing that if Habsburg power collapsed the future of Catholicism in Germany looked in doubt, drew together. Maximilian of Bavaria agreed to fight for his Habsburg rival, Emperor Ferdinand. So did Ferdinand's Spanish Habsburg cousin, Philip III. At the same time, the Protes-tant Union, bedeviled from the start by Lutheran-Calvinist squabbles, split over whether to back Frederick. The emperor bought off a key Lutheran prince, John George of Saxony. Maximilian hammered out a deal with other Protestants. Even within Bohemia, the new King Frederick was proving unpopular. A ma-jority of Bohemian Protestant nobles were Lutheran, and did not take well to the Calvinist Frederick and his plundering of Prague cathedral.[20]

Still Christian and Frederick pressed forward with their gamble to grab Bohemia from the Habsburgs and make it a Protestant kingdom. In November 1620 Catholic forces invaded Bohemia and crushed the revolt, decisively de-feating Christian's Protestant forces at the Battle of White Mountain outside of Prague. The demoralized Bohemian troops scattered. The following June, the Habsburgs publicly executed twenty-six Bohemian noblemen in Prague.[21] Protestantism was outlawed.

The Habsburgs then set out to punish the Palatinate for its impudence. The emperor placed Frederick V under an imperial ban, depriving him and his heirs of all of their lands. Catholic troops marched through Upper Palatinate west to Rhenish Palatinate and its capital Heidelberg. A few Protestant nobles now rallied to Frederick and won a battle at Wiesloch in April 1622. But these Protestant armies, lacking the support of any significant state, were driven to live off of the land. They began extorting food and supplies from German peasants. When the peasantry resisted, the troops turned savage, pillaging and burning. Some Protestant troops scattered, others went to fight elsewhere. Catholic troops besieged the capital city of Heidelberg in the summer of 1622, and on September 16 they stormed the city.[22]

The Calvinist Church of the Palatinate was destroyed. Frederick V fled to the Netherlands, where he lived until his death in 1632. Christian of Anhalt fled to Sweden. The Rhenish Palatinate itself, once prosperous, was laid waste.[23]

The lamentable story of the Electoral Palatinate is complex. It shows that an ideological state may for decades conduct itself prudently, pushing at soft spots and pulling back from hard ones, and achieve some successes. But the story also shows that under some leaders such a state may lose its prudence and take on foolish risks, holding when it should fold and bringing catastrophe upon itself and others. It is difficult to evade the conclusion that, in the end, the Palatinate's ruler became an irrational ideologue.

The Soviet Union:
Evolution of an Ideological State, 1917–89

The Bolsheviks who seized power in Russia in November 1917 always thought of themselves as leaders of a transnational movement. Once a faction of the Russian chapter of the Socialist International, in 1915 the Bolsheviks had broken with socialists in Europe who were not sufficiently militant and who acquiesced in the "bourgeois imperialist" First World War. The Bolsheviks happened to be Russian, for the most part, and the state they captured in 1917 was Russia. But they did not think of themselves as a Russian party. They were internationalists. They cared not for Russia, and even less for the old Romanov Empire, but for the workers of the world.

The Early Years: Radicalism Irrationally Pursued

Thus the Bolsheviks' chief task, as they saw it, was to facilitate similar revolutions around the world. Decades earlier Marx and Engels had predicted that Germany would be the first socialist country, and the Bolsheviks believed that Germany would fall shortly after Russia did, followed by other capitalist-industrial countries in a world revolution. Lenin and his ruling circle not only openly flouted the sovereignty of states upon which international society had been based for nearly three hundred years; they loudly sought to overturn it.[24] The early Soviet Union was radical in its goals and, it turns out, irrational in the means it employed.

In his autobiography Leon Trotsky relates the time when a comrade suggested to Lenin that he appoint the Trotsky head of the People's Commissariat for Foreign Affairs. "What foreign affairs are we now going to have?" asked Lenin. Still, he did appoint Trotsky to the post. Trotsky was elated because he thought the job would involve no work and he thus could pursue what really interested him. As he recalled later, "The Commissariat for Foreign Affairs meant freedom from departmental work for me. [A comrade] later in his memoirs gave a fairly juicy report of a conversation he had with me soon after the Soviet government was formed. 'What diplomatic work is there going to be with us?' I said to him, according to his account. 'Look, I'll just issue a few revolutionary proclamations to [foreign] peoples and shut up shop.'" Robert Service notes that Trotsky was "as good as his word in quickly publishing the Allies' secret treaties of 1915 and calling upon workers around the world to rise up against their governments."[25]

Indeed, the infant Union of Soviet Socialist Republics was quite radical, refusing to deal with sovereign governments—responsible for secret diplomacy, imperialism, and war—and purporting to speak directly to the proletariat across countries. "[T]he proletariat," wrote Trotsky, "is not interested in defending an anachronistic national 'Fatherland' . . . but in the creation of a new, more stable and powerful Fatherland, the republican United States of Europe, as the foundation for the United States of the World." World revolution was inevitable, they believed, and indeed without it their own revolution would have been doomed, because soon the capitalists and their armies were coming for them.[26]

The Bolsheviks' radicalism alarmed governments on both sides of the ongoing Great War in Europe. In January 1918 Robert Lansing, the U.S. Secretary of State, wrote to his boss, President Woodrow Wilson, that "Lenine [sic], Trotsky, and their colleagues are so hostile to the present social order in all countries that I am convinced nothing could be said which could gain their favor or render them amenable to reason."[27]

Pragmatic but Still Radical

The Bolsheviks had a problem, however: the Great War was still raging and the German army was threatening to cut to ribbons their young Soviet Union. While "Left deviationists" such as Nikolai Bukharin resisted, Lenin decided that the Soviet Union must act like a state among states—more precisely, to use the apparatus that they had inherited from the tsar whom they murdered. Lenin said that the revolution needed "breathing space," particularly during the transition from capitalism to socialism. Trotsky ended up conducting more foreign affairs than he had bargained for, founding the Red Army and negotiating the Treaty of Brest-Litovsk with a sovereign government, and a particularly reactionary one: Germany. Brest-Litovsk, signed in March 1918, gave the Bolsheviks that breathing space, but at the cost not only of vast territories but also their claim to have transcended the system of sovereign states.[28]

Even so, the Bolsheviks did not cease being ideological. They retained the goal of spreading revolution via the transnational proletarian class—the working men who, as Marx had said, "have no country."[29] It was not delusional of them to believe that the same conditions that had generated revolution in Russia would do so elsewhere. In January 1918 communists in Finland, inspired by the Bolsheviks, revolted and declared a workers' state. In November, just as the war was ending, Germany was rocked by revolution; in Berlin a Soviet Republic was declared, while in Munich a Bavarian Socialist Republic was announced. In January 1919 communists in Hungary proclaimed a Soviet republic there. In the same month Lenin announced the formation of the Communist International (Comintern), an association of parties across many countries led by the Bolsheviks.[30]

Yet, the world was pushing back against this radical foreign policy, not seen in a great power since the heady days of the French Jacobins in the early 1790s. The other European communist revolutions all failed. The crucial German case was especially consequential, as social democrats—the communists' former allies in the international workers' movement—ruthlessly put down the revolts. And in Russia itself, in 1918 French, British, American, and other groups invaded to try to drive the Bolsheviks from power.

Thus the Bolsheviks learned that they must moderate their means in pursuit of world communism. Given their goal of building communism, Lenin, Trotsky, and company would have been irrational to persist in their original radical tactics. The Soviet Union remained committed to spreading communist revolution, but soon evolved from a self-undermining entity to a prudent one, using traditional tools—an army, navy, and diplomacy—plus the Comintern to achieve its goals.[31]

It was Lenin's eventual successor, Joseph Stalin, firmly in charge of the Soviet Communist Party by 1924, who permanently settled the Soviet Union into its rational revisionist role. Stalin maintained the old slogan of "proletarian internationalism," but added "socialism in one country," signaling that the chief priority was building a new society within the Soviet borders. He married the two principles by redefining them so that they fit naturally. As he stated, "An internationalist is one who is ready to defend the USSR without reservation, without wavering, unconditionally; for the USSR is the base of the world revolutionary movement, and this revolutionary movement cannot be defended and promoted unless the USSR is defended."[32] In a sense, Stalin subordinated communist internationalism to the interests of the Soviet state.

But it would be a mistake to think that the Soviet Union became a "normal," power-seeking state that simply cloaked its quest for security in ideological language. In the words of political scientist Andrew Moravcsik, we must "take preferences seriously."[33] The Soviet Union continued to use its soft power—the appeal of communist ideas, transmitted via the Comintern—to exert leverage over other governments and more generally to improve its international environment.

As recounted in Lesson 1, there were in the West at the time diplomats, academics, merchants, bankers, and others who argued that Western governments could and should normalize relations with the Soviet Union. These self-styled pragmatists believed that Stalin—a dictator by the late 1920s—was a rational actor who would behave normally if treated normally. If ideology was wrecking Soviet-Western relations, they argued, it was not communist ideology but Western anticommunism that was the problem.

The problems with this kind of argument were two. First, it asserted that the West was ideological but the Soviet Union was not. Why would only one side be ideological? Second, it ignored or assumed away that the Soviet Union continued to have revisionist goals. Its very regime was a challenge to the legitimacy and hence stability of a number of European and Asian regimes. The Comintern, and more general appeal of Soviet communism among intellectuals and labor unions in the West, meant that Soviet power was not like other countries' power. Communist transnational strength is seen in the way it generated its opposite totalitarian number, fascism, first in Italy in the early 1920s, then in the 1930s in Germany and elsewhere in Europe and the Americas.[34]

Various Western powers did normalize relations with the Soviet Union—the United States was among the last, in 1933—and the Soviet Union joined the League of Nations in 1934. But Stalin's ongoing use of Soviet soft power—the allure of communism in dozens of countries—meant that the Western powers never could trust him and were wary of allowing Soviet wealth and power to grow. As the U.S. ambassador to Moscow wrote in 1935, "[T]here has been no decrease in the determination of the Soviet Government to produce world revolution. Diplomatic relations with friendly states are not regarded by the Soviet Government as normal friendly relations but 'armistice relations' and it is the conviction of the Soviet Union that this 'armistice' can not possibly be ended by a definite peace but only by a renewal of battle."[35] Thus when the French and British governments faced the rapid military rise of Nazi Germany after 1933, they were more inclined to try to cut a deal with Hitler than with Stalin.[36]

These problems of Soviet soft power and mistrust bedeviled relations between Stalin, on the one hand, and America's Roosevelt and Britain's Churchill, on the other, during the Second World War. The Western leaders generally understood that Stalin was defending Soviet interests, but those interests still entailed promoting communism, now by setting up "friendly"—read communist—governments in those lands that the Red Army liberated from the German army.

Stalin died in 1953, but the Soviet Union continued to be an ideologically shaped revisionist power. It continued to try to spread communism, particularly in the "Third World" of Asia, Africa, and Latin America. The Kremlin's drive to use communism as an instrument of Soviet power was partly responsible for the failure of Soviet-American détente in the 1970s, as the promotion of communism in Africa and then Afghanistan convinced many in the U.S. Congress that the Soviets were using détente to buy time so as to amass still more influence in the Third World.

All through the Cold War the Soviets probed possible weaknesses in American power and influence, and when they encountered resistance, as in Berlin in 1948 or Cuba in 1962, they pulled back and probed elsewhere. For America and the West, the problem with the Soviet Union was not that it was irrational; it was rather that it pursued its revisionist goals with remorseless and exquisite rationality.

Gorbachev Makes the Soviet Union a Status Quo Power

It was only when Soviet leaders finally abandoned communism themselves, and told their client regimes to do the same, that relations with Western countries could become genuinely normal. Mikhail Gorbachev and his circle of reformers, who assumed power in 1985, essentially abandoned the communist party's goal, honored since Lenin, of promoting communism at home and abroad. Gorbachev made the Soviet Union a status quo power. His ends came to match those of the United States and its Western democratic-capitalist allies, and the Western powers accordingly stopped thinking of the Soviet Union as a threat to their security. Even Ronald Reagan, America's most anticommunist president, came around.[37] We take up the fascinating story of the end of communism in Lessons 5 and 6.

The Revisionist That Succeeded: The United States of America, 1776–1950

No doubt most Americans would reject the notion that their country is ideological, in the manner of the Soviet Union or Iran (or, insofar as they have heard of it, the Electoral Palatinate). Surely, most would say, the United States is self-evidently rational.

But the argument we have been making implies that every country is, in a sense, ideological, because every country or every regime has some vision of the good society, both domestic and international. The United States has value-shaped ends or goals as much as these other states. Following Thomas Jefferson, Americans believe that their country is not ideological because they believe that the truths in the Declaration of Independence are self-evident. True they are, but if their truth were self-evident then U.S. counterterrorism and counterinsurgency would not need to win the "hearts and minds" of millions of people. Indeed, across history countless thinkers have thought that all persons are *not* equal. The truly self-evident truth is that American values are contested around the world. That means that to many around the world the United States is an ideological country, not a rational one.

Jefferson himself knew well that the young United States held a revolutionary set of ideas about how both domestic and international life ought to be ordered. America was a revisionist power. In the late eighteenth century the Western international system, based in Europe, was built upon the legitimacy of thrones. The only rightful states were *monarchical* states.[38] For more than a century, the crowned heads of Europe had been increasing their power by subduing the nobles who had been so powerful in the Middle Ages. Europe had republics dominated by nobles—Venice, the Netherlands, and Switzerland were the outstanding examples—but the great military powers were all monarchies, modeled on the successes of France's Louis XIV. Around this system had been built an ideology of royal sovereignty, seen in the writings of England's James I and of the Frenchmen Jean Bodin and Bishop Bossuet.[39]

As important, these monarchies sought empires—pieces of extra territory to rule and monopolize economically. Some European empire building in the eighteenth century took place in Europe itself, but most of it was in Latin America, Africa, and Asia. European monarchs commissioned private entrepreneurs and adventurers to claim new land for the purposes of economic exploitation. Under the system known as mercantilism, an imperial state (or metropole) would send colonists to subdue and govern a territory; the territory would export raw materials to the metropole; and the metropole would export manufactures back to the colony. Each imperial power claimed a monopoly on trade with its colonies, and so competition for territory could be fierce.

Mercantilism came under increasing criticism in Western Europe in the eighteenth century. In France the Physiocrats argued that agriculture, not the acquisition of precious metals or the development of manufacturing, was the engine of wealth. In Britain Adam Smith argued that political barriers to economic exchange actually impoverished nations; better to let people conduct commerce freely, without monopoly privileges within or among nations.[40]

These Enlightenment ideas influenced some of the founders of the United States, preeminently Jefferson and James Madison, the Virginians who later became leaders of the Republican (later Democratic) Party.[41] The Republicans wanted no part of either the centralization of power in a national state or European-style formal empires, which they identified in particular with Britain. They aimed for a republic of small independent farmers and believed that the dispersion of power both horizontally (among the president, Congress, and courts) and vertically (between the national and state governments) was necessary to preserve such a republic. They aimed for a world of freely trading independent nations, none monopolizing intercourse with any other.[42]

The Jeffersonians, then, intended to transform the international system by setting up a new kind of republic with a new kind of political economy, which would interact with other nations based on the common pursuit of wealth rather than the competitive pursuit of power. There were moments in the 1790s when the young United States contemplated taking radical steps to implement this vision—or, more precisely, when Jefferson and other Republicans pushed for highly risky policies to do so. Most of these moments concerned America's policy toward the war between France and Britain.[43]

In 1789 the French Revolution began. In 1792 the French ended their centuries-old monarchy and established a republic; they also declared war on Austria, Prussia, and Britain. Jefferson and company thrilled at these events, which seemed to confirm the American narrative of a democratic revolution sweeping the entire North Atlantic region.[44] In April 1793 a new minister from France, the young Edmond-Charles Genêt, arrived in Charleston, South Carolina. Rather than proceed directly to the national capital of Philadelphia to present himself to President Washington, as a new chief diplomat normally would do, Genêt took his time in the southern states, recruiting U.S. citizens to join the French in their war against Britain.[45] Genêt also wanted France to be able to arm privateers in U.S. ports to attack British merchant ships, and for the United States to subsidize France's war effort. In effect, he aimed to pull the United States into the war on the side of France.[46]

At first Jefferson himself—then secretary of state—was open to Genêt's proposals. But President Washington was not, and quickly proclaimed American neutrality in the Anglo-French war. Some Republicans attacked Washington in print; in the *National Gazette*, "Veritas" argued that neutrality meant abandoning America's ally France. To Genêt's astonishment, Jefferson went along with Washington, arguing that neutrality meant complete impartiality.[47] The Washington administration was to spurn America's sister republic again in 1794 with the Jay Treaty with Britain, which effectively favored Britain over France.[48]

The infant United States stepped back from a reckless pursuit of the vision of a world of freely trading republics in part because even Jefferson did not want war with Great Britain; it was clear that America was not ready for such an ordeal. But also significant was the presence of a competing force in U.S. politics, the alternative vision of Alexander Hamilton and the Federalists. The Federalists admired Britain's industry and power and wanted their young nation to imitate it with a strong presidency, a national bank, the development of industry, the use of debt, and a standing army. The Hamiltonians foresaw an American empire to rival that of ancient Rome.[49] Hamilton himself, as secretary of the treasury, exercised great influence over President Washington, and the president himself identified more with the Federalists.

As they became known as Democrats in the nineteenth century, Jefferson's ideological heirs retained their vision of a freely trading, chiefly agricultural republic that had no large military establishment or formal empire. But they were generally rational in pursuing that vision. President James K. Polk, a protégé of Andrew Jackson, wanted to expand U.S. territory so as to open up vast amounts of new farmland. Polk took the United States to war against Mexico knowing that the war could be won at acceptable cost; knowing that war against Britain could not be won at acceptable cost, Polk instead negotiated a settlement over the Oregon territory.[50]

At the same time, the heirs to the Federalists—the Whigs and then the Republicans—generally continued to be more accepting of the European-dominated international system and helped constrain any imprudence that the Democrats might have inclined toward. When in power, Whigs and Republicans developed America into an industrial power by protecting its manufacturers from European competition.[51]

Yet, American farmers maintained their attachment to free trade, and apart from a brief period in the 1890s, the United States never sought a formal empire outside of North America. Even its territories—Hawaii, the Philippines, Puerto Rico, and others—were allowed to trade with other countries. Its many military interventions in the Caribbean and Central America in the early twentieth century were certainly coercive, but the United States neither annexed new territory to its south nor restricted those countries' economic interaction with other countries. In the Western Hemisphere as in Asia, America worked for an "open door."

In the twentieth century America finally had sufficient power, in the form of industrially based wealth and growing military power, to begin implementing a kind of synthesis of the Jeffersonian and Hamiltonian visions of international relations. From Hamilton came the national power; from Jefferson the open world economy. Woodrow Wilson's Fourteen Points, announced during the First World War, envisaged free trade and the dissolution of formal European empires. Wilson's plan for a League of Nations proved too radical even for his own countrymen, particularly the Republicans. It was his fellow Democrat and protégé Franklin Delano Roosevelt who began to use American power to transform the international system in the 1940s.

Roosevelt badly wanted the aggressive empires of Nazi Germany and Japan stopped, but he was none too friendly toward the empires of Britain and France. The crucial Atlantic Charter, jointly issued by Roosevelt and British Prime Minister Winston Churchill in August 1941 (prior to U.S. entry into the Second World War), named as common goals the self-determination of peoples, the lowering of trade barriers, global economic cooperation, and freedom of the seas. Conspicuously absent from the charter was any mention of the right of Britain to keep its empire.[52] Roosevelt's successor Harry S. Truman and his advisors set up international institutions that addressed the chronic economic and security problems that had pushed the Europeans and Japanese to build formal empires. In effect, after the war the United States offered the old imperial powers a deal they could not refuse: give up your antiquated imperialism and open your economies; America will offer military protection and underwrite international institutions to lower the disruptions of economic openness.[53]

During the Cold War the United States did not consistently follow this program. The struggle against Soviet-style communism led Truman and subsequent administrations to support those old European empires against anticolonial Leftists in Asia and Africa. America itself intervened in all manner of ways, including with coercive force, in the Third World, leading to charges of imperialism. Yet, particularly following the fall of the Soviet Union and its alternative vision of international order,[54] the international system, seen broadly, is different today from what it has ever been. Formal mercantilist empires are a thing of the past. Goods and money move across more national borders more freely than ever. International institutions—the World Trade Organization, the World Bank, the International Monetary Fund, various United Nations organizations—constrain and enable sovereign governments. Technological and social changes are partly responsible, but so is U.S. hegemony—America's use of its power to induce, cajole, and coerce states to open their borders and, in some cases, become more democratic.

From the start, then, the United States had a distinctive global vision, but it was mostly prudent and patient in implementing that vision. Rather than take heedless risks to transform the international system, as some radicals wanted, U.S. leaders were content to expand in North America, forestall renewed European imperialism in Latin America, seek commerce with all foreign powers, and avoid alliances and wars. In the twentieth century America did take on some of the qualities of a European-style great power, but it used its newly attained power to implement elements of its old vision.[55]

Revisionist states are not necessarily irrational, nor are they doomed to fail. The American example shows that, if they are rational in pursuing their transformative goals for international life—if they correctly ascertain their relative power, monitor others' reactions to what they do, and respond accordingly—they may eventually succeed. The revisionist United States—a free-market republic—did not bring on general war or destroy itself, but slowly and prudently took advantage of opportunities to transform the international system. The world is a different place from what it was in 1800 or 1900: formal empires are virtually gone, barriers to foreign trade and investment have shrunk as well, and free-market democracy is the norm. By no means are these changes due solely to American efforts; many other states, general technological and social changes, and the great power struggles of the twentieth century also have been responsible. And the international system has not changed as radically as some Americans (or others) have hoped. But the United States has reshaped the world.

▨ ▨ ▨

History shows, then, that a state may act in ways that seem irrational to other states, yet appear rational once its goals are understood. It is the distance between those goals and those of other states that make the state appear irrational. The supposedly irrational state's goals are the product of an ideology, a plan for public (including international) order that embodies a vision of the good society and implies certain institutions and practices. *A state may, in other words, be a rational ideologue.* The Palatinate was such a state for roughly the half century after 1555. The Soviet Union settled into a rational-ideological policy in the 1920s and followed it for many decades.

The cases also show that an ideological state may sometimes act *irrationally*, that is, may use inefficient or even self-defeating means to reach its ideological ends. If we only considered the Soviet example, we might conclude that states always learn the lesson that moderation is the best policy and move from irrationality to rationality. The story of the Palatinate will not allow us that conclusion. This middle-sized power of early modern Europe went in the opposite direction. After many decades of rational revisionism, its leaders Frederick V and Christian of Anhalt got carried away with enthusiasm in the 1610s and took risks for their cause that even their fellow Protestants judged dangerous. The imprudent Frederick and Christian did not change the Palatinate's ideological goals. They simply were in a great hurry to achieve those goals, and lapsed into irrationality. In doing so, they helped bring on the Thirty Years' War and the destruction of their own state.

Important questions emerge from this history: *What causes a rational ideological state to become irrational? What causes the opposite movement?* Answering those questions is well beyond the scope of this book, but a good working hypothesis is that leaders play a large role. The most striking evidence of this is from the Palatinate's Christian of Anhalt, a risk-taking ideologue who persuaded Frederick V to do some very rash things. The Soviet case is less dramatic but still important. Lenin and Trotsky began as irrational from the perspective of international relations, but soon moderated. Yet it was Stalin—who was, ironically, paranoid concerning threats to his power from within his own communist party—who settled the young Soviet Union into its long-term stance of rational ideological state.

Back to Today: Islamists and Rationality

Are Islamist states rational? We begin by distinguishing such states' ends from their means.

Ends

By definition, Islamists share a general goal of having Sharia—whatever version, interpreted by whichever clergy—as the law of the land. Beyond that, their goals vary widely.

Saudi Arabia, the world's strictest Islamist regime, seems to aim at the survival and flourishing of the House of Saud on the Arabian Peninsula—home to the two holy mosques at Mecca and Medina—and, beyond that, influence among the world's Muslims via its Wahhabist networks. But the power of the Saudi dynasty depends upon its ability to sell oil, and it rules a vast desert kingdom with a small population. Vulnerable to invasion from their more populous neighbors, including Iran, Iraq, and Egypt, the Saudis many years ago decided to accept and support Western hegemony in the Persian Gulf and the Middle East more generally. Its economic and military cooperation with Washington has opened the Saudi dynasty to charges of hypocrisy and incoherence.[56] For decades it has managed to thrive despite those charges. Saudi Arabia is rationally pursuing the goal of maintaining the status quo in the Persian Gulf. It invited the United States to protect it from Iraq in 1990, contributed millions of dollars to the 1991 war against that country, and is pleased to have the U.S. Fifth Fleet headquartered in neighboring Bahrain.

The other main exemplary Islamist state, Iran, likewise seeks the preservation of its Islamic Republic. Iran's leaders, however, take a rather different view of the United States and its influence in the Middle East and Southwest Asia—and indeed, of the international system itself. Dehghani Firooz-Abadi, a political scientist and foreign policy official in Tehran, writes that Iran seeks an "evolution" of the international system through "structural reform," or an end to the domination of the great powers. Beyond that, Iran foresees an "evolution" of the system out of its "anarchic nature." Its ultimate goal is the "formation of an Islamic world society" "devoid of power relations, domination, suppression, and violence," in which all people would be free and equal under an "Islamic world government."[57]

No doubt other Iranian scholars would articulate the matter differently. But it is hardly controversial that the regional and world orders desired by Iran have contradicted sharply those that America wants. Even reforming presidents such as Mohammad Khatami and Hassan Rouhani have not accepted American hegemony. It will not do to assert that Iran simply has been resisting American power and that Islamist ideology is just a peculiar way of talking about self-interest. Iran's anti-Americanism is based upon and shaped by its version of Islamism, which is a rejection of the secularization that Shah Reza Pahlavi, an American client during the Cold War, was imposing on Persian society. Ideas and interests are entangled.[58] Suzanne Maloney, an American analyst, argues, that Iran's identity contains elements of nationalism, Islamism, and anti-imperialism, and the three coexist and can be mutually reinforcing.[59]

Iran, then, has been a revisionist state—just as the Palatinate was four hundred years ago, the Soviet Union was for most of the twentieth century, and the United States was until the 1940s. Owing to many factors, including its ideology, Iran has been deeply discontented not only with American policies but the very regional and international system in which it operates and which the United States sustains. Iran has wanted to change that system, and so many of its policies have been bound to mystify and repel the United States. Indeed, Flynt and Hillary Leverett, perhaps the most prominent American critics of U.S. policy toward Iran, are right about this much: the United States is ideological. What they miss is that all states are ideological, Iran included. The fundamental problem between Iran and America is that both countries are ideological, and their ideologies are incompatible.

As the leading American scholar of Iranian foreign policy in the late twentieth century, R. K. Ramazani, puts the contrast between Iranian and Saudi ideologies, "anti-Westernism versus pro-Western nonalignmentism."[60] Why the two Islamist exemplars have taken opposite views of American hegemony is a topic for another day. The vital question is this: If, as argued in this book's introduction, much of the Middle East is likely to be more Islamist in the coming years, will its Islamism be more like that of Saudi Arabia, or that of Iran?

Particularly because Islamism these days goes hand-in-hand with popular sovereignty, the smart money is on Iranian-style anti-Americanism. When out of power, Islamist parties tend to oppose American hegemony robustly and loudly. When they come to power, they tend to distance their countries' foreign policies from the United States. It is a difficult thing for many Americans to accept, but as far as the Middle East is concerned, more democracy probably means less love for the United States, partly because more democracy means more Islamism. Hamas, which rules Gaza, has proved much more anti-American than the secularist Palestinian Authority, which rules the West Bank.[61] As discussed in Lesson 3, Turkey under the moderate Islamist AK Party has remained a NATO member but its foreign minister has declared that it will be equally friendly to Iran, Russia, and Arab states as it is to the West.

So much for the goals of Islamist states. The questions remain: Will they pursue those goals rationally? Or will they be rash and self-defeating, perhaps bringing on war and destruction?

Means

It is easy to argue that at least one Islamist state was consistently irrational: Afghanistan under the Taliban. The regime of Mullah Omar isolated itself nearly completely by defying more powerful enemies. In trying to spread its peculiar, astringent brand of Islamism, the Taliban made itself obnoxious to its larger neighbors, including Iran, India, and Russia. Most brazenly of all, it hosted Osama bin Laden and his al-Qaeda network after they were ejected from Sudan in 1998, even as they continued in a self-proclaimed state of war against the world's only superpower, the United States. In the end, a U.S.-led force overthrew the regime in October 2001. The Taliban's effectiveness as a fighting force is not in question; at the time of this writing it continues to thrive in parts of Pakistan and Afghanistan and to fight NATO and Afghan troops. But the Taliban might yet be ruling Afghanistan outright itself had it not foolishly bound itself so tightly to al-Qaeda from 1998 to 2001.

Now we come to a harder case: Iran. Has it been pursuing rationally its ideologically shaped goals? Some experts say, in effect, "it depends." Clearly in its early months of existence, in 1979–80, the regime was imprudent.[62] Like the Russian Bolsheviks in 1917–18, the young Khomeini regime brazenly flouted diplomatic norms. It encouraged radical students to take hostage fifty-two Americans at the U.S. embassy in Tehran. It refused to deal diplomatically with a number of other states, and instead created the Islamic Revolutionary Council and called for their overthrow.[63] One of these regimes, that of Saddam Hussein in neighboring Iraq, responded by working in turn to overthrow the new Iranian regime. Iraq invaded Iran in September 1980, starting a war that lasted eight years and cost a million lives and thereby offering Saddam's first—but not his last—demonstration that secularists can pursue their ends irrationally as well. But Iran's regime baited Saddam into attacking by imprudently stirring up rebellion in Iraq.

Yet, at other times Iran has been more pragmatic. In 1984 Khomeini spoke against the export of revolution and called for the establishment of diplomatic relations with most countries. Iran ended the war with Iraq in 1988. It has built a strong association with Syria, a state with a secular Ba'athist regime similar to that of Tehran's archenemy Saddam Hussein of Iraq.[64] Most surprising have been occasions when Iran cooperated with the United States. During the 1991 Gulf War, when America led a multinational coalition against Iraq, Iran maintained contact with the United States and allowed the U.S. Air Force into its air space.[65] Following the al-Qaeda attacks of September 11, 2001, Iran officially denounced the terrorism and provided help of various sorts to the U.S. campaign to topple the Taliban in Afghanistan.[66] In 2013 its new President Hassan Rouhani began to negotiate with the United States and other powers over Iran's nuclear program.

Just as in the cases of the Palatinate four hundred years ago and the Soviet Union in the twentieth century, Iran's rationality seems to vary with its leadership. The zealous Ayatollah Khomeini, founder of the regime, was arguably irrational, engineering the taking of hostages at the U.S. embassy in 1979 and pushing for the export of the revolution. Other leaders, such as presidents Ayatollah Akbar Hashemi Rafsanjani and Mohammed Khatami, have downplayed revolution and sought to make Iran conform more to international norms.

Rafsanjani, president from 1989 to 1997, set up the Supreme National Security Council to separate foreign policy from domestic ideology. He took steps to block extremists from hampering the United States in the 1991 Gulf War, and at the end of his term he tried to induce Hezbollah into a cease-fire with Israel.[67] Khatami, president from 1997 to 2005, attempted even more, initiating a "Dialogue among Civilizations" to defuse ideological tensions with non-Muslim countries. Khatami also initiated a "Good Neighbor" policy to improve relations with Iran's Gulf neighbors, including rival Saudi Arabia. Under his presidency Iran established relations with the European Union.[68]

After Khatami left office in 2005, Iran moved back toward its more risk-taking, self-isolating strategy of the 1980s. President Mahmoud Ahmadinejad (2005–13) was a leader in Iran's so-called New Right movement. New Rightists blamed the failure to defeat Iraq back in the 1980s on the intervention of the West, and regarded the Rafsanjani and Khatami presidencies as setbacks to the Islamic revolution. While the New Right is itself divided between militants and moderates, all agree that Iran must press to become the leading power in the Persian Gulf.[69] That would have to come at the expense of the United States and Saudi Arabia.

Under Ahmadinejad Iran took on more risk through two related and persistent policy initiatives. First, it openly defied the United States, the European Union, and the UN's IAEA by continuing its nuclear program and refusing to comply with the IAEA's rules and requirements regarding disclosure. Iran's leaders insisted that their nuclear program is strictly for peaceful, civilian purposes; but their contrarian attitude and actions led many experts and government officials in the West to conclude that they were lying and bent on becoming a nuclear-armed state. Second, Iran explicitly threatened Israel. Ahmadinejad said more than once that the Jewish state will be "eliminated."[70] He hosted a conference in 2006 calling for research into whether the Nazi Holocaust actually occurred.[71] In the summer of 2012 Iran's Vice President Mohammad Reza Rahimi told an international conference that the Jews are responsible for the worldwide spread of illegal drugs.[72]

Even analysts who interpret all of this ideological talk and action as intended for domestic consumption must acknowledge that it was provocative and risky. Were Iran trying to bait Israel and the United States into bombing it, it could hardly have been more effective. Israel, in particular, was not shy about stating that it may carry out air strikes.[73] Of course, by the same token Israeli or U.S. bombing of Iran may have been irrational. But without question it would have been foreseeably self-defeating for Iran to *provoke* such a bombing campaign. Iran's nuclear program would have been set back by several years, Iran's grand vision of an Islamic world order free of American hegemony further than ever from realization.

There is a case, then, that Iran has had long bouts of irrationality—not in seeking great influence in accordance with its Islamist ideology, but in taking great risks to achieve that influence. But there is another way to look at the matter. Author Lee Harris argues that Iran has deliberately behaved in ways that violate Westerners' notions of reasonable and good behavior so as to keep the West off-balance. Iran has gambled, but there is nothing unusual in that.[74] In other words, Iran may have behaved rationally—taking on just enough risk to allow it to push ahead with its plan to become predominant in its region without provoking a U.S. or Israeli attack.

In the end, we are left with a circular argument: we will know if Iran is rational or not based on how things turn out. If Iran gets bombed, it was irrational; if not, it was rational.

Be that as it may, Iran's ideological rationality may well be a picture of the future. An Islamist Egypt or Libya or Syria or Palestine may act in ways that are so bewildering or repugnant to Westerners that Westerners will call them irrational. It is unlikely, given that these are ideological *states*, that a grand Islamist bloc will form and act in concert against the United States. The long-standing cold war between the two Islamist exemplars, Saudi Arabia and Iran, is evidence enough of that. But it is likely that some of the new Islamist states will be at least skeptical toward the U.S.-sponsored order in their part of the world, and will act so as to make life more complicated for America.

Calling states such as Iran irrational is a comforting self-deception. It is a self-deception because history makes clear that all states have ideologies and visions that shape their goals. It is comforting because it implies that they will fail. Ironically, America's own example suggests that ideological states may be rational, and sometimes ultimately succeed.

Lesson 5
The Winner May Be "None of the Above"

Success in Turkey can be an example for many nations. Supporting
a process of change that is evolutionary but gradual, that emphasizes
the importance of preserving values over institutions and relationships,
is the key to success in this region of the world. The Turkish democratic
ideal is not to have a mechanical democracy reduced to elections
and institutions, but rather an organic democracy that pervades
the administrative, social, and political arenas. We call
this "organic democracy "deep democracy."
—*Recep Tayyip Erdoğan, 2004*

Sharia leaves no room for democracy. . . . Not only do Islamic laws deny
freedom of speech and religion as well as equal rights under the law for
both men and women, Muslims and non-Muslims, there are laws that
punish sexual crimes with flogging, beheading, and stoning, and others
that make the creation of a democracy virtually impossible.
—*Nonie Darwish, 2012*

In the summer of 1989, as communism was beginning to crumble in Eastern
Europe, Francis Fukuyama published a famous article, "The End of History?,"
laying out the case that the human race's long struggle over the best way to
order society was finally over and that the winner was constitutional, free-

market democracy. With Marxism-Leninism exhausted and fascism long gone, no alternative to liberal democracy was left standing. The philosopher Hegel had insisted nearly two centuries earlier that History was a battle of ideas, and liberal democracy now had swept the field.[1]

Events over the next few years, including the fall of the Berlin Wall and the collapse of the Soviet Union itself, seemed to confirm Fukuyama's assessment. Fukuyama went on in a 1992 book to argue that liberal democracy won the war of ideas once and for all because it was the regime that best fit human nature—in particular, man's spiritedness and need for recognition.[2]

As Fukuyama acknowledged, liberal democracy had not yet triumphed in most Muslim societies. Subsequent years—in particular the endurance of Iran's regime and the terrorist attacks of September 11, 2001—led many to wonder if the Muslim world might be stubbornly continuing to participate in History. Yet, the Arab Spring that began in December 2010 gave hope to many that Fukuyama might be right about Islamic societies as well. The revolts across so many Arab countries were clearly popular, and much of the rhetoric and leadership was liberal.

On the other hand, subsequent events in Egypt, Libya, Tunisia, and elsewhere made clear that many of the people who wanted the old Arab authoritarian regimes gone may want popular rule, but are not liberal—that is, they do not want the regime of individual rights and secular government cherished by most Westerners. Some experts say that if democracy wins in the Arab world, it will not be Fukuyama's liberal democracy, but some kind of Islamic democracy, along the lines described and implemented by the Justice and Development (AK) Party in an important non-Arab state, Turkey.

In the prolonged contest between Muslim secularism and Islamism, will one ideology and regime type eventually win? If so, what will the winner be? Or might there be no winner? Is "Islamic democracy" possible? What would it look like? Is it sustainable? Do Islamists embrace democracy only as a tool to gain power? Is Erdoğan's Turkey a model of Islamic democracy?

Answering these questions requires deep analyses of the changing discourse and goals of various Islamists, the distribution of power among them, their relations with other actors and institutions in their societies, and a host of other factors. A number of capable scholars are conducting such analyses. But as with other questions about political Islam, looking back at the West's own history also can help us. Western history shows that a transnational ideological struggle such as that between secularism and Islamism can end in one of three ways.

Suppose that one ideology—say, Islamism, which had the wind in its sails in the early twenty-first century—vanquishes the other. Secularist regimes would continue to experience increasing domestic turmoil; some would be overthrown, perhaps some others would voluntarily dissolve themselves. No doubt Islamist regimes would be diverse and compete as they do now. But political, social, and economic order would be markedly different in Muslim societies than in the West or Asia. We can call this outcome *victory*.

Suppose instead that secularists and Islamists somehow ceased to place such a high priority on the issue or boundary that divides them. Suppose that Muslims continued to disagree on whether the state should enforce Sharia, but stopped caring very much whether or not it did so. The situation would be something like that in Europe today between monarchies and republics: these regime types endure but, in marked contrast to the nineteenth century, few Europeans care or even notice. In this equilibrium the Islamist-secularist contest would end because the contestants would have changed the subject. We can call this outcome *transcendence*.

Finally, suppose that Islamists and secularists began to adopt some of one another's institutions and practices. Such might happen if the two sides agreed to a pluralist model of law, in which criminal law had secular sources but family law derived from Sharia. A hybrid regime might be a multiparty democracy whose constitution did not rule out a stronger role for Sharia or the clergy if the electorate wanted it. We can call this outcome *convergence*.

Each of these three outcomes has a precedent in Western history. The most familiar case, the twentieth-century contest among communism, fascism, and liberal democracy, ended in victory: the last of the three unambiguously triumphed over the others. This was what Fukuyama called the End of History—the triumph of democratic capitalism over communism in the late twentieth century.

Another of the cases ended in transcendence. A new regime type emerged that rendered the old ideological differences irrelevant. This was the melting away of the religiopolitical strife in early modern Europe. Europeans remained Catholic and Protestant, but it no longer made much difference politically. Religious differences lost most of their political salience under a new regime type, secularism.

Still another of the cases ended in convergence. A hybrid regime took shape that fused elements of each of the formerly competing ideologies into one. Convergence happened in the 1860s in Europe, as monarchists and republicans laid aside their differences and built regimes sometimes called liberalconservative.

This lesson narrates all three types of ending—victory, transcendence, and convergence—and considers which of the three the Islamist-secularist contest seems to be moving toward. The signs at present point to convergence, a hybrid Islamist-secularist regime that Westerners may find counterintuitive but that may just work in many Muslim societies.

Victory: The Triumph of Democratic Capitalism—
Late Twentieth Century

One still occasionally sees them: earnest young people, or not-so-young people, wearing "Mao More Than Ever" T-shirts; lectures organized on various university campuses on globalism and the class struggle; Occupy protesters who focus on global financial capital. But Marxism, in its various forms, lacks the power it once had. It may some day experience a global comeback, but so far it has failed to capture either the workers it claims to serve or the intellectuals who were its traditional vanguard. (Even Thomas Piketty, academic economist and rock star of the global Left, disavows any debt to Marx.)[3]

Marxism's problem was clear back in the early 1990s. The regime type most explicitly traced to Karl Marx's writings, communism, had manifestly failed. The Soviet Union collapsed in 1991. Marxism-Leninism and its variants simply provided no sustainable plan for ordering society. Revolution Books in Cambridge, Massachusetts, Manhattan, Berkeley, Chicago, and other American cities continued to sell their products and lend a frisson of radical chic to the cities populated by the knowledge classes. Various transnational communist groups continue to this day to form, dissolve, anathematize one another, and recombine, their cumbersome names always helpfully abbreviated: the CWI, ICC, RIM, ISO, and so on.[4] A reconstituted Fourth International of Trotskyists is still out there.[5]

Consider the disciples of Chairman Mao Zedong, founder of the People's Republic of China. Maoist networks continue to exist in the United States, Peru, Colombia, Turkey, Iran, Afghanistan, India, Nepal, and the Philippines. Of these, the Filipino New Peoples' Army, the Naxalites in India, and the Shining Path in Peru continue to fight to overthrow their countries' regimes. In most other countries Maoists are peaceful, although they continue to argue that the traumas their movement visited upon China decades ago were worthwhile. In the United States Maoists try to persuade people that the Cultural Revolution (1964–76)—the catastrophic effort by the Chinese Communist Party to coerce the Chinese population into perpetual revolution—was actually a good thing.[6]

Maoism, however, is not what it used to be. Maoists did co-govern Nepal in 2008–9, and the guerrillas in Asia and South America continue to kill people and vex governments. But the ideology is nothing like the widespread threat to regimes that it was in the 1960s and 1970s. The FARC in Colombia remains dangerous, but most other radical Left groups are notable only for their obscurity.

Of the old communist states, there remain two self-impoverishing exemplars: North Korea, a Stalinist hereditary dictatorship, known chiefly for its temper tantrums, famines, pear-shaped hereditary leaders, and periodic attempts at nuclear extortion; and Cuba, reliant on the tourism of wealthy anti-American Westerners, with a regime acknowledged not to work even by its father and icon, Fidel Castro, in 2010.[7]

Time was, of course, when transnational communism was not to be dismissed as ragtag collections of oddballs, thugs, and romantic intellectuals. Communism once was a specter haunting not only Europe but the entire world, a movement whose adherents had moral fervor and invincible confidence, that made dictators and democrats alike tremble. Communist parties ruled many countries and bid fair to take over many more. Other Leftists who rejected communism's hard edges, such as dictatorship and forced famine, were sufficiently impressed to cooperate with communists—to see them as using dubious methods in pursuit of worthy ends—and to align their countries with the Soviet Union. From the 1920s through 1970s, communists and many of their enemies were convinced that communism was going to triumph over democratic capitalism.[8]

Transnational communism already was in a crisis by the early 1980s. The crisis was evident in the persistent stagnation of the Soviet economy and the embrace of capitalism by communist China.

The market reforms that Deng Xiaoping began in China in 1979 were a signal that state socialism was not fulfilling its promise to raise standards of living and make great the nations that implemented it. In the Soviet Union itself, economic growth had never recovered to the impressive levels of the 1950s. The period of Leonid Brezhnev's rule was to become known in the late 1980s as the "years of stagnation," and with good reason. As British historian Willie Thompson, a communist himself, writes, "The year 1981 was supposed to have been the year when, according to Khrushchev's boast at the 22nd Congress, the USSR would overtake the USA in material consumption, not to speak of other indicators of public welfare. All that had, of course, been quietly forgotten, and the continuing dependence of the Soviet Union on US grain imports were [sic] a humiliating reminder of just how inferior in that capacity it was to a country with a much smaller agricultural sector."[9]

The late U.S. senator Daniel Patrick Moynihan has written that, in the late 1970s, he noted telltale Soviet statistics indicating acute manpower shortages; a ten-year and widening gap between male (sixty-four) and female (seventy-four) life expectancy; and a steep rise in the infant mortality rate from 22.9 deaths per 1,000 births in 1971 to 31.1 deaths in 1976. "In a word," Moynihan writes, "communism was dead."[10] All in all, Brezhnev had led the Soviet Union into what Western writers were to call "imperial overextension," an overextension that was partly a function of state socialism's intrinsic incapacities.

In Africa, Latin America, and East Asia, countries that adopted Marxism-Leninism generally fared much worse than their counterparts that adopted economic liberalism. As David Lane writes, "Capitalism on a world scale has proved to be more successful as a system of production and consumption than anticipated by a succession of communist leaders from Lenin to Brezhnev. . . . [T]he 'developmental model' of state socialism had positive effects in Eastern Europe and the Third World immediately after the Second World War. But from the 1980s the rise of the capitalist South-East Asian economies such as Taiwan, Malaysia and South Korea provided an alternative for the developing societies of the Third World."[11] Fred Halliday adds, "In the end . . . it was the pressures of the West, above all the demonstration effect of capitalist economic success, which brought the Soviet system, and that of its defected allies, down."[12] As an example, Zbigniew Brzezinski points out that in the 1980s Tanzania, which had adopted state socialism, was economically stagnant and actually reducing industrial output, while neighboring Kenya, which had adopted more market mechanisms, enjoyed modest overall and industrial growth.[13]

Compounding the problem for Third World communists was the increasing scarcity of Soviet aid. In the 1970s Moscow had begun to target aid to strategic countries such as Angola and Ethiopia. No longer was massive aid available to any Third World regime that was moving toward Marxism-Leninism. Mikhail Gorbachev, who took office in 1985, further cut aid to foreign communist parties and regimes. By then, Moscow was telling clients in Africa and Asia, including Mozambique, Angola, Ethiopia, and Vietnam, to integrate into world markets and try to attract foreign investment, "clearly signaling thereby," as Brzezinski writes, "that the Kremlin was not about to foot their development bills." Gorbachev informed the Cubans that they should improve their economic situation by conciliating the United States.[14]

At the same time, the spectacular successes of those states that had opened their economies, such as South Korea, Taiwan, and Chile, demonstrated that following the development advice of the West paid handsomely. Neo-Marxist dependency theory, which had prescribed socialist revolution and economic isolation from the United States and the West in general, was failing on its own terms.

The crumbling of communism did not mean the triumph of a simple, homogeneous regime type. Liberal-democratic free-market states are by no means all the same. In particular, an "Anglo-Saxon" model, practiced in the United States, Great Britain, and other Anglophone countries, is often contrasted with a "Continental" model, exemplified by France, Germany, and other European states. The Anglo-Saxon model allows less state control over the economy than the Continental.[15]

These differences, however, are about policies, not regimes. The British or U.S. constitution could accommodate moves toward more state control, and indeed each did so in the 1930s and 1940s. The French or Dutch constitution could accommodate moves toward less state control, and indeed each did so in the 1980s and 1990s. These differences were present throughout the post–World War II period. It remains the case that there was a global competition between two basic ideologies, and one of them won. And that tells us that Islamism or secularism could in principle triumph in the Middle East in the coming years or decades. Sometimes, one side wins.

Transcendence: The Dutch Changed the Subject in the Seventeenth Century

Sometimes neither side wins. Instead, a new regime type emerges from the contention. That is the story of the emergence of secular regimes in the West several centuries ago.

In one sense, the secularism that for many decades has been contending for supremacy in the Middle East is unique to that world. It is directed specifically against traditional Islamic regimes, which are shaped by their own notions of how the sacred and the profane relate. In another sense, however, Muslim secularism is very much like Western secularism and indeed is related to it historically. In the introduction to this book we saw how the modernizers in the late Ottoman Empire, and Atatürk, founder of modern Turkey, consciously tried to imitate the secular West in hopes that they would strengthen their societies and make them competitive with those of the West.

But how did Western secularism come about? It was the result of our first Western ideological struggle, that between political Catholicism and political Protestantism in early modern Europe. Secularism was not itself a contender—at least, not until quite late in the contest. It emerged as a third option but one that transcended the others, that effectively changed the subject from "Which branch of Christianity will be integral to this regime?" to "How can the regime be made indifferent toward the contest among the various branches of Christianity?"[16]

The so-called confessional states of sixteenth-century Europe not only had an established church intimately tied to the secular rulers and institutions, but also handicapped or disallowed alternative Christian and non-Christian practices and groups. Most Europeans believed that an intolerant state was the only type that was sustainable; the question was whether it would be Catholic or some kind of Protestant (Lutheran, Calvinist, Anglican, or other). That was because of a norm dating to the Middle Ages: in Latin, *religio vincula societatis* ("religion is the bond of society"). For a society to cohere—for subjects to remain loyal to rulers—all must hold to a common religion under a common religious authority. Medieval Europeans believed that religion was Roman Catholic Christianity—hence the periodic bouts of Jewish persecution—and early Protestants believed the bonding religion was their alternative version of Christianity. The intimacy between church and state, in the minds and practices of most people, meant that the spread of a rival religion *really was* a threat to rulers.

By the late seventeenth century, the old norm of *religio vincula societatis* had begun to fade in most European societies. Religious dissidents had begun to prove that they were not going away but also that they could be loyal subjects or citizens. In turn, that meant that it made more sense for Protestant rulers to tolerate Catholics, and for Catholic rulers to tolerate Protestants. The growth of one branch of Christianity no longer threatened rulers who adhered to a different branch.

To be sure, toleration was not new. But it had always been provisional and temporary, and everyone knew that it was. Religious toleration had been tried in various European lands almost from the outset of the Reformation. Princes and city councils had sometimes declared that religious minorities could practice their faith in peace, within certain limits, in exchange for guarantees of fealty to the rulers and the law. The Holy Roman Emperor Charles V agreed to a so-called religious peace on several occasions between 1520 and 1555, tolerating Lutheranism so long as Lutheran princes would fight with him against the Turks or French or the pope. King Henry IV of France issued the Edict of Nantes in 1598, granting the Huguenots (Calvinists) limited toleration. But Charles, Henry, and other monarchs always reserved the right to rescind toleration and resume persecution. France's Louis XIV infamously struck down the Edict of Nantes in 1685, leading to a renewed slaughter of Huguenots and the flight of thousands to Protestant lands. In France as elsewhere, religious freedom was not really an institution; it was at the pleasure of the ruler, and dissenters could not depend upon it.[17]

The Dutch Show the Way

The first country to change that, to build a tolerant *constitutional regime*, was the United Provinces of the Netherlands or the Dutch Republic. At the time of its birth in 1581, the United Provinces would not have been an obvious candidate to exemplify anything, except perhaps how to defy the world's mightiest empire (Spain). The seven northern provinces of the Low Countries that joined forces in 1579 against the Spanish Crown, the United Provinces was small and, considered solely in geographic terms, highly vulnerable. And indeed, foreign friends and foes continued to fight on Dutch soil for many more years after the Dutch declaration of independence.

Nor was the United Provinces, in its early decades, particularly tolerant. The bigotry of the infant Dutch Republic appears ironic to us today, since much of the motivation for Dutch independence was the bigotry of the Spanish Crown. In 1562, when the Netherlands were still ruled by Spain, King Philip II brought the notorious Inquisition there in response to the growth of Calvinism.[18] The Inquisition triggered a Dutch revolt in 1567. Nine years later, with the Pacification of Ghent, it appeared that all provinces of the Netherlands would unite to declare independence from Spain. But many Dutch remained Catholic, especially in the southern provinces. The Dutch intensely debated whether to implement, for the sake of anti-Spanish unity, a religious peace (*Religionsfrieden*) in which all Dutch Christians would be able to practice their religion.[19] But the Calvinist leaders of the northern provinces rejected the idea both on principle and because they suspected Dutch Catholics of being a Fifth Column for Spain.[20] The southern Catholic nobility responded in May 1579 by forming the Union of Arras (with roughly the same borders as modern Wallonia in Belgium) and aligning with the Spanish. In turn, the northern, mostly Protestant nobility formed the Union of Utrecht.[21] In 1581 the Utrecht Union formed the United Provinces, and in 1585 they declared themselves a republic.[22]

The Union of Arras, ruled by Spain, did not tolerate Protestantism; the Dutch Republic did not tolerate Catholicism. Massive self-sorting between the two unions took place, as an estimated 150,000 Protestants fled the Union of Arras for the new Dutch Republic over the next forty years, reinforcing the republic's Protestant character.[23] The Dutch state did not engage in anything like a Calvinist Inquisition; indeed, Calvinist doctrine regarded efforts by the state to convert people as a usurpation of God's sovereignty.[24] But public worship and other expressions of non-Reformed belief were forbidden. Only members of the Reformed church could hold political office. Many thousands more—the *Liefhebbers*, literally, "Lovers"—attended preaching but did not take communion.[25] Dutch intolerance showed itself particularly with the trial and imprisonment of a number of so-called Remonstrants—who asserted that man has a free will—in the early seventeenth century.[26]

The trauma of the Remonstrants' struggle triggered a prolonged debate in Dutch society over religious homogeneity. Old arguments in favor of tolerance—that true belief can never be coerced, that heterodox believers can be loyal citizens, that dissent was here to stay—began to have more purchase. City dwellers were the first to relax restrictions. In Amsterdam and Rotterdam, non-Calvinists found themselves allowed to practice openly. A Lutheran church opened, as did a Remonstrant one in 1630; in 1638–39 a Jewish synagogue opened. Even Catholics were finding that they could worship in certain regions.[27] From 1650 or so the Reformed faithful ceased harassing Catholics.[28]

Toleration did not increase in a steady, straight-line fashion. As dissenters grew bolder and more innovative, Dutch rulers sometimes pushed back. Under the leadership of Johan de Witt, the regents of Holland disallowed anti-Trinitarian teaching in 1653 and three years later set strict rules on the propagation of the religious ideas of the French philosopher René Descartes.[29] Still, during the de Witt years it became increasingly more difficult for leaders to crack down on most religious minorities.

What caused the United Provinces to set out on this irreversible path of toleration? The ordinary Dutchman seems to have practiced "live and let live" out of sheer pragmatism, to get on with his fellows. But such is often the case with the laity. Many Reformed pastors, who enjoyed significant societal influence, dearly wanted the state to favor the dominant faith more than it did. But the magistrates refused to do so. So let us restate the question: Why did Dutch leaders so favor toleration, when other European rulers at the same time with similar incentives opted to rescind toleration or never to try it to begin with? Historians disagree. Some attribute it to the earlier influence of Erasmus, the Dutch Catholic humanist of the preceding century; others, to the disruptive effects of intolerance on a commercial republic.[30] It is clear that Dutch rulers were greatly concerned to maintain domestic tranquility.[31] C. P. Hooft, burgomaster of Amsterdam, said early in the century that trying to eradicate non-Calvinist practice would spark a civil war and open the door to Spanish reconquest.[32]

In any case, whereas monarchs had granted toleration but reserved the right to withdraw it, the Dutch Republic made toleration into a self-reinforcing institution. As the United Provinces gained an international reputation for tolerance, it attracted various types of religious minority from the southern Netherlands (still ruled by Spain) and elsewhere in Europe. Many of these refugees brought with them, as economic historian Angus Maddison puts it, "capital, skills, and international contacts."[33] The industry and wealth of these newcomers made any enforcement of Calvinist belief still more difficult. Dutch wealth and power became a hostage to toleration.

In Lesson 6, our final lesson, we shall see how the Dutch example—a small state punching well above its weight—inspired imitation throughout Europe in the late seventeenth and eighteenth centuries. The English in particular were bothered by the commercial and naval successes of the Dutch—bothered enough to fight several trade wars with them—and English writers began to ask what the Netherlands' secret was. One of the answers they settled on was religious toleration. The Dutch Republic was officially Calvinist, and most Dutch remained religious. But over the course of the seventeenth century the state became progressively indifferent toward whether citizens were Calvinist or Arminian, or even Catholic or Jewish. English success with toleration in turn impressed the French, so that in the eighteenth century France too began to practice religious toleration.

Here, then, we have a second pathway through which an ideological struggle ends. A new regime type that effectively transcends the other two emerges through practice and gains support and articulation, then imitation. Secularism did not eliminate Catholicism or Protestantism from Europe. It did not even disestablish churches. It simply changed the subject.

Convergence: The End of Monarchism versus Republicanism, 1870s

The third pathway by which a prolonged ideological struggle stops is through construction of a convergent or hybrid regime. Whereas transcendence involves a new regime that sets aside the old bone of contention, convergence entails a new regime that combines elements of the old by creatively finding ways to square the circle. Suppose that in the 1980s the Soviets had adopted multiparty democracy but kept state socialism, and the Americans had adopted state socialism and kept multiparty democracy. Or suppose that in the seventeenth century the Dutch had somehow come up with a set of doctrines and practices that combined Calvinism with Catholicism. (Actually, it is fair to say that that is precisely what the English did in what became known as Anglicanism—explicitly Protestant in its doctrinal statements and rejection of papal authority, but retaining Catholic elements in its liturgy and church organization. The Anglican model, however, did not catch on elsewhere.)

Something like that did happen in the nineteenth century in Europe, in the final stage of the long contest between monarchism and republicanism. This time it was not the Dutch or the Americans who pioneered the solution, but the British.

Liberal Conservatism Triumphs in the 1870s

For many decades after the 1760s three ideologies contended for supremacy: absolute monarchism, constitutional monarchism, and republicanism. The main battlefield was, again, Europe, but the Americas also were infected with the struggle. The contest began in the 1770s with revolutions in the Netherlands and British North America. It endured for a century, sometimes dormant, sometimes very much awake. But this struggle, too, eventually ended. By the end of the nineteenth century, Europe still had monarchies and republics, but few people cared about these differences. Just as the political salience of Calvinism and Catholicism had diluted in most of Europe by the early eighteenth century, the questions of the extent of monarchical power, and whether there should be a monarch at all, were close to irrelevant by the late nineteenth. Italy was a constitutional monarchy, but did not thereby threaten the (nominally) absolute monarchy of Austria-Hungary. Republicanism in France did not threaten constitutional monarchy in Britain.

These differences in form lost salience because in fact these regimes were not nearly as different as they had been before. They were by no means identical; in the newly united Germany only the monarch could dismiss a government, whereas in Britain only parliament could. But they all fell into a fairly narrow range, relative to their wide differences in previous decades. By the 1870s, across societies, those who ruled and those who aspired to rule had reached a new settlement. Most of those who had sought revolution, and most of those who ruthlessly suppressed them, began to make significant concessions to one another. Historian Michael Broers writes, "The revolutions of 1848–51 [changed] the face of European political life forever. . . . They shattered the existing political order in every country where serious disorder occurred. Instead of creating new radical regimes influenced by nationalism or socialism . . . they gave birth to a new form of conservatism, able to absorb elements of liberalism, nationalism, and even socialism, and to transform them almost beyond recognition."[34] An early example was Piedmont, the leading state in the Italian Peninsula. Charles Albert, Piedmont's king, was an absolute monarch who felt his throne wobble during the revolutions of 1848. In order to retain power and achieve stability in Piedmont, Charles Albert granted a constitution. Following the Risorgimento (resurgence) or unification of Italy, Charles Albert became king of the new nation in 1861. He was persuaded that keeping his fragmented nation together required a continuation of the same regime, in which the monarch was constrained by law. The 1848 constitution of Piedmont became the *Statuto* of Italy.

In the years that followed other European powers followed suit, each in its own fashion. Austria's Emperor Francis Joseph was, like his Habsburg forebears, a committed absolutist. But, likewise concerned to keep his realm together, in 1867 he allowed his chancellor, Friedrich von Beust, to set up the Dual Monarchy (with Hungary as co-equal partner) and granted both the Austrian and Hungarian assemblies more power. Prussia's Emperor William held similar attitudes, as did his chancellor, Otto von Bismarck. Upon uniting Germany by conquest in 1866–71, they too granted a national legislature (the *Bundesrat*) extensive powers. Finally, in France the Emperor Napoleon III, who had dissolved the Second Republic in 1851, began to allow the national legislature more power in 1861 and in 1870 promulgated a new constitution that made his ministers responsible to that body.[35]

Even Alexander II, tsar of all the Russias, was planning to meet halfway those demanding liberal reforms. Having suffered several attempted assassinations by anarchists, the tsar and his minister Mikhail Loris-Melikov proposed a popularly elected legislature and other changes. But Alexander was assassinated on the day he signed orders to begin the reforms—March 13, 1881.[36] His son and successor Alexander III proved uninterested in reform, as did his grandson Nicholas II. The brutal and catastrophic ending of the Romanov's stubborn dynasty in 1917 demonstrates the wisdom of all of those European rulers who submitted to reform in the preceding decades.

The historian J. A. S. Grenville sums the matter up: "Before 1848, parliamentary assemblies worthy of the name were the exception rather than the rule. France and Britain were the leading constitutional European states. By 1878 the participation of elected parliaments was recognized virtually everywhere except in Russia as an indispensable element of good government. In Vienna, Berlin, Budapest, Rome, Paris and London, the parliamentary assemblies were acquiring increasing power; some parliaments were already elected on the basis of universal manhood suffrage."[37] The prolonged ideological struggle was over, and middle-class revolution was a thing of the past. Some have called this new regime *liberal-conservative*. It was liberal inasmuch as it embodied some of the reforms that constitutionalists and republicans had long favored: equality under the law, decreased privileges for Church and nobility, an executive constrained by an elected legislature. It was conservative inasmuch as it protected many elements of traditional order against the demands of radical republicans and socialists. The liberal-conservative regime could accept reform but was predisposed to defer to custom.

What triggered these changes? As with the religiopolitical conflict of earlier centuries, the story is complex. But two developments were crucial. First, after 1848 it was increasingly clear to ruling elites that the social and economic changes brought by commercialization were not going away. Those changes entailed the growing self-consciousness and political assertiveness of the commercial classes—those whose wealth derived not from inherited land but from the production of goods and services. With its growing wealth, education, and aspirations, the middle class was not going to stop demanding more power.

As we saw in Lesson 2, the victors over Napoleon in 1814–15 were convinced that they could suppress revolution by using force and secret police. But over the next forty-three years three waves of revolution were to roll across Europe—in the early 1820s, the early 1830s, and 1848. The last wave was the most dangerous, bringing down the corrupt monarchy in France and the reactionary ministries in Austria and Prussia.

But the middle classes had to compromise as well. They softened their demands because 1848 scared them as well. In that year they found themselves sharing the barricades with people from other stations in life and with other, still more radical goals for society. It was just before revolution erupted in Paris that Karl Marx and Friedrich Engels published *The Communist Manifesto,* which opened, "A specter is haunting Europe—the specter of communism."[38] The revolutions of 1848 were not communist—guildsmen trying to restore the old-regime economy were at least as evident as were factory workers[39]—but they did move the problem of the infant working class into greater prominence. Historian Eric Hobsbawm notes that one statesman, Count Cavour of Piedmont, had predicted in 1846 that a truly radical revolution, one that threatened private property, would drive many constitutionalists and republicans into becoming conservatives. Something like that happened in 1848. "From the moment the barricades went up in Paris," Hobsbawm writes, "all moderate liberals . . . were political conservatives."[40]

Lesson 6 will finish the story, which involves the impressive national performance of nineteenth-century Great Britain—a country with few special natural endowments but that had by far the world's wealthiest society and history's largest empire. Britain, moreover, had escaped the waves of revolution in the 1790s, 1820s, 1830s, and 1848. Cavour and other conservatives on the Continent began to conclude that Britain's constitutional monarchy, which was resistant to revolution precisely because it allowed for gradual reform, was the key.

For now, however, the lesson is clear. A third pathway toward the end of a grand, transnational ideological struggle is sometimes available: a new combination of elements of one with elements of another, amounting to a new hybrid.

How Might the Islamist-Secularist Struggle End?

Victory

The ongoing contest among Muslims could end like the communism-liberal democracy contest ended in 1989—with victory by one side. If so, which side appears more likely to win? From the first stirrings of the contest until the early 1970s, a victory by secularism appeared likely. These were the decades of Atatürk's Turkey, the Pahlavi dynasty in Iran, Jinnah's Pakistan, Nasser's Egypt, Ba'athism in Syria and Iraq, and PLO dominance over the Palestinians. The secularists themselves tended to think of Islamists as atavists with no appeal to the young and no future. Indicative is the *Time* cover story of November 4, 1974, on the shah of Iran, which touted Iran as the Middle East's rising power and made no mention at all of any Islamist revival movement.[41]

The Islamist resurgence that began after Israel's defeat of three Arab neighbors in June 1967, and was accelerated by the 1979 Iranian Revolution, has seemed to some to presage the opposite: a victory by political Islam. In recent years the safe bet, some say, has been on those who insist that "Islam is the answer" to all of the Muslim world's troubles. To be sure, secular regimes survive in many Muslim states, including Indonesia, the world's largest. But in the Arab world, Islamism broadly conceived seems to have captured and held the imagination of elites and general citizens alike, young and old, rural and urban.

It has proven difficult even for some academic experts on the Middle East to come to terms with the enduring appeal of Islamism. As we saw in Lesson 1, Westerners reflexively sell political Islam short because it violates our sense that social progress (as we conceive of it) cannot be reversed—that "you can't turn back the clock." But in fact Islamists see their movement as progressive, and secularism as "turning back the clock" to times of ignorance and paganism. It is worth stressing again that Islamism has been underestimated since it emerged in the 1920s. The mid-twentieth-century Muslim secularists—Atatürk and his imitators—naturally downplayed Islamism's viability; doing so validated their own modernizing project to themselves and to the wider world.

The Arab Spring of 2010–12 at first gave confidence to experts who had long argued that Islamism was (again) a fading movement; since the uprisings were popular, they could not be Islamist, by definition. Thus did one analyst declare that the Arab world was now "post-Islamist."[42] That was before any elections had taken place. The elections in Tunisia (a 40 percent plurality for the Islamist al Nahda Party) in October 2011,[43] and those in Egypt two months later (37 percent for the Muslim Brotherhood's Freedom and Justice Party, and another 24 percent for the ultra-conservative al Nour Party)[44] altered the mood among liberals, Arab and Western alike. References to an "Islamist Winter" became more common."[45]

In fact, as Western history demonstrates in abundance, an ideology that gives birth to institutions and practices can alter the world to its advantage, so to speak, and last much longer than we might guess. Absolute monarchy seemed doomed to liberals in Europe in the 1790s, but proved resilient, perhaps superior, over the next few decades and lived on for nearly another century. Or, to turn things around, absolutists after 1815 thought that liberalism was unsustainable because it degenerated into monstrosities like the presumptuous and rampaging Bonapartism that had dominated France after the French Revolution. We all tend to believe that our ideology—insofar as we are aware that we have one—is not only the most just but also the most viable, and we sell short its alternatives. But we must not let notions of the inevitable universal triumph of liberal democracy cloud our view of trends. Even if the Fukuyama of 1989 was right, and liberal democracy is destined to triumph the world over, destiny can be a long time in coming. As hard as it is for secular people to fathom, Islamism may prove viable in today's world.

Of course, as discussed in Lesson 4, Islamism is far from monolithic. A triumph for Islamism in general would not settle which Islamism—Sunni or Shia, moderate or extreme, monarchical or republican, and so on—would predominate. The victory of liberal democracy in the 1990s has not meant an end to ideological disagreement and competition within and across democracies. But the end of secularism as a viable model in the Middle East would be, to say the least, significant.

Transcendence

The Islamist-secularist struggle might instead end as the Catholic-Protestant political struggles did many centuries ago—by moving on or changing the subject. In the late seventeenth and early eighteenth centuries, Europeans slowly transcended their politico-religious differences by detaching religious differences from questions of political loyalty. Catholics and Protestants remained faithful to their respective churches and doctrines, but over time ceased linking political institutions or power with questions of Christian dogma or practice. A Catholic could be a loyal subject of the Dutch Republic; a Protestant, of the French king.

One problem with transcendence as a resolution in the Middle East is that secularists already claim to have arrived at this solution. In a sense, they are correct. In early modern Europe, transcending the Catholic-Protestant political struggles meant becoming secular—not in the sense of abandoning religion, but in the sense of making the state indifferent toward questions of fidelity to any particular set of religious doctrines. One of the starker statements is in the seventeenth-century philosopher Thomas Hobbes's famous book *Leviathan*. Political order, argues Hobbes, is not about building a righteous society or the Kingdom of God, but about securing individuals against violent death. Hobbes reduced religious fidelity to obedience to the sovereign, who was put in charge of religion.[46] Indeed, twentieth-century Muslim secularists borrowed, directly or not, from such Western ideas about the purpose and securing of public order. They did so, as we saw in this book's introduction, because they thought Islam's traditional mixture of politics and religion had held the Middle East back and that secularism had helped Western countries achieve global dominance.

Any transcendent solution, then, could not mean secularism, for that would mean victory for one of the contestants rather than changing the subject. How, then, might a transcendent resolution between Islamists and secularists look?

Muslims, elites and average people, would need to stop seeing the question of how much Islam should shape or determine laws and institutions as a life-or-death matter. They would not need to become indifferent between

Islamism and secularism. But they would need to see the contest in something like the way most Americans see debates over taxes. Some Americans believe that high (or low) taxes would endanger the very constitutional order upon which the country is based. Most, however, see questions of tax cuts or increases as policy questions that do not implicate the regime. This majority has strong views and preferences on taxes, and may vote based upon those. But if they lose an election or congressional vote, they do not begin to mobilize for revolution or emigrate. Even if they see that they may not win for a long time to come, they endure the loss and focus on the other issues they care about.

Just so, if secularists and Islamists were to transcend their regime contest, each group would see the other's victories as regrettable but less than catastrophic. Religion-and-state questions would be just some of a variety of questions about which elections or laws were decided. If Islamists took power and began to alter the laws, secularists would be disappointed, even outraged, but they would not go underground, form revolutionary cells, and so on. Instead, secularists would accept the government as legitimate. The same would go for Islamists when secularists gained power and began to move laws and policies in their preferred direction. Both sides would need to adopt this "policy change, not regime change" attitude.

Some may protest that questions of religion and state are just qualitatively different from questions such as taxation. As explained in this book's introduction, I am abstracting from the content of the ideologies under consideration, and it may be that we are confronting one of the limits of this abstraction. How God and the state relate surely is more fundamental than whether the top marginal income tax rate is 25 percent or 35 percent.

In the world of politics, however, what qualifies as a religion-and-state issue can shift over time. Consider what has happened to Sabbatarian laws in many European countries, prohibiting certain businesses from operating on Sundays. These laws originated in the traditional Christian teaching that the Ten Commandments should be codified in secular law. By the late twentieth century, the percentage of Europeans who were believing Christians had dropped significantly. Sabbatarian laws remained, but their justification had changed: it was no longer a matter of obeying God, but of mandating a day off for workers. At the same time, opposition to Sabbatarian laws had changed: it was based no longer on hostility to religiously derived laws, but instead on a desire to increase consumer choice. Whether one was religious or not, in other words, had less and less bearing on whether one favored Sabbatarian laws.

Is such a "change-the-subject" regime plausible in the Middle East today? Can secularists and Islamists scale back their aspirations and trust one another enough to transcend their decades-old struggle? In fact, in many countries Islamist parties are tolerated. Political scientist Nathan Brown has shown that in countries where such parties are legal, they tend to moderate their methods and policy platforms (although they also leave themselves the option of reverting to extremism, perhaps because they are unsure of how long they will remain legalized).[47]

It stands to reason that a transcendent resolution could be more palatable and hence sustainable if it involved compromises over questions of religion and law. Secularists and Islamists might trust one another more if each got a bit of what it wanted when the other dominated. That leads us to the final type of resolution, convergence.

Convergence

The third possible outcome is this: the Islamist-secularist contest could resolve as the West's long monarchical-republican contest did in the late nineteenth century. Convergence would produce a hybrid regime and ideology. In the 1860s and 1870s, absolute monarchists and republicans, equally alarmed by the rise of a common enemy, socialism, worked out new bargains in state after state.

How would such an outcome look in the Middle East? Convergence would entail secularists' and Islamists' striking a new bargain, at least implicitly, under which the regime would have elements of both ideologies. The main site of conflict has concerned the source of the laws. Pure Islamists insist that law derive directly from the sacred texts, as interpreted by clergy; pure secularists insist that law derive from reason uninformed by putative divine revelation. Stated in those ways, the two positions are mutually exclusive. But it is conceivable that the two could apportion areas of law by mutual agreement, with secularists having greater say over some areas of law and Islamists over others.

Indeed, a majority of the world's majority-Muslim countries already have some kind of hybrid regime, in which the sources of law are both Sharia and secular civil law.[48] In Malaysia, for example, family law—covering marriage, divorce, women's rights, and so on—derives from Sharia, whereas other areas of law do not. In Lesson 1 we saw that during the Islamic revival of the 1970s many secular regimes, including those of Egypt and Pakistan, enacted Islamic law in some areas. Part and parcel of these political bargains has been a new acceptance among Muslim intellectuals who have identified as secularists of Islam as a legitimate source of law. Some of these intellectuals recast the religion as a cultural heritage that Muslim societies cannot and should not cast aside. Others have themselves become Islamists. These intellectuals have outlined, in various ways, paths toward hybrid secular-Islamist regimes.[49] Muslim scholars have shown how some conceptions of constitutionalism and democracy are compatible with Islam.[50]

The trouble is that that same Islamic revival left many Islamists dissatisfied with hybridity and demanding full Sharia. That is part of what we mean when we say that the Muslim world is still going through a clash of ideas. Although secularists have moved in an Islamist direction, such that there are few pure secularists left in the Middle East, it is not enough for many Islamists. In Libya, Egypt, Syria, Iraq, Pakistan, and Muslim regions of African states such as Nigeria, Mali, and Chad, significant minorities—perhaps majorities in some cases—genuinely want full-blown Sharia. These countries could only equilibrate into hybrid Islamist-secularist regimes if enough Muslims accepted them as such. That, in turn, would entail the demobilization of military Islamist parties seeking total Sharia.

Still, some Islamists in some states have moved toward the center as they have been offered the opportunity to compete in elections.[51] In 2011–13 Egypt's Freedom and Justice Party, the political wing of the Muslim Brotherhood, took pains to portray itself as moderate by, for example, accepting religious and ideological pluralism. That effort ultimately failed, but Tunisia's Ennahda Party similar effort enjoyed greater success.

Analysts such as Daniel Pipes argue that Islamists can never be democrats; Islamism and democracy are mutually exclusive. If this claim is true by definition, such that any Islamist who adopts democratic principles is declared no longer an Islamist, it is not very useful. We want to know if people who hold that law should derive from Sharia may be willing to compromise and tolerate other views *on a permanent basis*. And of course, it is impossible to say just how robust is the commitment by various Islamists to democracy, compromise, and toleration. A leading Egyptian Islamist, Yusuf al-Qaradawi, calls himself a democrat but explicitly sees democracy as a way to achieve an Islamist society. The commitment is not to democracy but to Sharia.[52] Were Qaradawi and Islamists of his stripe to find that democracy did not result in Sharia after all, one must ask what would become of their allegiance to democracy. At the same time, secular democrats who profess a willingness to allow religion a role in public life may be willing to suspend or overturn democracy if religion has *too* great a role. Something like this seems to have happened in Egypt during the summer of 2013, when secular liberals applauded the army for ousting a democratically elected Islamist government that was casting serious doubt on its stated commitment to compromise.

So an Islamist-secularist convergence may prove unsustainable. On the other hand, in the 1820s or 1840s in Europe, monarchists and republicans had similar deep suspicions of one another. Their ideologies were mutually exclusive and so any move toward moderation by one would be dismissed by the other. By 1870, however, in most of Europe, both sides had moved toward the center. Each had shed some of its dogmas and ceased to define itself in opposition to the other. The resulting bargains were not easily struck, but once struck they stuck.

It would be not only unimaginative but also ahistorical to rule out of hand the possibility of a durable Islamist-secularist hybrid. Western history teaches that ideologies have a number of components, and which components are emphasized in a given time and place depends on who the "other" is in that time and place. Even where religion and secularism are concerned, what may appear an incoherent impossibility in 1960 or 1990 may appear a natural fit in 2020. Western history also teaches that, historically speaking, liberal democracy does not have purely secular origins. It owes a great deal to Catholic conceptions of natural right, Calvinist notions of covenant, and other elements in the soil of Christendom out of which it grew.[53] If Western democracy is not as secular as many suppose, Islamic democracy may not need to be either.

How likely such a hybrid is to win, and what its content would be, however, are not only matters of intellectual argument. Our final lesson is that the outcome of a prolonged ideological contest depends in large part upon the relative performance of the states that exemplify the ideologies. It is to that lesson that we now turn.

Lesson 6
Watch Turkey and Iran

Whether you like it or not, history is on our side. We will bury you.
—*Nikita Khrushchev to Western diplomats 1956*

My idea of American policy toward the Soviet Union is simple, and
some would say simplistic. It is this: We win and they lose.
—*Ronald Reagan to Richard Allen 1977*

Khrushchev in 1956 and Reagan in 1977 agreed on one thing: the competition
between the Soviet Union and the United States was about more than just
which state had more power. It was about which social system was superior. As
historian Melvyn Leffler later put it, the Cold War was a struggle "for the soul
of mankind."[1] The Cold War was at once a contest between two superpowers
and a contest between two ways of ordering society. The two contests were
intertwined.

In 1987, a decade after Reagan's statement to his friend Richard Allen, the
struggle's resolution was becoming clear. The United States had won and the
Soviet Union had lost—and that was tantamount to saying that democratic
capitalism had won and communism had lost. In the end, the Marxist-Leninist
model for ordering society, entailing state control of the production of resources and a monopoly on power by single party, did not work. More to the
point, communism failed when compared to its chief competitor, the Western
model of democratic capitalism, which entailed (mostly) market control of the

economy and competition for power among political parties. And this conclusion took hold among political elites in most of the world precisely because in the 1980s it became manifestly clear that the United States was outperforming the Soviet Union. The outcome of the ideological contest turned on the outcome of the international contest. That the United States outperformed the Soviet Union meant, to all concerned, that democratic capitalism has outperformed communism. The fate of each ideology was hostage to the successes and failures of the states that exemplified it.

In fact, the importance of what we can call *exemplary countries* is evident in all three of the historical ideological contests we have been examining in this book. The reason for this is straightforward. An ideology is a set of claims about best way to order society: Calvinist is better than Catholic; republican, than monarchical; fascist, than communist. And "best" means, among other things, that societies that implement the ideology will do better—be stronger, richer, more just, more cultured—than those that do not. These alleged advantages are a great part of any ideology's appeal, to elites and masses alike. Centuries ago, advocates of established Catholicism maintained that Catholic states would have more obedient subjects, and fewer rebellions, than Protestant ones. Partisans of constitutional monarchy claimed that their kind of state was less vulnerable than absolute monarchies to the destructive whims of kings. Liberal democrats asserted that their favored regime was more technologically innovative than Marxist-Leninist societies.

And, advocates claim, these putative advantages will show up in international competition. Catholic states, constitutional monarchies, liberal democracies—each, say its partisans, will win more wars and generally be wealthier, more powerful, and stabler than countries that exemplify alternative, competing ideologies.

The same kind of implied test is evident when it comes to Islamism and secularism in the Middle East. The Young Turks of the early twentieth century, and Atatürk as well, believed in secularism because they believed that traditional Islam was holding back Muslim societies, rendering them unable to compete with European countries. It was the old ways, said the secularists—the powerful clergy, the emphasis on piety, the resignation to the supposed will of Allah—that rendered Muslims vulnerable to Western imperialism. Islamists have made the opposite claim: the weaknesses of Muslim societies—their persistent poverty and humiliation—is owing to the adoption of the impious institutions of the West; "Islam is the solution" to all the problems Muslims face.

The implications are clear: secularists and Islamists alike claim that states that put *their* principles into practice—set up and keep the right institutions, exemplify their ideology—will outperform those that put the opposing, wrong principles into practice. These claims invite a real-world test. If Islam is the solution, then pious societies will be strong, wealthy, and not subservient to the West. If Islam—or at least Islamism—is not the solution, then Islamist societies will end up weak, divided, and subservient.

These predictions and boasts are not just a matter of rhetoric. In practice, states—or the elites who run them—do pay close attention to which models work and which do not. Just as firms imitate successful techniques and avoid failed ones, states imitate successful regimes and avoid failed ones. Elites do so because, reasonably enough, they would rather learn from the mistakes of others than to make those mistakes themselves. Scholars have noted that institutions "diffuse" through the international system by emulation of success.[2]

Hence history's final lesson: *A good indicator—probably the best we have— of which ideology will triumph in the Middle East is the relative performance of various state exemplars.* What qualifies a state as an exemplar? In a literal sense, every state exemplifies its regime type. History shows, however, that some states present themselves as exemplary: their governments and perhaps some leading subjects or citizens note publicly that they regard their country as a virtuous example of its regime. States that loudly announce themselves in this way tend to be regarded as such by foreigners. Exemplary states invite others to judge them, and others generally accept the invitation.

For the Muslim Middle East, Turkey was the chief exemplar of secularism from its founding in 1923 through the early 2000s. As discussed elsewhere in this book, Kemalism and its offshoots in the Arab and Persian worlds has all but died out, and so there is no strongly secularist exemplar in the Middle East. Ironically, Turkey today under the AK Party has moved in an Islamist direction and seems to have settled on a hybrid Islamist-secularist regime, which it proudly exemplifies.

As for Islamism, undiluted, Iran seems to be the best exemplar. Although its Shia Islam is a minority branch of Islam, the Islamic Republic has drawn admiration from many Sunni Muslims—including in the Muslim Brotherhood—since its founding in 1979. Saudi Arabia's form of Sharia is harsher, but that regime's reputation has suffered from its hypocrisy and long-standing participation on American hegemony.[3]

At the end of this lesson we focus, as many Muslims are doing, on Iran and Turkey for clues as to the future of Islamism and secularism. First, we look back once more at Western history, which clearly shows the importance of exemplary states to the outcome of prolonged ideological struggles.

The Netherlands, England, and the Rise of Secularism

In Lesson 5 we saw that the struggle between Catholic and Protestant theocracies many centuries ago ended with the triumph of a new type of regime—a *tolerant* or *secular* regime.[4] Secularism in the West emerged in the seventeenth century, and became predominant in the eighteenth. Its uniqueness, as regarded political power, lay in its indifference to changes in the religious composition of society. Where a Catholic sovereign had once seen the growth of Protestantism in his realm as a threat to his authority, now he could see it as something regrettable but irrelevant to his influence and power.

The new secular regime achieved this indifference toward religion by abandoning the old notion that "religion is the bond of society" (*religio vincula societatis*) and looking instead to other societal bonds—loyalty to the Crown, or constitution, or nation. It could be monarchical or republican, but regarding religion, this new regime was tolerant in practice and, increasingly, in law. In these early centuries the secular regime was still confessional, in the sense that it gave privileges to one church over others. But it allowed freedom of practice to dissenting churches, adherents of other religions, and (eventually) adherents of none.

All during the religious strife of the sixteenth and seventeenth centuries, various monarchs tried toleration as a provisional measure (modus vivendi). Holy Roman emperors, kings of France, and others sometimes decreed that dissenters were free to practice their religion, usually within strict limits. The important thing about these decrees is that they were just that: decrees, reversible by the monarch when he thought it necessary. And all of them eventually were reversed. The most famous came late in the period, in 1685, when Louis XIV of France rescinded the Edict of Nantes and thereby reignited persecution of the Huguenots (Calvinists).

One reason why even many Catholics in Europe condemned Louis for this reversal was the sense many had that religious persecution was no longer acceptable or productive. Today we regard this sense as moral progress, and so it is. But the story of how more and more Europeans came to favor toleration is a story of national power and wealth—specifically, that of a much smaller and younger country, a country that punched well above its weight during these decades: the United Provinces of the Netherlands.

Lesson 5 recounted how the Dutch were the first to institutionalize secularism—that is, to make toleration into a sort of rule that everyone accepted or at least accommodated themselves to. The emergence of secularism was gradual and came only after much strife between Catholics and Protestants and then among Protestants themselves. But by the early seventeenth century toleration was becoming ensconced there.

Table 6.1.
European merchant fleets and armies, 1670

Country	Merchant fleet	Army
Netherlands	568,000	110,000
England	260,000	15,000
France	80,000	120,000
Russia	NA	130,000
Spain	250,000	70,000

Source: Maddison, The World Economy, 78–79.

Lesson 6 points us to the apparent outcome of Dutch secularism. With a population of only 1.8 million in 1700—compared to 9 million in Britain and 19 million in France—the Netherlands was a bona fide great power.[5] It sent ships to the Indian Ocean, Japan, North America (what is now New York), Brazil, and the Caribbean; Dutch ships captured Spain's entire silver fleet off of Cuba in 1628. The young Netherlands surpassed Portugal as Europe's biggest trader with Asia. It channeled some of its wealth into its army and navy. Table 6.1 compares the Dutch merchant fleet and army to those of other European powers in 1670.

The young republic made rapid strides in science and higher learning as well. When under Spanish rule, the northern Netherlands had only one university (Leuven, founded in 1425). The Dutch Republic founded many more— Leiden (1575), Franeker (1585), Harderwijk (1600), Groningen (1614), and Utrecht (1634). As the biggest, Leiden attracted students from other countries.[6] The seventeenth century was to be known as the Netherlands' Golden Century, as this tiny state became financially and economically dominant in Europe and a naval power of consequence.

England Imitates the Netherlands

Dutch wealth and power naturally attracted the notice of foreigners who wanted to know what this little country's secret was. The causes of Dutch national success are complex, and certainly go beyond the state's religious toleration. But it is significant that many Europeans at the time attributed the Netherlands' success in part to secularism. In particular, religious dissenters in other countries, who were looking for arguments to use back home, stressed that the Dutch way of managing permanent religious diversity contributed to national strength. Thomas Helwys, the English founder of the Baptist denomination, moved to the Netherlands in 1608 because of the greater toleration there and was persuaded that rulers should never persecute anyone because of religion.[7] "Behold the Nations where freedome of Religion is permitted, and you may see there are not more florishinge and prosperous Nations under the heavens then they are," wrote Helwys.[8] William Bradford and a group of English Separatists went to the United Provinces during the same period, settling until 1619, when they moved on to what is now Plymouth in Massachusetts.

To be sure, other foreigners took a dim view of Dutch ways. Most violent in his consternation was Louis XIV of France, who set out (and ultimately failed) to put the United Provinces in its place and overturn its republican, Protestant regime. Even many European Protestants rejected Dutch toleration. Jean-Baptiste Stouppe was a French Huguenot who had pastored a church in London and spied for the Puritan leader Oliver Cromwell. In 1672 Stouppe was an officer in a French force that invaded the Netherlands. Attacked in print for fighting for the Catholic Louis against the Protestant Netherlands, Colonel Stouppe responded with *La Religion des Hollandois* (1673), in which he asserted that this was no Protestant country: "there are Roman Catholics, Lutherans, Brownists, Independents, Arminians, Anabaptists, Socinians, Arians, Enthusiasts, Quakers, Borelists, Muscovites, Libertines, and many more . . . I am not even speaking of the Jews, Turks, and Persians."[9] Stouppe noted with horror that the Dutch allowed the free-thinking Jewish philosopher Benedict Spinoza to publish his work, in which he argued that religions were created for social or political purposes. "A few years ago [Spinoza] wrote a book in Latin, whose title is *Theological-Political Treatise*, in which his principal goal seems to be to destroy all religions, particularly the Jewish and Christian ones, and to introduce libertinage, atheism, and the freedom of all religions." The Dutch allowed Spinozism to flourish, Stouppe thought, because they put commerce ahead of religion.[10]

It is ironic that Stouppe the soldier appealed to religious fidelity, whereas Helwys the preacher appealed to national power. In the event, the Dutch army repulsed Stouppe's army in 1678. For that and other reasons, practical men of affairs found Helwys's arguments more persuasive.

One who took Helwys's arguments further was Sir William Temple (1628–99). Englishman, man of letters, accomplished diplomat, Temple was an admirer of the United Provinces and a close friend of De Witt and of William of Orange, the Dutch Stadholder (head of state).[11] Temple published his *Observations upon the United Provinces of the Netherlands* in 1673, during one of the Anglo-Dutch wars over trade. The book was almost entirely sympathetic to the Dutch, and Temple devoted an entire chapter to religion. Temple noted that trying to change a nation's religion by force will involve "Violence, Oppression, Cruelty, Rapine, Intemperance, Injustice, and, in short, the miserable Effusion of Humane Blood, and the Confusion of all Laws, Orders, and Virtues, among Men."[12] He could not understand "how those who call themselves, and the world usually calls, religious men come to put so great weight upon those points of belief which men never have agreed in, and so little upon those of virtue and morality, in which they have hardly ever disagreed; nor why a state should venture the subversion of their peace and their order, which are certain goods, and so universally esteemed, for the propagation of uncertain or contested opinions." It was not so in the United Provinces, where even Catholics were unofficially allowed to practice openly. Thus "it is hardly to be imagined how all the violence and sharpness which accompanies the differences in religion in other countries seems to be appeased or softened here [in the Netherlands], by the general freedom which all men enjoy, either by allowance or connivance; nor how faction and ambition are thereby disabled to color their interested and seditious designs with the pretenses of religion, which has cost the Christian world so much blood for these last hundred and fifty years."[13] So long as Dutchmen were loyal to the state and did not foment unrest, they could worship as they pleased; and this toleration enhanced the wealth and power of the Netherlands.

Temple had company in England. The economist William Petty published *Political Arithmetick* in 1690, containing an analysis of the Dutch marvel. With a population only one-tenth that of France, the Dutch merchant fleet was "nine times that of the French, its foreign trade four times as big, its interest rate about half the French level, its foreign assets large, those of France negligible." Aside from its physical advantages, such as accessible waterways, Petty argued, were Dutch institutions: the legal system and clear property rights encouraged commerce, and taxes (actually high) were levied on spending rather than income. And, Petty noted, Dutch religious tolerance attracted skilled and entrepreneurial immigrants. Petty's contemporary, Gregory King, noted that the United Provinces' per capita fiscal revenues in 1695 were two and a half times larger than those of France or England, enabling it to fight wars more efficiently.[14]

Arguments in favor of toleration had been batted about England for many decades. Only now, in the late seventeenth century, were they getting a serious hearing. In the decades before Temple, Petty, King, and others published their observations, England and Scotland had passed through their vicious civil wars (1642–51) between High Church monarchists and Puritan republicans. After the restoration of the Stuart dynasty, there remained intolerant Anglicans who had concluded from the Civil War that religious dissent must be suppressed. A coalition of Whigs and Tories in Parliament still believed the medieval rule of *religio vincula societatis*: a united England must have a single version of Christianity enforced by the state.

But this old view was increasingly on the defensive. The first to push back against it were the Stuart kings themselves. Charles II (r. 1660–85) leaned Catholic and converted to the Church of Rome on his deathbed; James II (r.

1685–88), his brother and successor, was openly Catholic. Unabashedly wishing to re-Catholicize England, James tried to remove the Anglican Church's special status but found himself blocked by Parliament. In 1687 James sidestepped Parliament with a Declaration of Indulgence, declaiming that recent history had shown that religious diversity in England was "invincible."[15] The following year James reiterated his Declaration, with a justification that sounds much like those of Helwys and Temple: "We must conclude, that not only good Christians will join in this, but *whoever is concerned for the increase of the wealth and power of this nation.* It would, perhaps, prejudice some of our neighbours who might lose part of those vast advantages they now enjoy, if liberty of conscience were settled in these kingdoms, which are above all others most capable of improvements and of commanding the trade of the world."[16] In other words, the Dutch advantage lay in part in its religious toleration; were England to follow suit, it would level the playing field.

As every student of English history knows, Anglicans of all stripes suspected that James was using toleration to re-Catholicize England and make himself an absolute monarch like his patron Louis XIV of France. In 1688 James found himself dethroned, exiled to France, and replaced by none other than the Dutch Stadholder, William of Orange. Ironically, but unsurprisingly, England's new King William III quickly pushed Parliament toward the same religious policy as James had: toleration. William did this both because he was Dutch, and because he needed to counter propaganda from Louis XIV that he intended to banish Catholicism from the British Isles.[17]

Once enthroned in England, William found that Parliament was still not ready for full toleration. The resulting compromise was the grudging Toleration Act of 1689, which upheld Anglican privileges but allowed Protestant dissenters—Quakers, Presbyterians, Baptists, and Independents—to preach and build chapels. Catholics and Jews were not included in the Toleration Act, but William used his royal prerogative to instruct judges not to inhibit their religious practices.[18] Full religious freedom was not to come to Britain until the early nineteenth century, when non-Anglicans finally were allowed to hold public office and to be members of the universities in Cambridge and Oxford. But the importance of 1689 is indisputable. In that year England became another exemplar of the new political regime of religious toleration—and one even more compelling than the United Provinces.[19]

France Imitates England

The story continues, as English success in the early eighteenth century forced still more Europeans to consider the merits of secularism. The contrast between England and France could hardly have been starker. In 1685 Louis XIV had revoked the Edict of Nantes, France's eighty-seven-year-old official toleration of

Huguenots. Louis ordered the destruction of Protestant churches, the exile of Protestant clergy, and the forced baptism of Protestant children.[20] From France's powerful armies *dragonnades* formed to enforce the persecutions. Protestant emigration was forbidden, but by 1700 an estimated three hundred thousand Huguenots had left France for England, the Netherlands, Germany, North America, and elsewhere.[21] Louis revoked the Edict of Nantes less out of devotion to Rome or the Catholic hierarchy than out of the old conviction that a united society rested on religious conformity throughout his realm. And the Revocation, as it became known, was popular in France, from bishops down to peasants.[22]

But the cruelty and suffering that the Revocation triggered horrified Protestant Europe. Over time, this revulsion fed back into France itself. Also altering French opinion was the clear evidence that the Revocation had actually weakened, not strengthened, France. In 1689 the Marquis de Vauban, Marshal of France, assessed the Revocation as a net loss for the realm: valuable Huguenot men and money left the country, as did many good seamen and soldiers, perhaps as many as six hundred officers and twelve thousand enlisted men. And, Vauban added, the Revocation was a gift to William of England, Louis's chief rival, in that it made him the international champion of the outraged Protestant half of Europe.[23] Gottfried Wilhelm Leibniz, the German philosopher and mathematician, later wrote that the Revocation was a turning point in European history. "Insofar as it is possible to insist upon a date to determine the movements of thought, it is true to say that 1685 marks the culmination of the victorious efforts of the Counter-Reformation: after that comes the turn of the tide. . . . It is now necessary to apply ourselves more to combating Atheism and Deism than our own heresies."[24]

Leibniz meant that, for growing numbers of European elites, the savagery that followed the Revocation undermined the credibility of orthodox Christianity itself. In eighteenth-century France ideas such as those of the Jewish Spaniard-turned-Dutchman Spinoza began to take hold among elites. Among the most influential was the French thinker Voltaire, who visited the Netherlands in 1722 and England in 1726. In 1723 Voltaire published *La Henriade*, a paean to Henry IV, who had issued the Edict of Nantes back in 1598. In *Lettres philosophiques* (1733) Voltaire's observations of England read like the observations the Englishman Temple had offered on the Netherlands sixty-one years earlier: "England is properly the country of sectarists. *Multæ sunt mansiones in domo patris mei* (in my Father's house are many mansions). An Englishman, as one to whom liberty is natural, may go to heaven his own way. . . . If one religion only were allowed in England, the Government would very possibly become arbitrary; if there were but two, the people would cut one another's throats; but as there are such a multitude, they all live happy and in peace."[25]

Voltaire and other French elites also began to write worriedly about how Great Britain (formed in 1707 from England and Scotland) was now outpacing France in wealth and power. France's rulers did not embrace the deism of Voltaire, but as the eighteenth century progressed, the Crown all but ceased to enforce Catholic orthodoxy.[26]

Little by little, secularism won. Most Europeans remained devout Christians, but the link between religious conformity and political power was loosened. Revolutionaries no longer sought to change a country's established religion; governments were no longer threatened by the growth of a rival branch of Christianity. And this profound change took place in large part because states that began to practice official toleration—first the Netherlands, then England—demonstrably outperformed those—France, Spain, Austria, and others—that did not.

Great Britain and the Triumph of Liberal Conservatism, 1870s

Two centuries later, the decades-long struggle among absolute monarchy, constitutional monarchy, and republicanism ended in a loose hybrid of these three—sometimes called liberal conservatism or constitutionalism. Most European countries reformed themselves into a regime that retained a strong centralized executive—monarch or president—but allowed an elected legislature to constrain that executive. The triumph of liberal conservatism was partly caused by the manifest superiority of the state that best exemplified it: Great Britain.

The 1848 revolutions that swept over the Continent and toppled governments and dynasties barely touched Britain. As a constitutional monarchy, opposed to both the French Revolution and the reactionary policies of the absolutists, Britain had long stood alone among the powers. British constitutionalism emerged out of the same tumultuous seventeenth-century events that made Dutch secularism more plausible for the English. Tied up with the religious conflicts in England, Scotland, and Ireland were conflicts over absolute monarchy, insisted upon by the Stuart kings, and the republicanism favored by the Puritans. With the invasion of William of Orange in 1688 the traumatized nation decisively returned to its historic and messy kind of monarchy, in which sovereignty was deliberately ambiguous: it resided in "the King in Parliament." England's unwritten constitution sought to maintain a balance among Crown, nobility, and commoners.[27]

While Dutch and British secularism gradually won over the eighteenth century, Britain's constitutional monarchy did not. Until the 1770s most European elites continued to bet on France's model of absolute monarchy. It was not at all clear during the transnational struggle of the 1770s through 1860s which ideology would win. But toward the end of the struggle, more and more absolutists began to recognize the superiority of a reforming conservative regime—regardless of what it was called. In 1830–31 revolution toppled the Bourbon dynasty in France and caused regimes in the Netherlands, Germany, Italy, and Poland to totter. Britain was far from calm; radicals agitated for revolution in British cities too. But in the end British radicalism was not so radical after all. Precisely because they were freer to speak and write openly, many radical elites chose to join mainstream politics; the writings of John Stuart Mill and William Cobbett were reasoned considerations of such questions as universal suffrage, questions out of bounds in many countries on the Continent.[28] And British institutions yielded different results as well. While most rulers on the Continent were suppressing liberals and radicals, Britain was passing its Great Reform Act of 1832, expanding the franchise and effectively transferring power from Crown to Parliament.

Camillo Benso, Count of Cavour, was one influential political elite who admired Britain's regime. A nobleman from Piedmont, the leading state in the Italian Peninsula, Cavour became a leading European politician and journalist in the 1840s and 1850s. Within Piedmontese politics, Cavour began as a liberal, believing in the increasing progress of the human race toward rationality. His early opponents were the absolutists and advocates of the old privileges of Church and nobility: the Habsburgs, the popes, the large landholders. But Cavour also rejected the radicalism of the Italian republicans such as Giuseppe Mazzini and Giuseppe Garibaldi; these, he argued, would destroy social order just as the Jacobins had done in France in the 1790s. Cavour admired the work of the French writer Alexis de Tocqueville, whom he met in London in 1835, for its qualified endorsement of democracy. Cavour favored *le juste-milieu*, the "appropriate middle" or "happy medium," exemplified in the July Monarchy in France (1830–48) and, most of all, in Britain's robust regime.

An argument he had with Tocqueville reveals Cavour's reasons for admiring British institutions. Where Tocqueville predicted a violent revolution in England owing to deep class divisions, Cavour (prophetically) predicted peaceful reform. In the words of one historian, "Cavour's deep respect for the English led him to assume that they had sufficient moral and political forces to enable them to avoid the trauma of revolution. His admiration stemmed from his belief that the English always weighed up what was practically possible, and did not follow utopian dreams. They talked less, he said, than other nations, but they did more."[29] Cavour's native Piedmont was an absolute monarchy, however, and in the years that followed, Cavour became notorious for openly praising British institutions.[30] The revolutions of 1848 finally gave

Table 6.2.
Relative shares of world manufacturing output, 1830 and 1860

Country	1830	1860
Great Britain	9.5	19.9
Russia	5.7	7.0
France	5.2	7.9
Prussia	3.5	4.9
Austria	3.2	4.4

Source: Kennedy, *The Rise and Fall of the Great Powers*, 149.

Cavour and his confreres their opportunity to push Piedmont in a constitutional direction. They helped King Charles Albert see his way to submit to a written constitution in order to ward off a republican revolution.[31] As prime minister (1852–61), Cavour helped engineer the Risorgimento (Resurgence) or wars of Italian unification; united Italy inherited the Piedmontese constitution and Cavour as its first prime minister.

The British model recommended itself to other Europeans not only because it had proved so resilient in the face of revolutionary discontent. A small island nation, Britain had become the world's richest state, possessing the largest manufacturing capacity in its day and the largest empire in all of history. Table 6.2 gives trends in the relative shares of world manufacturing output over the course of the nineteenth century.

As for overall wealth, here again Britain outperformed all others. Table 6.3 lists overall gross domestic product (GDP) and, in parentheses, per capita GDP in 1820 and 1870.[32] It makes clear that Britain pulled ahead of all rivals in both categories, and was particularly impressive in the per capita figure.

Table 6.3.
GDP and GDP per capita of major European powers, 1820 and 1870

Country	1820	1870
Great Britain	36.2 million (1,707)	100.2 million (3,191)
Russia	37.7 million (689)	83.6 million (943)
France	38.4 million (1,230)	72.1 million (1,140)
Prussia	26.3 million (1,058)	71.4 million (1,876)
Austria	4.1 million (1,218)	8.4 million (1,863)
Netherlands	4.2 million (1,821)	10 million (2,753)

Source: Maddison, *The World Economy*, 184–85.
Note: GDP per capita values are in parentheses.

This was the period of Pax Britannica, the Peace of Britain, when the Royal Navy kept the sea lanes open and Britain kept any one country from dominating the Eurasian land mass. Political economists today recognize Victorian Britain as the world's economic hegemon—the power that supplied the public goods necessary to the smooth functioning of the global economy.[33] Like the Netherlands in the seventeenth century, Britain in the nineteenth was an astonishing success, outperforming larger nations with more impressive natural endowments. Foreigners wanted to know how the British did it. The answers were many and complex. But Britain watchers settled on the things they could control, and one of those was the way they handled radicalism. The old British formula of co-opting and moderating it, once considered dangerous to the aristocracy and unacceptably slow to the middle class, now seemed the best option.

The United States and the Superiority of Democratic Capitalism, 1980s

The end of the ideological spasms of the twentieth century was more like the last case, except that the result was even clearer. One contender, democratic capitalism, simply won. Fascism had had its *Götterdämmerung* in 1945, with the utter defeat of Nazi Germany, leaving communism and liberal democracy to fight on. Four decades later, the stagnant Soviet Union was starting to imitate the Western model, as were most other communist states. By the time of the Soviet collapse in 1991 communism had been an empty husk for several years.

As we saw in earlier lessons, it was not always clear that communism would lose, much less that it would do so in the 1980s. In the 1950s and 1960s Soviet growth rates outpaced American. In the 1970s Westerners were preoccupied with economic stagflation—a new, miserable combination of high inflation and unemployment—and Americans in particular with the lost war in Vietnam and the traumas of Watergate. But it was in that decade that Soviet leaders began to recognize that their own system had stagnated. Table 6.4 compares GDP, GDP per capita, and average annualized GDP growth between the two superpowers in 1970 and 1980. Figure 6.1 depicts comparative GDP growth graphically, plotting per capita over time for each superpower. (The vertical scale is logarithmic, rather than linear, for convenience).

The difference in the American and Soviet numbers and curves may not appear dramatic, but they tell an important story. The United States started the 1970s wealthier and finished wealthier, and the Soviet Union grew as well, both in total and per capita. But the Soviet economy grew at a somewhat slower pace, and it was already well behind the American. Note that in the graph, the

Table 6.4.
Economic growth in the superpowers, 1970s and 1980s

	United States 1970–80	Soviet Union 1970–80
GDP	3.1 trillion–4.2 trillion	1.3 trillion–1.7 trillion
GDP growth (decade)	35.5%	30.7%
GDP per capita growth (decade)	23.6%	15.3%

Source: Data set from the Maddison Project, http://www.ggdc.net/maddison /maddison-project/home.htm.

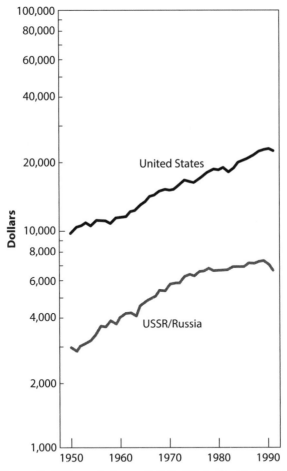

Figure 6.1. Per capita GDP growth (logged), United States and Soviet Union, 1950–90
Source: Maddison, *The World Economy*, 133.

Soviet curve is dramatically steeper in the 1950s, and slightly steeper in the 1960s, than the American; but in the 1970s the Soviet becomes flatter while the American, notwithstanding the 1973 recession, continues to climb at nearly the same slope as in the 1960s.

Although U.S. and Western economic growth slowed in the 1970s, leading to a publishing boom on American decline, Soviet decline at the time was much more severe (and more hidden). It is strange to contemplate, but the decade of Watergate, defeat in Vietnam, leisure suits, and disco music saw the United States finally pull decisively away from the Soviet Union.[34]

These relative national growth trends mattered because they defied the strong expectations of the Soviets and most communists around the world—and the fears of Westerners—in the 1950s and 1960s. In those years, America's economy was growing rapidly, but the Soviet economy was growing even more rapidly. The more time passes, the harder it is for those of us who teach international relations to convince our students that the Soviet Union was once a real superpower, terrible to behold. In 1956 Soviet Premier Nikita Khrushchev proclaimed, "We will bury you!" (i.e., will be present at your funeral). In 1961 he predicted that within twenty years the Soviet economy would surpass the American. In the end, of course, it was the Soviet Union that was buried, in 1991. But thirty years earlier, Khrushchev's hectoring was all too realistic and intimidating. What happened between then and now was the 1970s, when the growth trends in the two countries crossed, and the 1980s, when the Soviet Union reformed itself out of existence.

The story of the Soviet abandonment of communism is well-known. In late 1984 the Central Committee of the Soviet Communist Party, desperate to reverse the continuing trends, selected Mikhail Gorbachev, a leading reformer, as the next party chairman. Gorbachev's reforms went well beyond what most of his elite supporters had envisaged. He and his circle began by encouraging free debate over policy—*glasnost* or openness—and went on to push a restructuring or *perestroika* of the Soviet economy. The reformers' goal was, roughly, a social-democratic Soviet Union, not a U.S.-style capitalist democracy. What matters for our purposes is that Gorbachev and his circle were abandoning Marxism-Leninism for something closer to a Swedish model of political economy.

Soviet desertion of the communist cause choked off transnational communism in two ways. First, Gorbachev literally ceased material aid to communist parties elsewhere. The Bulgarians, the Cubans, Marxist-Leninist guerrillas in Angola and El Salvador, even the Provisional Irish Republican Army—all were told that they would have to go it alone.[35] Some Leftist groups turned to crime to fund themselves.

Second, Soviet failure demoralized communists and dissuaded other Leftists from aligning with communists. In earlier decades, the Soviet Union's impressive successes—its rapid industrialization in the 1930s, its defeating of Nazi Germany in the 1940s, its high growth rates and world-class space program in the 1950s and 1960s—inspired imitation in much of the world, particularly what became known as the Third World. Here, countless elites believed, was the best model for state building, one that brought to a mostly agrarian, impoverished society crushed beneath a despot's heel (Russia in 1917) security and prosperity—even superpower status—while maintaining an equitable distribution of wealth. By the mid-1980s, it was clear that the Soviets no longer believed in their own system. The Soviet Union had failed, and with it Marxism-Leninism.

Back to the Present: Islamism and Secularism

If we want to know how the Islamist-secularist contest, now in its tenth decade, will turn out, Western history directs us to the states that exemplify competing ideologies and their relative performances. Participants and observers will, over time, judge the best regime type for Muslim societies based upon which seems to bring the most wealth and power.

Which Muslim states, then, exemplify the contending ideologies? Map 6.1 depicts regime types across the Muslim world as of 2009.[36]

The question is not "Which states do Muslims most admire?" but rather "Which states do Muslims think exemplify, for good or ill, Islamism and secularism?" The answers are not straightforward. Saudi Arabia has always presented itself as the model Islamist polity. It practices a strict form of Sharia, and is located on the original homeland of the Arabs, who gave Islam to the world. The Saudi king has the official title Guardian of the Two Holy Mosques, those in Mecca and Medina. For decades the Saudi state has propagated throughout the world its Wahhabist version of Islam, via well-endowed mosques and schools (madrassas). Gilles Kepel writes that in the 1970s in particular, new Saudi oil wealth gave the country regional prestige. "To Muslims," he writes, "the successes of Saudi Arabia and her allies in the oil war had a symbolic significance, and were generally seen as a sign from God heralding the coming triumph of Islam over the whole world."[37]

But it is not at all clear that Saudi Arabia enjoys exemplary status among many Muslims outside of its borders. The first serious assault on its Islamist credentials came with the 1979 revolution in Iran. Ayatollah Khomeini and his fellow Shia-Islamists made a credible bid to assume the position of Islamist exemplar, and indeed the Egyptian Muslim Brotherhood—the powerful Sunni-Islamist entity that had been supported by the Saudis—embraced the new Iranian regime and even considered declaring Khomeini imam of a new

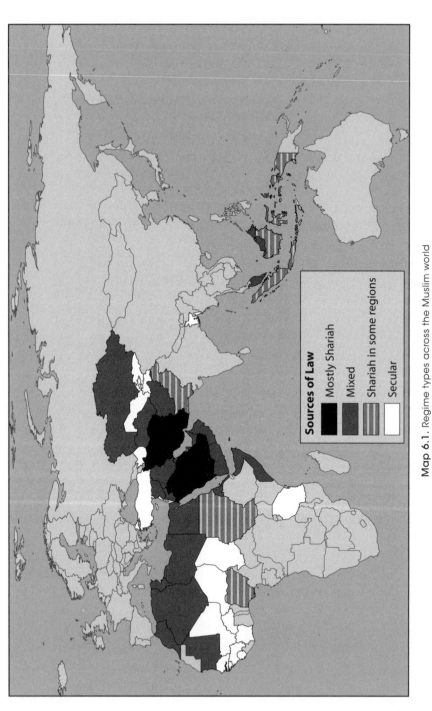

Map 6.1. Regime types across the Muslim world

Source: John M. Owen IV, *The Clash of Ideas in World Politics: Transnational Networks, States, and Regime Change, 1510–2010*, Princeton, Princeton University Press, 2010.

caliphate.[38] The second major assault came from Osama bin Laden in the 1990s. Bin Laden, once a Saudi subject supported by Saudi resources in Afghanistan in the 1980s, turned against his king in 1991. When Iraq conquered Kuwait in August 1990 and appeared poised to invade the kingdom, bin Laden offered the services of his mujahideen to protect his country. He believed that inviting the Americans to protect the Arabian Peninsula would be a gross impiety. When the Saudi government turned him down, bin Laden broke with them; eventually exiled, bin Laden formed al-Qaeda and for several years thereafter tried to overthrow the Saudi regime. For all of their vehement disagreements, the Shia-Islamist Iranians and Sunni-Islamist al-Qaeda agree that Saudi Arabia is a fraud, corrupt, hypocritical, a willing tool of the Western infidels.

Other Islamist regimes have sought pride of place as exemplar. Sudan under Hassan al-Turabi tried to assume exemplary status in the 1990s, as did the Taliban when they ruled most of Afghanistan. Sudan and Afghanistan, however, are peripheral states, lacking wealth and size.

Iran as Exemplar

Unquestionably a leading—and perhaps the chief—Islamist exemplar is the Islamic Republic of Iran. Iran's leaders have consistently proclaimed their republic to be *the* model polity for Shia and Sunni alike. At least some of their policies seem designed to buttress this claim. That is why they have directed much of their propaganda since 1979 against Saudi Arabia, which had long enjoyed its status as the exemplar of Islamism. Iran has emphasized Islam in general over Shia Islam, and Muslim solidarity over Persian ethnicity. The fatwa by Ayatollah Khomeini against the novelist Salmon Rushdie in 1989 was an attempt by Khomeini to burnish Iran's Islamist credentials. Iran's energetic militancy against Israel may be seen in a similar light; while Saudi Arabia talks of the plight of the Palestinians but continues to align with the United States, Iran acts: it openly defies America and funds Hamas and Hezbollah.

How, then, is Iran performing? On the whole, the news is mixed. Iran begins with some advantages. Its population is seventy-eight million. It ranks fourth worldwide in oil exports. It sits atop the Persian Gulf, location of the highest concentration of oil production in the world. Owing in part to modernization under the Pahlavi regime, Iran has an industrial economy, good infrastructure, and relatively rich human capital.

Of course, a country endowed with natural advantages can underperform. Iran under its Islamist regime has made strategic mistakes—goading Iraq into attacking it in 1980 was the main one—but in recent years it has performed impressively along many fronts. Its economy is the world's twentieth largest; the only Muslim states with larger economies are Indonesia (sixteenth) and Turkey (seventeenth), both of which are larger.[39]

Most impressive has been Iran's strategic progress. It has combined skill, ideological and ethnic affinity, and luck to build a network of alliances. It has enjoyed influence in Lebanon owing to its sponsorship of Hezbollah, the Shia-Islamist organization that essentially governs the southern part of the country and some sectors of the capital Beirut. Connecting it to Hezbollah has been Iran's close relationship with the Assad regime in Syria, based in a Shia offshoot, the Alawites. Iran also has provided support to Hamas, the Sunni-Islamist Pales-tinian group that rules the Gaza Strip. Iran's regime has enjoyed the sympathy of many of the Shia majorities in tiny Bahrain and in Saudi Arabia's Eastern Prov-ince. Perhaps most important are developments in neighboring Iraq since 2003. Ironically, the American-led war rid Iran of its archenemy Saddam Hussein; and the establishment of majoritarian democracy has empowered Iraq's Shia major-ity, one of whose leading political parties was founded in Iran.[40] All told, Iran has been attempting to construct a Shia Crescent stretching from the Indian Ocean to the Mediterranean Sea.[41] Propelling its influence in Iraq, Lebanon, and else-where is the al-Quds Force, a transnational entity that trains and arms guerrillas in other countries and reports directly to the Ayatollah Khamenei.[42]

Second, and related, for many years Iran has been the leading source in the Middle East—and perhaps the world as a whole—of articulate and reso-nant anti-Americanism. Mahmoud Ahmedinejad, Ali Larijani, Ali Khamenei, and others have proved able to exploit predictable but unfocused resentment against U.S. hegemony. Iran's anti-hegemonic credentials are partly responsi-ble for its regime's historic prestige among Sunni-Islamist groups such as the Muslim Brotherhood and its offshoots. Other governments can be sharply critical of American policy—Venezuela, and sometimes Russia and China—and even call for the return of a "multipolar" world. But those governments continue to do business with the United States. Iran has been able to claim an anti-American purity denied to all but North Korea.

Third, Iran has defied international demands that it halt its nuclear pro-gram. Even if negotiations with the Western powers and Russia produce an Iran that is not actively producing and deploying nuclear weapons, Iran has made clear that it insists on the right to process nuclear fuel for civilian use.[43] It may prove difficult to prevent Iran from developing a "breakout" nuclear capability, that is, enough lightly enriched uranium that it could develop a bomb within a few months.[44] A study by political scientist Matthew Fuhrmann shows that countries with civilian nuclear programs are much more likely eventually to develop military ones.[45] It would appear risky to bet against Iran's joining the nuclear club at some point.

Iran has weaknesses. Its ambitions are resisted by adversaries near and far. Near adversaries include Israel and Iran's Gulf neighbor Saudi Arabia, much smaller in population but with more oil reserves, high-technology defenses, and

U.S. protection. Far adversaries include the United States. Even countries that profess no hostility toward Iran, such as Russia, China, and those of Western Europe, have resisted in various ways its nuclear program. Perhaps Iran's chief problem is its regime's domestic legitimacy. The protests following the dubious elections of May 2009, which nearly toppled the regime, reveal just how little acceptance Khamenei has among at least young urban Iranians. In the aftermath of this threat the regime moved in a more authoritarian direction, with the Republican Guard and hard-line clergy closing ranks against the reformers. This centralization of power could extend the life of the regime, but Iran's institutions seem brittle.

Related, Iran's legitimacy in the Arab world in particular has suffered since the eruption of the Arab Spring. A June 2011 poll of publics in six Arab nations—Morocco, Egypt, Saudi Arabia, Lebanon, Jordan, and the United Arab Emirates—showed a sharp reversal of long-standing pro-Iranian sentiment. Whereas Arab publics had once admired Iran for its defiance of the United States and welcomed its nuclear program, the 2011 poll showed widespread worry that Iran is not a force for peace and stability in the Middle East. (Saudis were the most anti-Iran, Lebanese the most pro-Iran.)[46] Most damaging was Iran's unstinting support for the Assad regime in Syria; as Assad's forces killed thousands of (mainly Sunni) Syrians, Tehran extended it rhetorical and material support.[47] Figure 6.2 depicts the trend.

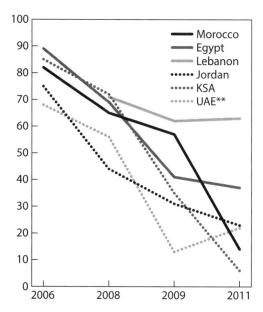

Figure 6.2. Opinion about Iran in various Arab states, 2006–11
Source: Zogby, "Arab Attitudes toward Iran, 2011."

The reasons for the shift, according to pollster James Zogby, probably have to do in part with the Arab Spring. "The region is now looking at a different direction. They are looking inwards and not looking [at] who is defying the US the most. The US has become almost irrelevant in this period." Iran's interference in Iraq, Bahrain, Lebanon, and other places came to be seen less as a challenge to America than as a challenge to Arab self-determination.[48]

Notwithstanding these reversals in its soft power, some trends concerning Iran's actual and potential hard power remained positive. Iran's Islamist regime has made a habit of foiling expert predictions of its impending collapse. Iran may find ways of adjusting its behavior so that it regains its lost popularity.

And what of secularism? Which state is its champion? It is not clear that there remains in today's world a secularist Muslim exemplar. Such purely secular regimes as remain, as shown in Map 6.1, tend to be in Saharan Africa and Central Asia, regions on Islam's periphery. Other putatively secular states have either moved in an Islamist direction in recent years by allowing some areas of law to derive from Sharia, or (as in the case of Indonesia) by allowing some provinces or regions to be governed by Sharia. This broad re-Islamizing trend began in the 1970s, as the religious revival across the region compelled secularist rulers to move in an Islamist direction so as to safeguard their legitimacy. Saddam Hussein's Iraq also moved slightly in an Islamist direction in the 1980s, as did Pakistan under Zia ul-Haq. Egypt, the most populous Arab country, was the main secularist exemplar to Arabs under Nasser, but under Anwar Sadat its constitution, too, began to include elements of Sharia.[49] The military takeover in July 2013 wrenched the country back in a secularist direction from its brief experiment in democratically elected Islamist government. At the time of this writing, Egypt's regime is too unsettled to qualify it as exemplifying any type.

In Lesson 5 we saw that few Muslim elites believe any longer that the strong secularism of Atatürk or Nasser is feasible. Liberals, socialists, and other modernizers have increasingly come to accept that any legitimate regime in a majority-Muslim society must in some way recognize Islam's special role in shaping laws and institutions. In the twenty-first century the leading alternative to Islamism appears to be no longer a wholesale rejection of any influence of religion on politics and the state, but a hybrid regime. The hybrid is taking different forms in different countries. Tunisia after the Arab Spring appears to have in place one promising example. By no means is a final form yet in place anywhere. It is clear, however, that for many Muslims, particularly in the Middle East, the model of a secular-Islamist hybrid is—ironically—the birthplace of Muslim secularism: the Republic of Turkey.

Turkey as Exemplar

Constitutionally the secular Kemalist republic it has always been, Turkey has been governed since 2002 by the Justice and Development Party (AKP), an organization "with Islamic roots" but one that works through constitutional means and disavows any attempt to coerce Turks into embracing Sharia. The AKP, led by Recep Tayyip Erdoğan, insists that it is democratic and indeed it has liberalized Turkish law so as to strengthen Turkey's bid to join the European Union.[50] Erdoğan has laid out his vision of "conservative democracy," a "concept of modernity that does not reject tradition, a belief of universalism that accepts localism, an understanding of rationalism that does not disregard the spiritual meaning of life, and a choice for change that is not fundamentalist."[51] Erdoğan and Abdullah Gül, the AKP's other main leader, compare their vision for Turkey to that which Christian Democrats for their societies in Europe and Latin America. They claim to accept secularism, but an Anglo-Saxon version, in which the state avoids interfering with religious practice, rather than the Gallic version, in which the state is supreme over religion.[52]

In concrete terms, Turkey's shift from Kemalism to conservative democracy has meant legislative reforms in both a democratic and an Islamist direction. New laws have increased respect for the "social, cultural and political rights of all Turkish citizens irrespective of religious and ethnic origin"; reduced the military's role in politics; and increased freedom of expression.[53] It surprises many Westerners to learn that, in Turkey at least, democracy and Islamism do not necessarily pull in opposite directions. Increasing rights and freedoms has entailed overturning the old Kemalist law prohibiting women from wearing religious head coverings.[54] The increased public expression of traditional Islam in Turkey has alarmed many Kemalists. More recently, Erdoğan's increasingly coercive policies toward dissent have worried democrats and human rights activists. The net effect is serious concern that the AKP has used liberal means in the service of unchanged Islamist ends.[55]

In any case, Turkey under the AKP is certainly no Iran, and is widely seen in the terms in which Erdoğan presents it. During the Arab Spring, Arab and non-Arab elites debated extensively the "Turkish model," with many arguing that it was the best available for their own countries.[56]

How is this hybrid experiment faring? Economically, Turkish success has been striking. Possessing the world's twenty-sixth largest economy when the AKP took power in 2002, it has risen to seventeenth largest. Its GDP grew in 2010 by 8.2 percent (by 2013 the rate had slowed to 3.8 percent). The inflation rate in 2002 was over 70 percent; in 2013 it was 7.6 percent.[57] Turkey was not immune from the global recession of 2008–9, but it altered its exporting patterns in a significant way: in 2007 its main customers were in the European Union; since then its exports to the Middle East have risen 20 percent.[58]

In the realm of high politics, Turkey has not pursued the same strategy as Iran: it has not set itself against the United States (or the United Nations), and indeed has remained a member of NATO, which it joined in 1952. But Turkey nonetheless has begun to cut a more independent path than before—and its efforts have met with some success. Traditionally a key partner of the United States and Israel, Turkey under the AKP has shifted from a concerted effort to join the European Union to a more eastward and southward focus. An important moment came in early 2003, when some AKP members of parliament voted against a resolution to allow U.S. forces to pass through Turkey on the way to invading Iraq.[59] In 2009 Ahmet Davutoğlu became foreign minister. As part of his "zero problems" policy, Davutoğlu has put Turkey on a decidedly autonomous path. He has sought to improve ties with Turkey's Muslim neighbors. In 2010 Turkey, along with Brazil, attempted to mediate between the Western countries and Iran over Iran's nuclear program. Turkey has tried to improve relations with Syria and Libya as well. The most striking change has been in Turkey's relations with Israel. In May 2010 Turkey's government allowed an Islamist charity, IHH, to organize a flotilla to attempt to break an Israeli blockade of Hamas-ruled Gaza; the resulting Israeli raid killed nine Turks, and Turkey recalled its ambassador over the incident. Erdoğan's rhetorical support for Hamas and condemnation of Israel have been robust.[60]

It is abundantly clear that, in the Middle East at least, Muslims tend to ascribe prestige to countries that demonstrate independence from the United States, Europe, and Israel—the conglomeration of states that form "the West." Like Iran, Turkey has succeeded in doing so in recent years. Unlike Iran, it has done so in a fairly risk-averse fashion. Turkey is not pursuing a nuclear program, and no one is talking about Israel or America bombing Turkey. Turkey also played the Arab Spring better than Iran: whereas Iran refused to condemn its friend Bashar al-Assad for violently suppressing rebels in Syria, Turkey reluctantly but firmly did so. Turkey spoke out against Libya's Qaddafi regime for its brutality in 2011. Turkish political stock was high in the Arab world after the Arab Spring, as Figure 6.3 shows. Figure 6.4 decomposes what Arabs think about Turkey.[61]

In September 2011 Erdoğan sought to capitalize on his personal popularity in the Arab world by embarking on a tour of Egypt, Libya, and Tunisia. Erdoğan was received as a hero, his anti-Israel rhetoric as gospel.[62]

Turkey, like Iran, has weaknesses. The chief one may be the government's ongoing struggle with the Kurds, who compose roughly 18 percent of the country's population. In October 2011 Kurdish raids from northern Iraq were met with attacks by ten thousand Turkish troops.[63] Another weakness is turmoil

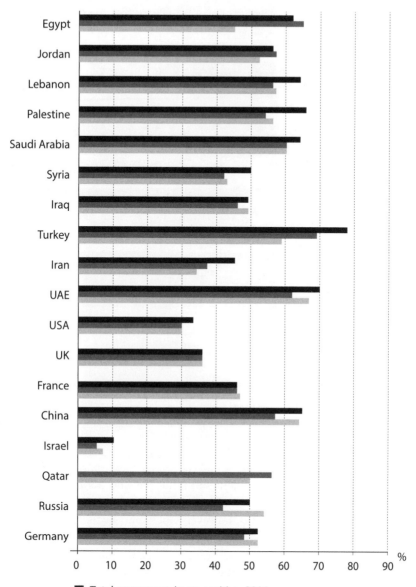

Egypt
Jordan
Lebanon
Palestine
Saudi Arabia
Syria
Iraq
Turkey
Iran
UAE
USA
UK
France
China
Israel
Qatar
Russia
Germany

0   10   20   30   40   50   60   70   80   90   %

■ Total agreement / very positive, 2011
■ Total agreement / very positive, 2012
▨ Total agreement / very positive, 2013

Figure 6.3. Turkey: Popular but fading, 2011–13
Source: Akgün and Gündoğar, *Perception of Turkey*, 9.

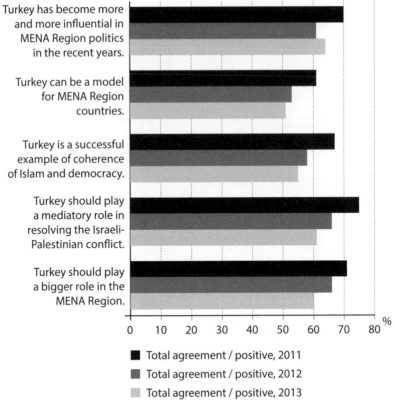

Figure 6.4. Analysis of Arab opinion of Turkey, 2011–13
Source: Akgün and Gündoğar, *Perception of Turkey*, 20.

and intrigue among Turkey's Islamists. Erdoğan's former political ally Fethullah Gülen, who lives in Pennsylvania but influences the National Police and various networks and schools in Turkey, once helped him tame Turkey's army, guardians of Kemalism. In 2013, however, Gülen and Erdoğan fell out, and fear of Gülen's movement has helped prod Erdoğan's lurches toward authoritarianism.[64] Signs have emerged that Erdoğan is befriending the same army he once brought to heel.[65] However the intra-Islamist rivalry resolves, the AKP already has damaged Turkey's democratic credentials.[66]

Still, through most of the AK Party's years in power, Turkey has had the wind in its sails. The Arab Spring seems to have helped it and, on the whole, hurt Iran. Projecting current trends portends well for Turkey and its incipient model of Islamic democracy.

Were Egypt, the largest Arab state and once the font of Arab secularism, to settle on a stable, long-term regime, it would doubtless attain exemplary status as well, at least for Arab states. It would appear that some kind of authoritarian regime has emerged from the years of turmoil since early 2011. That regime may be strongly secular, excluding Islamists from power. Or it eventually may find a place for the Muslim Brotherhood or other Islamists.

Nothing is for certain, of course. But the United States, and the rest of the world, needs to be preparing for a Middle East, and perhaps a Southwest and even Southeast Asia, in which countries are at once more Islamist and more democratic.

Conclusion
What to Do and What Not to Do

Political Islam matters, and it is not going away any time soon. It is a powerful ideology and social movement, running deep within and across most Muslim countries today and among minority Muslim populations in Europe, the Americas, Africa, and Asia. A source of hope to millions, an atavistic nightmare to millions of others, Islamist networks are implicated in both existing and emerging regimes and in political and social turmoil of many types, from terrorism to rebellion and repression to political parties to foreign policy. By no means are all Muslims Islamists, nor are all Islamists violent extremists. The Middle East would have strife and stress without Islamism. But this multiform, shape-shifting ideology has helped knot a set of problems that might otherwise be separate. Islamism affects the lives of most Muslims as well as the ideas and interests of their governments—and of governments of non-Muslim countries, including those in the West.

To grasp Islamism in all of its complexity, there is no substitute for the deep study of Muslims and Islam on their own terms—their theologies, cultures, and histories, including subjugation to outside imperialism. But it also is vital to understand how transnational ideologies work in general. Doing that requires that we look at the history of the West itself, with its long periods of transnational ideological conflict. Much like ideological movements in the West, political Islam emerged as a reaction to the status quo; is healthiest when embattled; mystifies outsiders; and is progressive on its own terms. Ideologies such as Islamism cannot be understood apart from their competition with alternative ideologies. Thus we have paid particular attention to those historic competitions and what they tell us about Islamism's prolonged struggle with secularism.

Seeing the Western past in the Muslim present can be at once reassuring and alarming. It helps make some sense of the often-ferocious rivalries among Islamists to recall that, during the Protestant Reformation, Calvinists and Lutherans could be worse enemies with each other than either were with Catholics. It is comforting to know that people who hold strongly to an ideology and its triumph are also people with interests and egos who act, in a tactical and instrumental sense, rationally. Yet, it is unsettling, to say the least, to recall that the Protestants also could coalesce against their Catholic enemies as those enemies coalesced against them, and that in a time and place when state rulers were consolidating power, that helped lead to general war. Even rational human beings can end up deeply polarized and in a very dangerous situation.

This book is written for policy makers, students, and citizens of countries grappling with how to respond to the ideological and political dynamics of the Middle East. In this brief conclusion, I offer a few conclusions for American foreign policy specifically. The United States remains engaged in most Muslim countries, militarily, economically, and socially, as no other outside country does. Notwithstanding its much-studied ongoing loss of global economic clout, America remains the world's only military superpower and likely will remain so for many years to come.[1] In very general terms, what ought America to do in the Middle East? What ought it not to do?

America Cannot Fix This—Yet Cannot Withdraw

The Middle East is beset with a tangle of problems, and one thread in the tangle is Muslims' own crisis of legitimacy, seen in the prolonged ideological contest between Islamism and secularism. An outside superpower cannot unknot the problems. That may seem obvious, but it was not obvious to all in the first few years following September 11, 2001. Then the idea took hold among some in the Bush administration and more widely that America had it in its power to remake the Middle East, and quickly. It was the "unipole" and exemplified the only viable set of ideas for ordering society. Three thousand of its people had just been murdered by a handful of men in thrall to backward ideas, made attractive by the gruesome regimes under which they lived. What Muslims in the Middle East and Southwest Asia needed and wanted was freedom; freedom would make them and their societies productive and peaceful; and America must act swiftly so as to bring it to them while it had the ability. As President George W. Bush said in his second inaugural address in January 2005, "it is the policy of the United States to seek and support the growth of democratic movements and institutions in every nation and culture, with the ultimate goal of ending tyranny in our world."[2]

As the great enemy of tyranny Edmund Burke might have forecast, Afghanistan and Iraq chastened this hubris. The United States had to use military force in both countries for many years, suffering great human and material losses and reaping ambiguous results. The Iranian Green Movement of 2009 and the Arab Spring of 2010–12 show that millions of Muslims do want freedom. But it is clear that by "freedom" many do not mean what Americans mean—or, at the very least, most Muslims do not trust the United States to help them achieve freedom.

Had American policy makers absorbed the lessons of the West's own history of ideological conflict in the months after 9/11, they would have been more skeptical about their country's ability transform the Middle East. The past shows that regional ideological struggles have a logic of their own. Such struggles always trigger much foreign intervention. But foreign interventions do not end the struggles: they perpetuate them. Four centuries ago, various Habsburg emperors fought to eradicate Protestantism, but they only made the Protestants more anti-Catholic and attracted counter-intervention. Two centuries ago, Napoleon used massive force time and again to eradicate both the "old regime" and republicanism in Europe; he failed utterly.

Why intervention does not end ideological strife is a complicated matter, but it is in part because people in ideologically polarized times and places believe that no one, including the outsider, is neutral. For them, interveners are not transcending the contest, but participating in it. Indeed, insiders on all sides tend to believe that the benevolent outsider is helping their enemy. Thus intervention invites resistance and aggravates ideological tension. In the end, Muslims must settle their legitimacy crisis themselves, and no one can control precisely when that will be.

Still, Bush's goal of "ending tyranny in our world" is only a maximal version of what we saw in Lesson 4 is a strong tradition in American foreign policy ideology to transform global order to the benefits of others and itself. America is an ideological country that has, by and large, acted rationally to shape the international system in its favor. Since the Second World War the United States has succeeded in large part through an active strategy of promoting, within and among states, self-government and the rule of law.[3] For most of its history, however, America promoted these institutions by example. The Middle East's endemic resistance to forcible U.S. intervention means that America should lean toward this older strategy of what political scientist Jonathan Monten calls "exemplarism"—a point to which I return below.[4]

Such is far from saying that the United States should withdraw from Muslim regions, militarily or economically, or even that it ought never to intervene militarily. It might be tempting to throw up our hands and say that we do not understand the Middle East, already have too much to answer for, and can only make matters worse by staying. If we cannot affect the outcome of the Muslims' long legitimacy crisis, should we not simply leave and let Muslims sort things out?

To do that would be to set aside the ongoing interests the United States has in much of the Middle East, particularly North Africa and Southwest Asia. This is not the place to join the already robust and interminable debates about the future of world oil markets or the extent to which America ought to support various Israeli policies.[5] It suffices here to make a logical point: that the United States cannot decide the contest between Islamism and secularism implies nothing about whether the United States has vital interests in the Middle East or other predominantly Muslim regions. Whether Washington withdraws, retrenches, maintains the status quo, or indeed increases its presence in the Middle East depends on more than the ideological contest that is our main concern here.

Be Flexible

By and large, it does not pay to treat Islamism as monolithic. A clear lesson of history is that treating an ideological group as a monolith helps to make it one. What I called in Lesson 4 a hedgehog strategy—seeing Islamism as "one big thing"—does provide moral and strategic clarity. It supplies the advantages of having a stable, known enemy at all times. When one treats everyone as wearing either a white hat or a black hat, the murky compromises and the hypocrisy go away.

Politics, however, is seldom about absolute and permanent friends and enemies. Certainly domestic politics in any country is more typically characterized by compromise and shifting coalitions based upon common issue-specific goals and interests. The trouble with acting the hedgehog and treating Islamism as monolithic is that sometimes profitable opportunities to divide and conquer, or even to enter a sustained period of cooperation with moderate ideologues, are available. Often it pays to play the fox, as the United States actually did during the Cold War, exploiting and widening fissures among communists and socialists.

Do Not Hope for Too Much

On the other hand, playing the fox—trying to locate and cultivate moderates—has significant hazards. One is the risk of forgetting that there usually are irreconcilables, hard-core ideologues who are themselves hedgehogs and will not change. A fox dealing with hedgehogs on his own side should remember that the foxes on the other side likely are struggling with hedgehogs of their own. Identifying who is fox and who is hedgehog on the other side is as important as it is difficult. The Truman administration in the late 1940s outfoxed Stalin in Western Europe. It found reliably anticommunist, pro-American elites in various parties.

Another hazard of flexibility is forgetting that the moderates with whom one is dealing still hold an ideology that they take seriously. Just because you can work with them does not mean that they are "like you." In the Second World War the West allied with Stalin against Hitler, and some Westerners—including Franklin Roosevelt himself—came to believe that Stalin cared little or nothing about communism per se and could be dealt with in the long term. That proved an expensive misreading. Centuries earlier, Charles V, Holy Roman emperor and militant Catholic, convinced some Lutherans to fight against other Lutherans; he successfully played divide-and-conquer and came to believe that his allies actually did not care about Lutheranism. Charles was wrong, and paid a high price.

Moderate, pragmatic, democratic Islamists are still Islamists. They remain committed to bringing about Sharia in their societies, and often other societies as well. Islamists' views on the rights of women and of religious minorities—Christians, Jews, Bahais, and others—on education, and on other issues will always contrast sharply with the liberal views of Western democracies. Islamists' anti-Semitism—their refusal to recognize Israel, the denial by many of the Holocaust—must remain an especially sturdy handicap to cooperation.

The West's history shows that states with opposing ideologies—conflicting views of the best social order—need not be enemies but can never be close friends. If Americans hope for relations with Turkey or Egypt or Iran comparable to the close relations they have with Canada or Great Britain, or even the more dysfunctional but still familial relations they have with France, they are bound to be frustrated and may overreact to that frustration.

Be Who We Are

Finally, Americans should remember that, although they cannot resolve the Muslims' ideological contest by force, they can have a virtuous indirect influence on how Muslims themselves resolve it. The United States can influence the outcome by preserving its example and image of a constitutional democracy with an attractive society—by using what Joseph Nye calls its "soft power"—and by quietly helping those in Muslim countries who find constitutional democracy attractive and want it in their own societies.[6]

Lesson 6 concerned the processes by which prolonged, region-wide ideological struggles end. The long competition between Islamism and secularism will end just as ideological fights in the West ended: when states exemplifying one regime type manifestly outperform exemplars of rival ideologies. In the seventeenth century the Netherlands punched far above its weight economically and militarily, and foreigners concluded that one reason was its regime of religious toleration, which freed it from domestic strife and attracted talented émigrés. England and later France adopted this new regime and allowed religious minorities to practice their faith. In the nineteenth century Great Britain increased its economic lead over its rivals, developed the world's largest empire, and escaped various waves of revolution that rolled over most of Europe. Those rivals concluded that Britain's moderate, reforming brand of liberal conservatism was responsible, and by the 1870s most were imitating it. In the 1980s the United States was manifestly outperforming the Soviet Union and it was clear that the Soviets were not going to close the gap. Throughout the world elites concluded that communism had failed and that democratic capitalism was the surest route to national development.

There are signs that the winner of the Islamist-secularist contest may be an emerging hybrid, an Islamic democracy comparable to Christian Democracy in Europe and Latin America. That hybrid may prove unsustainable, however, or the states exemplifying it (at present, Turkey) may end up performing poorly. How ought Americans to think about the end of the Muslims' long legitimacy crisis? Is there anything the United States and other outside powers can do to influence developments? Or is any attempt to influence the outcome liable to be perceived as imperialistic and to backfire?

It is not clear which contending ideology would be friendlier to America and its interests. Americans tend to think that secularists are friendlier and Islamists more hostile, but as we have seen, that is not necessarily so. Islamist Saudi Arabia remains one of America's most solid partners in the Arab world. In the 1980s Islamists cooperated with the United States to defeat the Soviets in Afghanistan. Many secularist regimes—Nasserism in Egypt, Ba'athism in Syria and Iraq, the PLO—have been anti-American. How hostile either ideology is to the United States at any given time and place seems to depend on other conditions. One recent study suggests that secularists and Islamists alike tend to be more anti-American in societies where they are competing with each other most fiercely; where one is clearly predominant, it tends to be less hostile to U.S. interests.[7]

That said, for reasons of principle, Americans should want a regime type for Muslims that is just, fair, and conducive to human flourishing. We may argue over how secular or Islamist such a regime may be for Muslims in the twenty-first century. We should agree that it be, in general terms, a *constitutional democracy*. A constitutional state is constrained by law and avoids dense concentrations of power in any one person or office. In practical terms, this means that the executive (which controls the means of coercion) is checked by a legislature, courts, or both. A democracy, broadly conceived, is a state constrained by the popular will. The executive and legislature must be accountable to the people via regular competitive elections.

The countries that make up the West, as well as many in Asia and Africa, are constitutional democracies. Constitutionalism also has a history in the Islamic world,[8] and some of the roots of democracy may be found there as well.[9] No doubt constitutional democracy will look different in Muslim countries than it does in America and the rest of the West. Western constitutional democracies are also *liberal*, that is, the constitutions that constrain them prize individual rights against the state. In recent decades Western liberalism has come to value individual autonomy against traditional religious institutions and practices as well. Islamist constitutional democracy would be incompatible with this relatively new Western liberalism.

So liberalism may not be an available outcome for devoutly Muslim societies. Yet, the United States can do two things to nudge constitutional democracy—more or less Islamist—along in the Middle East.[10] The first is to engage in public diplomacy, or diplomacy aimed at the people and non-state institutions in Muslim societies. The call for better public diplomacy is not new, and indeed was renewed after the September 2001 terrorist attacks.[11] The George W. Bush administration hired Karen Hughes, a talented political operative, to be undersecretary of state for public diplomacy. Her tenure shows just how difficult public diplomacy can be, as Muslim opinion of the United States fell during the years that she held the office.[12]

Public diplomacy entails conveying, through media, academic exchanges, commercial ties, and other means, the attractiveness of one's society. It is far from foolproof. Sayyid Qutb, one of the leading Islamist thinkers of the twentieth century, sometimes called the grandfather of al-Qaeda, spent two years studying in the United States in the 1940s. Far from finding American society attractive, he was repulsed and set himself to combating liberalism in his native Egypt. But public diplomacy can gradually build affinity and trust among peoples, such that they respond favorably to one another's national policies and extend to one another the benefit of the doubt."[13]

The second thing the United States can do is simply to remain the attractive society that it always has been—to be true to itself. Well into its third century, America remains a global exemplar of constitutional democracy. It has demonstrated the viability and superiority of a regime that is suspicious of concentrated power, that holds leaders accountable, that has deep divisions and disagreements but invariably conducts competitive elections and transfers power peacefully.

For America to be itself consistently and thoroughly is a tall order when national security is threatened. The very legitimacy crisis in Muslim countries that we have been analyzing in these pages continues to place America's security at risk. In extreme cases, temporary violations of the U.S. Constitution may be justified. After leaving the White House, Thomas Jefferson wrote that his highest duty as president was not to the Constitution but to preserving the nation. "To lose our country by a scrupulous adherence to written law, would be to lose the law itself, with life, liberty, property and all those who are enjoying them with us; thus absurdly sacrificing the end to the means."[14]

What has sustained America's republic is that its habit of using Jefferson's *in extremis* argument sparingly and temporarily. Unconstitutional concentrations of power in the executive have been both rare and short-lived. The Alien and Sedition Acts of 1798 and suspensions of habeas corpus by Abraham Lincoln and Woodrow Wilson were all during times of high external or internal threat, and none lasted for very long.

One of the challenges of our time—a time when we are reminded of the threat of catastrophic terrorism every time we pass through a tiresome and intrusive airport security apparatus—is figuring out how, without taking on too much risk, to redisperse the power that has been concentrated in the executive branch of the federal government since the dark days of September 2001. Barack Obama entered office in January 2009 pledging to abolish torture and free all terrorism suspects from Guantanamo Bay Prison. As his second term began in 2013, he had done neither. Warrantless wiretapping continued, and drone strikes on civilian populations in Afghanistan, Pakistan, and Yemen— even on American citizens in those places—had become more common than ever. These policies all are designed to make America more secure at minimal cost. But as they persist and become institutionalized, they damage not only the nation's constitutional order, but also that order's appeal and credibility in the Middle East. America's constitutional democracy comes to look like the regimes that Muslims have suffered under for many decades.[15]

A second and perhaps more stubborn challenge is how to remain a constitutional republic, guaranteeing freedom for all, when American society is so deeply divided over cultural and ideological questions. Cultural polarization— blue *versus* red America, progressive *versus* traditional, secular *versus* religious—is already far along.[16] At issue is the very notion of liberalism itself, as noted above: Is the individual to be protected chiefly from the state, as conservatives (or classical liberals) hold? Or from society—nonstate entities such as corporations, churches, even their families—as many of today's liberals maintain? Who or what threatens individual liberty is at the heart of debates over secularism and may be the most polarizing and paralyzing question America faces today.[17]

At the end, then, we return to the similarities between the ideological conflict in the Middle East and the culture wars in the United States. America has met the challenge of deep difference many times. On two occasions, both concerning racial relations—when slave and free states confronted one another, and when some states denied black Americans full rights—the challenge was met through the victory of one side via federal coercion. But more typically, the United States has managed its cultural diversity through a collective determination among its people to be at once pluralistic and civil. As difficult as pluralism and civility are for both red and blue today, that is the way for America to be truest to itself. If secular and religious Americans can respect one another, avoid believing each other to be dangerous, and avoid being dangerous to each other—engage in what philosopher Nicholas Wolterstorff calls dialogical pluralism—America also can set an example that is germane to the Middle East's ongoing struggle.[18] One place to start, fitting for Americans and relevant to Muslims everywhere, would be with the chief drafter of the U.S. Constitution, James Madison, who wrote in 1785: "It is the duty of every man to render to the Creator such homage and such only as he believes to be acceptable to Him. This duty is precedent, both in order of time and degree of obligation, to the claims of Civil Society."

At the beginning of the Cold War, George Kennan, a senior U.S. diplomat, advised his country to "contain" Soviet communism rather than capitulate to or crusade against it. Containment entailed not only military and economic strength, not only diplomacy, but also soft power—the attractiveness of a good example. Crucial, he wrote in 1947, was "the degree to which the United States can create among the peoples of the world generally the impression of a country which knows what it wants, which is coping successfully with the problem of its internal life and with the responsibilities of a World Power, and which has a spiritual vitality capable of holding its own among the major ideological currents of the time."[19]

Kennan knew that the United States could do this, but knew that it might not, and he saw with a clear eye what would happen if it did not. He understood then what Americans should understand today: that their ability to negotiate their country's internal divisions and their confidence in their constitutional democracy have consequences for the wider world. Now, as then, what happens within America is not just about America.

NOTES

Preface

1. Having once been roundly scolded by Brazilian colleagues for excluding Latin America from the West, I include the entire Western Hemisphere, inasmuch as it all shares the classical, Christian, and Enlightenment heritage of Europe.
2. John M. Owen IV, *The Clash of Ideas in World Politics: Transnational Networks, States, and Regime Change, 1510–2010* (Princeton: Princeton University Press, 2010).

Introduction: It Did Happen Here

1. I Peter 1:10.
2. John Mackintosh, *The Story of Scotland from the Earliest Times to the Present Century* (New York: G.P. Putnam's Sons, 1890), 132–33. "Shaveling" was a pejorative term for a man with a tonsure, the special haircut of a religious man. "Gainstand" was Scots English for "stand against."
3. Quoted in Owen, *Clash of Ideas*, 100.
4. For a magisterial analysis of the effects of the Protestant Reformation on transnational and international politics in Europe, see Daniel H. Nexon, *The Struggle for Power in Early Modern Europe: Religious Conflict, Dynastic Empires, and International Change* (Princeton: Princeton University Press, 2009).
5. Throughout this book I use the phrase "Arab Spring," which suggests analogies with similar chains of events in Western history. I am mindful that many experts prefer alternatives such as "Arab Uprisings."
6. Rick Coolsaet compares jihadists to nineteenth-century anarchists; see Coolsaet, "Anarchist Outrages," *Le Monde Diplomatique* (September 2004), http://mondediplo .com/2004/09/03anarchists, accessed on December 14, 2010. Norman Podhoretz compares Islamism to fascism; see Podhoretz, *World War IV: The Long Struggle Against Islamofascism* (New York: Random House, 2007). Richard N. Haass compares the Middle East to early modern Europe in "The New Thirty Years' War," *Project Syndicate* (July 21, 2014), http://www.project-syndicate.org/commentary/ richard-n--haass-argues-that-the-middle-east-is-less-a-problem-to-be-solved-than -a-condition-to-be-managed, accessed on July 24, 2014. Many have compared the Arab Uprisings of 2011 to the 1848 revolutions in Europe; see Jonathan Steinberg, "1848 and 2011: Bringing Down the Old Order Is Easy; Building a New One Is Tough," *Foreign Affairs* (September 28, 2011); John M. Owen IV, "Why Islamism Is Winning," *New York Times* (January 7, 2012), A19; Sheri Berman, "Marx's Lesson for the Muslim Brothers," *New York Times* (August 10, 2013), SR6; Kurt Weyland, "The

Arab Spring: Why the Surprising Similarities with the Revolutionary Wave of 1848?" *Perspectives on Politics* 10, no. 4 (2012), 917–34.

7. Ahmed H. al-Rahim, "Whither Political Islam and the 'Arab Spring'?," *Hedgehog Review* 13, no. 3 (2011), 8–22.

8. Owen, *Clash of Ideas*, 213, 216.

9. Paul Salem, *Bitter Legacy: Ideology and Politics in the Arab World* (Syracuse: Syracuse University Press, 1994), 39–44.

10. Jeffrey Legro argues that a fundamental change in official or national ideas requires not only a crisis for the old ideas but the presence of alternative ideas with significant social support. See Legro, *Rethinking the World: Great Power Strategies and International Order* (Ithaca, N.Y.: Cornell University Press, 2005).

11. Sheri Berman, "Islamism, Revolution, and Civil Society," *Perspectives on Politics* 1, no. 2 (2003), 257–72.

12. Gilles Kepel, *The Revenge of God: The Resurgence of Islam, Christianity, and Judaism in the Modern World* (University Park: Penn State University Press, 1994).

13. E.g., Mark Juergensmeyer, *Global Rebellion: Religious Challenges to the Secular State, from Christian Militias to al Qaeda* (Berkeley: University of California Press, 2009); Peter L. Berger, ed., *The Desecularization of the World: Resurgent Religion and World Politics* (Grand Rapids, Mich.: Eerdmans, 1999).

14. Kepel, *Revenge of God*, 98–99, 192–98. For a thorough treatment of the global religious revival and its political ramifications, see Monica Duffy Toft, Daniel Philpott, and Timothy Samuel Shah, *God's Century: Resurgent Religion and Global Politics* (New York: Norton, 2011).

15. Quoted in Owen, *Clash of Ideas*, 202.

16. Sayyid Qutb, *Signposts along the Road* (1964), quoted in Roxanne L. Euben and Muhammad Qasim Zaman, eds., *Princeton Readings in Islamist Thought: Texts and Contexts from al-Banna to Bin Laden* (Princeton: Princeton University Press, 2009), 137.

17. "Most Muslims Want Democracy, Personal Freedoms, and Islam in Political Life," Pew Research Center (July 10, 2012), http://www.pewglobal.org/2012/07/10/most-muslims-want-democracy-personal-freedoms-and-islam-in-political-life/, accessed on December 19, 2012.

18. U.S. Central Intelligence Agency, *CIA World Factbook*, https://www.cia.gov/library/publications/the-world-factbook/geos/le.html, accessed on December 19, 2012.

19. "Muslims Believe U.S. Seeks to Undermine Islam," World Public Opinion (April 24, 2007), http://www.worldpublicopinion.org/pipa/articles/brmiddleeastnafricara/346.php?lb=brme&pnt=346&nid=&id=, accessed on December 13, 2010. Notably, Indonesia was the outlier, with bare majorities favoring the two propositions.

20. Michaelle Browers, *Political Ideology in the Arab World: Accommodation and Transformation* (New York: Cambridge University Press, 2009), 19–47.

21. "Nuclear Weapons: Who Has What at a Glance" (Washington, D.C.: Arms Control Association, November 2012), http://www.armscontrol.org/factsheets/Nuclearweap onswhohaswhat, accessed on January 19, 2013.

22. This book does not focus on the Sahel. For a recent survey of Muslims and Christians in that region, see "Tolerance and Tension: Islam and Christianity in Sub-Saharan

Africa," Pew Forum on Religion and Public Life (April 2010), http://www.pewforum
.org/files/2010/04/sub-saharan-africa-full-report.pdf, accessed on May 16, 2014.

23. "Muslim Publics Share Concern about Extremist Groups" (Pew Research Global Attitudes Project, September 10, 2013), http://www.pewglobal.org/2013/09/10/muslim
-publics-share-concerns-about-extremist-groups/, accessed on January 14, 2014.

24. Assaf Moghadam and Brian Fishman, "Introduction: Jihadi 'Endogenous Problems,'" in Moghadam and Fishman, eds., *Fault Lines in Global Jihad: Organizational, Strategic, and Ideological Fissures* (New York: Routledge, 2011), 6–8.

25. Benjamin Wallace-Wells, "The Lonely Battle of Wael Ghonim," *New York* (January
22, 2012), http://nymag.com/news/features/wael-ghonim-2012-1/, accessed on December 28, 2013.

26. See, e.g., Amr Hamzawy, "Two Sorrowful Scenes at a Church Funeral," *Atlantic
Council* (November 8, 2013), http://www.atlanticcouncil.org/blogs/egyptsource/two
-sorrowful-scenes-at-a-church-funeral, accessed on December 30, 2013. See also
Marwan Muasher, *The Arab Center: The Promise of Moderation* (New Haven: Yale
University Press, 2008).

27. Mia Bloom, *Dying to Kill: The Allure of Suicide Terror* (New York: Columbia University Press, 2005).

28. Robert A. Pape, *Dying to Win: The Strategic Logic of Suicide Terrorism* (New York:
Random House, 2005).

29. In social science language, Pape samples on the dependent variable. Scott Ashworth,
Joshua D. Clinton, Adam Meirowitz, and Kristopher W. Ramsay, "Design, Inference, and the Strategic Logic of Suicide Terrorism," *American Political Science Review* 102, no. 2 (2008), 269–73.

30. Robert A. Pape and James K. Feldman, *Cutting the Fuse: The Explosion of Global
Suicide Terrorism and How to Stop It* (Chicago: University of Chicago Press, 2010).

31. For a more general critique of these and other books, see Martha Crenshaw, "Explaining Suicide Terrorism: A Review Essay," *Security Studies* 16, no. 1 (2007), 133–62.

32. This is so even though Saddam Hussein, the late dictator of Iraq, had nothing to do
with the September 11 attacks. Friends and foes of the G. W. Bush administration
agree on one thing: no 9/11, no Iraq War.

33. Owen, *Clash of Ideas*, 202–4. In social-scientific jargon, these events appear endogenous, connected by feedback loops. For a clear social-scientific treatment of feedback effects, applied in particular to international relations, see Robert Jervis, *System Effects: Complexity in Political and Social Life* (Princeton: Princeton University
Press, 1998).

34. On suicide terrorism and networks, see Michael C. Horowitz, "Nonstate Actors and
the Diffusion of Innovations: The Case of Suicide Terrorism," *International Organization* 64, no. 1 (2010), 33–64.

35. "Terrorism, Poverty, and Islam," *Indonesia Matters* (October 6, 2006), http://www
.indonesiamatters.com/742/terrorism-poverty-islam/, accessed on November 11,
2010.

36. Russell L. Ackoff and Johan P. Strümpfer, "Terrorism: A Systemic View," *Systems
Research and Behavioral Science* 20, no. 3 (2003), 292.

37. They refer to Gerald P. O'Driscoll, Jr., Kim R. Holmes, and Mary Anastasia O'Grady, *Index of Economic Freedom* (Washington, D.C.: Heritage Foundation, 2002).

38. United Nations Development Program, *Arab Human Development Report: Human Security* (New York: United Nations, 2009), 11, 113, available at http://www.arab-hdr .org/contents/index.aspx?rid=5. The HPI was formulated by the UN Development Program, which sponsors the reports.

39. David Stringer, "Poverty Fueling Muslim Anti-West Tendencies: Study," *Huffington Post* (May 7, 2009), http://www.huffingtonpost.com/2009/05/07/poverty-fueling -muslim-an_n_199192.html#, accessed on November 11, 2010.

40. "After Earlier Growth, Decline in Freedom Seen in Middle East in 2007" (press release, Freedom House, January 18, 2008), http://www.freedomhouse.org/template .cfm?page=70&release=613, accessed on November 18, 2010.

41. United Nations Development Program, *Arab Human Development Report*, 2. The Arab Spring that began in late 2010 rendered that statement problematic, at least for a short while.

42. E.g., *AHDR 2009*, 14–15.

43. Ira M. Lapidus, *A History of Islamic Societies*, 2nd ed. (New York: Cambridge University Press, 2002), 761–63.

44. Fareed Zakaria, "The Politics of Rage: Why Do They Hate Us?," *Newsweek* (October 14, 2001), http://www.newsweek.com/politics-rage-why-do-they-hate-us-154345, accessed on January 16, 2014.

45. World Bank, "Replicate the World Bank's Regional Aggregation," http://iresearch .worldbank.org/PovcalNet/povDuplic.html, accessed on November 19, 2010.

46. See Alan Krueger and Jitka Malečková, "Education, Poverty, and Terrorism: Is There a Causal Connection?" *Journal of Economic Perspectives* 17, no. 4 (2003), 119–44; and the survey in Tim Krieger and Daniel Meierrieks, "What Causes Terrorism?," *Public Choice* 147, nos. 1–2 (2011), 3–27.

47. http://www.thereligionofpeace.com/, accessed on November 8, 2010; http:// chromatism.net/bloodyborders/, accessed on November 9, 2010.

48. E.g., Spencer, *Religion of Peace? Why Christianity Is and Islam Isn't* (Washington, D.C.: Regnery, 2007); and Spencer, *The Truth about Muhammad: Founder of the World's Most Intolerant Religion* (Washington, D.C.: Regnery, 2006).

49. "Speech Geert Wilders New York, Four Seasons (Monday Feb 23, 2009)," http:// www.geertwilders.nl/index.php?option=com_content&task=view&id=1535, accessed on December 1, 2010.

50. David Cohen, "Violence Is Inherent in Islam—It Is a Cult of Death," *Evening Standard* (London) (February 7, 2007), http://www.islamophobia-watch.com/islamopho bia-watch/2007/2/7/violence-is-inherent-in-islam-it-is-a-cult-of-death.html, accessed on November 8, 2010.

51. J. David Goodman, "Police Arrest 5 in Danish Terror Plot," *New York Times* (December 29, 2010), http://www.nytimes.com/2010/12/30/world/europe/30denmark .html?ref=danishcartooncontroversy, accessed on January 16, 2014.

52. Robert Mackey, "Israeli Minister Agrees that Ahmadinejad Never Said Israel 'Must

Be Wiped off the Map,'" *New York Times* (April 17, 2012), http://thelede.blogs.ny times.com/2012/04/17/israeli-minister-agrees-ahmadinejad-never-said-israel-must -be-wiped-off-the-map/, accessed on January 16, 2014. Then president Ahmadinejad evidently said that Israel would disappear, but he was not announcing that Iran would destroy the country.

53. Samuel P. Huntington, *The Clash of Civilizations and the Remaking of World Order* (New York: Simon & Schuster, 1996), 254–58. See also Davis Brown, "The Influence of Religion on Armed Conflict Onset" (Ph.D. diss., University of Virginia, 2012).

54. Lapidus, *History of Islamic Societies*, 22–34.

55. David Cook, *Martyrdom in Islam* (New York: Cambridge University Press, 2007), 14–15.

56. Jonathan Fox, "Two Civilizations and Ethnic Conflict: Islam and the West," *Journal of Peace Research* 38, no. 4 (2001), 459–72.

57. Karen Barkey, "Islam and Toleration: Studying the Ottoman Imperial Model," *International Journal of Politics, Culture, and Society* 19, nos. 1–2 (2005), 5–19.

58. E.g., "Khatami Condemns 9/11 Terror Attacks," Reuters, September 10, 2006, http://gulfnews.com/news/world/usa/khatami-condemns-9-11-terror-attacks-1.254539, accessed on November 9, 2010.

59. For another treatment of how ideological struggles affect the Middle East, see Mark L. Haas, *The Clash of Ideologies: Middle Eastern Politics and American Security* (New York: Oxford University Press, 2012).

60. Yuen Foong Khong, *Analogies at War: Korea, Munich, Dien Bien Phu, and the Vietnam Decisions of 1965* (Princeton: Princeton University Press, 1992).

61. Richard E. Neustadt and Ernest R. May, *Thinking in Time: The Uses of History for Decision Makers* (New York: Simon & Schuster, 2011).

Lesson 1 Don't Sell Islamism Short

1. Charles Kurzman and Ijlal Naqvi, "The Islamists Are Not Coming," *Foreign Policy* (January–February 2010), http://www.foreignpolicy.com/articles/2010/01/04/the _islamists_are_not_coming, accessed on October 20, 2010.

2. "Saving Faith," *Economist* (July 15, 2010), http://www.economist.com/node/16564186, accessed on December 23, 2013.

3. Olivier Roy, "This Is Not an Islamic Revolution," *New Statesman* (February 15, 2011), http://www.newstatesman.com/religion/2011/02/egypt-arab-tunisia-islamic, accessed on January 14, 2014.

4. Fareed Zakaria, "Egypt's Real Parallel to Iran's Revolution," *Washington Post* (February 7, 2011), http://www.washingtonpost.com/wp-dyn/content/article/2011/02/06 /AR2011020603398.html, accessed on January 14, 2014.

5. "And the Winner Is . . . ," *Economist* (December 20, 2011), http://www.economist.com /node/21541404, accessed on January 14, 2014.

6. Shadi Hamid, "Did Religious Parties Really Lose the Iraqi Elections?" *Democracy Arsenal* (blog), April 4, 2010, http://www.democracyarsenal.org/2010/04/did-reli gious-parties-really-lose-the-iraqi-elections-.html, accessed on October 15, 2010.

7. Shadi Hamid, "Underestimating Religious Parties," *Democracy Arsenal* (blog), April 5, 2010, http://www.democracyarsenal.org/2010/04/underestimating-religious-parties .html, accessed on October 15, 2010.

8. Robert Nisbet extends the progress narrative back through three thousand years of Western history. Nisbet, *History of the Idea of Progress* (Piscataway, N.J.: Transaction, 1980).

9. Steven Pinker, *The Better Angels of Our Nature: Why Violence Has Declined* (New York: Viking, 2011).

10. Immanuel Kant, "Idea for a Universal History with Cosmopolitan Intent," in *Perpetual Peace and Other Essays*, ed. Ted Humphrey (Indianapolis: Hackett Press, 1981).

11. G. W. F. Hegel, *Lectures on the Philosophy of World History*, trans. H. B. Nisbet (New York: Cambridge University Press, 1975).

12. Herbert Butterfield, *The Whig Interpretation of History* (New York: Norton, 1965).

13. Partial text in English at http://pages.uoregon.edu/sshoemak/323/texts/augsburg .htm, accessed on October 20, 2010.

14. Hajo Holborn, *A History of Modern Germany: The Reformation* (New York: Knopf, 1961), 243.

15. Richard Stauffer, "Calvin," in *International Calvinism, 1541–1715*, ed. Menna Prestwich (Oxford: Clarendon, 1985), 15–38; Holborn, *History of Modern Germany*, 257–59.

16. An excellent social and political treatment is in Michael Walzer, *The Revolution of the Saints: A Study in the Origins of Radical Politics* (Cambridge, Mass.: Harvard University Press, 1965).

17. Menna Prestwich, "The Changing Face of Calvinism," in Prestwich, *International Calvinism*, 3–4.

18. Text at http://www2.stetson.edu/~psteeves/classes/edictnantes.html, accessed on October 19, 2010.

19. Holborn, *History of Modern Germany*, 305–6.

20. Geoffrey Parker and Simon Adams, eds., *The Thirty Years' War*, 2nd ed. (New York: Routledge, 1997), 178.

21. Nexon, *Struggle for Power*. William T. Cavanaugh, *The Myth of Religious Violence: Secular Ideology and the Roots of Modern Conflict* (New York: Oxford University Press, 2009), notes that "religion" cannot be held responsible for these wars because "religion," in the abstract sense of "not secular," is a modern construct; indeed, it was constructed in the aftermath of these very wars by secularists who wanted to discredit any mingling of sacred and profane. I would put the matter somewhat differently. These wars are properly called ideological, because of the principle held by most Europeans at the time that social stability required religious uniformity. Absent that (ideological) conviction, the growth of Protestantism would not have implicated the distribution of power or triggered political violence.

22. Michael Broers, *Europe after Napoleon: Revolution, Reaction, and Romanticism, 1814–1848* (Manchester: Manchester University Press, 1996), 13–14.

23. Alan Cassels, *Ideology and International Relations in the Modern World* (New York: Routledge, 2002), 43–44.

24. Ibid., 44–45.

25. Frederick B. Artz, *Reaction and Revolution, 1814–1832* (New York: Harper, 1934), 3.

26. Eric Hobsbawm, *The Age of Revolution 1789–1848* (New York: Vintage, 1996), 91.

27. E. H. Carr, *The Twenty Years' Crisis, 1919–1939: An Introduction to the Study of International Relations* (1946; repr., London: Macmillan, 2001); see esp. the final chapter.

28. John Maynard Keynes, *General Theory of Employment, Interest, and Money* (London: Macmillan, 1936).

29. Seymour Martin Lipset and Gary Wolfe Marks, *It Didn't Happen Here: Why Socialism Failed in the United States* (New York: Norton, 2000), 74.

30. On the differences and interactions among socialists and social democrats in the 1930s and 1940s, see Daniel T. Rodgers, *Atlantic Crossings: Social Politics in a Progressive Age* (Cambridge, Mass.: Harvard University Press, 1998); Norman Birnbaum, *After Progress: American Social Reform and European Socialism in the Twentieth Century* (New York: Oxford University Press, 2001).

31. Lincoln Steffens, *The Autobiography of Lincoln Steffens*, vol. 1 (New York: Harcourt Brace, 1931), 799.

32. "Quintus Fabius Maximus Verrucosus," *Encyclopædia Britannica*, http://www.britannica.com/EBchecked/topic/199706/Quintus-Fabius-Maximus-Verrucosus, accessed on November 4, 2010.

33. Sidney Webb and Beatrice Webb, *The Decay of Capitalist Civilisation*, 3rd ed. (London: Fabian Society, 1923), 3–4.

34. David Caute, *The Fellow-Travellers: Intellectual Friends of Communism* (New Haven: Yale University Press, 1988), 86–89.

35. Robert Conquest, *Reflections on a Ravaged Century* (New York: Norton, 2001), 93–96. For a full treatment, see Conquest, *The Harvest of Sorrow: Soviet Collectivization and the Terror-Famine* (New York: Oxford University Press, 1987).

36. Webb and Webb, *Soviet Communism: A New Civilisation?*, 3rd ed. (New York: Longmans, Green, 1944), 463–71. The passages in question are unchanged from the first edition of 1935.

37. Caute, *Fellow-Travellers*, 4.

38. Ian Hunter, *Malcolm Muggeridge: A Life* (Vancouver: Regent College Publishing, 2003), 76–85. The quotation is from Muggeridge, *The Green Stick*, 257. For Muggeridge's articles, see http://www.garethjones.org/soviet_articles/soviet_and_the_peasantry_1.htm.

39. Juan Linz, "The Crisis of Democracy after the First World War," in *International Fascism: Theories, Causes, and the New Consensus*, ed. Roger Griffin (London: Arnold, 1988), 180.

40. Eugen Weber and L. L. Snyder, *Varieties of Fascism: Doctrines of Revolution in the Twentieth Century* (New York: Van Nostrand, 1964), 28–43.

41. Adolf Hitler's National Socialist German Workers' Party (NSDAP) deviated from the Italian model—chiefly in its obsession with racial hierarchy—and many scholars consider national socialism to be its own movement. But Nazism clearly overlapped with fascism significantly, and the two displayed great affinity in their statism, imperialism, anticommunism, and rejection of democracy.

42. Philip Coupland, "H.G. Wells's Liberal Fascism," *Journal of Contemporary History* 35, no. 4 (2000), 542–43. Coupland argues that Wells continued to seek liberal ends but thought that, under current circumstances, fascist means were needed to reach those ends.

43. Max Wallace, *The American Axis: Henry Ford, Charles Lindbergh, and the Rise of the Third Reich* (New York: Macmillan, 2004), 155 (italics mine).

44. Ibid., 158.

45. Ibid., 197.

46. Quoted in ibid., 118–19.

47. Anne Morrow Lindbergh, *The Wave of the Future: A Confession of Faith* (New York: Harcourt, Brace, 1940), 40.

48. Wallace, *American Axis*, 279–96.

49. For more on this narrative of progress as applied to the Muslim world, see Michaelle Browers and Charles Kurzman, eds., *An Islamic Reformation?* (Lanham, Md.: Lexington Books, 2004); John M. Owen IV and J. Judd Owen, eds., *Religion, the Enlightenment, and the New Global Order* (New York: Columbia University Press, 2011).

50. Kepel, *Revenge of God*.

51. Gilles Kepel, *Jihad: The Trail of Political Islam* (London: I.B. Tauris, 2006), 375–76.

52. Olivier Roy, *The Failure of Political Islam* (Cambridge, Mass.: Harvard University Press, 1996), viii–xi.

53. Olivier Roy, "Islamism's Failure, Islamists' Future," *Open Democracy* (October 30, 2006), http://www.opendemocracy.net/faith-europe_islam/islamism_4043.jsp, accessed on October 12, 2010.

54. M. Hakan Yavuz, "Cleansing Islam from the Public Sphere," *Journal of International Affairs* 54, no. 1 (2000), 21–42; Angel Rabasa and F. Stephen Larrabee, *The Rise of Political Islam in Turkey* (Santa Monica, Calif.: RAND, 2008), 32–27.

55. Hassan Bashir, "How the Roots of Revolution Began to Grow," in *The Roots of the Islamic Revolution in Iran: Economical, Political, Social and Cultural Views*, ed. Hassan Bashir and Seyed Ghahreman Safavi (London: Book Extra, 2002), 17–18.

56. "Iran: Oil, Grandeur and a Challenge to the West," *Time* (November 4, 1974), http://www.time.com/time/magazine/article/0,9171,945047,00.html, accessed on April 9, 2012. I am grateful to Houchang Chehabi for alerting me, many years ago, to this cover story.

57. Robert Jervis, *Why Intelligence Fails: Lessons from the Iranian Revolution and the Iraq War* (Ithaca, N.Y.: Cornell University Press, 2011), 25.

58. Peter L. Berger, "The Desecularization of the World: A Global Overview," in Berger, *Desecularization of the World*, 1–4. See Huntington, *Clash of Civilizations*, 56–78.

Lesson 2: Ideologies Are (Usually) Not Monolithic

1. Janet Tassel, "Militant about 'Islamism,'" *Harvard Magazine*, January–February 2005, 38–47.

2. Podhoretz, *World War IV*, 14.

3. Charles Kurzman, *The Missing Martyrs: Why There Are So Few Muslim Terrorists* (New York: Oxford University Press, 2011).
4. Youssef N. Aboul-Enein, *Militant Islamist Ideology: Understanding the Global Threat* (Annapolis, Md.: Naval Institute Press, 2010), 1–2.
5. Brendan O'Reilly, "The False Monolith of Political Islam," *Asia Times* (December 17, 2011), http://www.atimes.com/atimes/Middle_East/ML17Ak01.html, accessed on July 19, 2012.
6. Daniel Pipes, "The Scandal of U.S.-Saudi Relations," *National Interest* (Winter 2003), http://www.danielpipes.org/995/the-scandal-of-us-saudi-relations, accessed on July 20, 2012. Also challenging America's friendship with Saudi Arabia is former CIA analyst Robert Baer, *Sleeping with the Devil: How Washington Sold Our Soul for Saudi Crude* (New York: Random House, 2004).
7. On divide and conquer strategies in international relations more generally, see Timothy W. Crawford, "Preventing Enemy Coalitions: How Wedge Strategies Shape Power Politics," *International Security* 35, no. 4 (2011), 155–89; Yasuhiro Izumikawa, "To Coerce or Reward? Theorizing Wedge Strategies in Alliance Politics," *Security Studies* 22, no. 3 (2013), 498–531.
8. Isaiah Berlin, *The Hedgehog and the Fox: An Essay on Tolstoy's View of History* (New York: Simon & Schuster, 1951).
9. Qaradawi, in a speech broadcast on Al Jazeera TV on January 28, 2008, said that Allah used Hitler to punish the Jews and that "Allah willing, the next time will be at the hands of the believers." As translated by the Middle East Media Research Institute, http://www.memritv.org/clip/en/2005.htm, accessed on December 18, 2013. On apostasy, see "Qaradawi's Ruling on Major and Minor Apostasy," *Islamopedia Online* (October 22, 2010), http://www.islamopediaonline.org/fatwa/al-qaradawis -200-7-ruling-apostasy, accessed on July 28, 2014.
10. On the complexity of Saudi-Israeli relations, see Chemi Shalev, "With New BFFs Like Saudi Arabia, Who Needs Anti-Semitic Enemies?," *Haaretz* (October 27, 2013), http://www.haaretz.com/blogs/west-of-eden/.premium-1.554722, accessed on January 18, 2014.
11. Arthur Herman, *Metternich* (London: Allen & Unwin, 1932), 34.
12. Quoted in Henry A. Kissinger, *A World Restored: Metternich, Castlereagh and the Problems of Peace, 1812–22* (Boston: Houghton Mifflin, 1957), 202–3.
13. Paul W. Schroeder, *The Transformation of European Politics 1763–1848* (New York: Oxford University Press, 1994), 602.
14. Perhaps the leading normative text was Jean Bodin's *Six Books of the Commonwealth* (*Les six livres de la République*), published in 1576. For commentary, see Mario Turchetti, "Jean Bodin," in *Stanford Encyclopedia of Philosophy* (2010), ed. Edward N. Zalta, http://plato.stanford.edu/entries/bodin/#4, accessed on August 14, 2012.
15. Owen, *Clash of Ideas*, 137–38.
16. J. H. Leurdijk, *Intervention in International Politics* (Leeuwarden, Netherlands: Eisma BV, 1986), 238.
17. C. W. Crawley, "International Relations, 1815–1830," in *The New Cambridge Modern History*, vol. 9, *War and Peace in an Age of Upheaval, 1793–1830* (New York: Cambridge University Press, 1965), 684.

18. Parker and Adams, *Thirty Years' War*, 14–15.
19. Andrew Pettegree, "Religion and the Revolt," in *The Origins and Development of the Dutch Revolt*, ed. Graham Darby (New York: Routledge, 2001), 67–83; Prestwich, "Changing Face."
20. Peter Marshall, *The Magic Circle of Rudolf II: Alchemy and Astrology in Renaissance Prague* (New York: Bloomsbury, 2009), 3–4.
21. Holborn, *History of Modern Germany*, 296–302.
22. A helpful glossary is at http://www.cyberussr.com/rus/insults.html, accessed on August 17, 2012.
23. Barbara C. Malament, "British Labour and Roosevelt's New Deal: The Response of the Left and the Unions," *Journal of British Studies* 17, no. 2 (1978), 136–67.
24. Pietro Nenni, "Where the Italian Socialists Stand," *Foreign Affairs* 40, no. 2 (1962), 216–18.
25. Parties and Elections in Europe, http://www.parties-and-elections.eu/italy2a.html, accessed on August 15, 2012.
26. Zachary Karabell, *Architects of Intervention: The United States, the Third World, and the Cold War, 1946–1962* (Baton Rouge: Louisiana State University Press, 1999), 37–49.
27. The Christian Democrats received 48.5 percent, while the Popular Front was runner up with 31 percent. Parties and Elections in Europe, http://www.parties-and-elections.eu/italy2a.html, accessed on August 15, 2012.
28. Geoffrey Pridham, *Political Parties and Coalitional Behaviour in Italy* (New York: Routledge, 2013), 42–53; James Edward Miller, *The United States and Italy, 1940–1950: The Politics and Diplomacy of Stabilization* (Chapel Hill: University of North Carolina Press, 1986), 147–50.
29. Michael A. Ledeen, *West European Communism and American Foreign Policy* (Piscataway, N.J.: Transaction, 1987), 80–83.
30. Parties and Elections in Europe, http://www.parties-and-elections.eu/france2.html, accessed on August 15, 2012.
31. Jonathan Fenby, *The General: Charles de Gaulle and the France He Saved* (New York: Simon & Schuster, 2010).
32. S. William Halperin, "Leon Blum and Contemporary French Socialism," *Journal of Modern History* 18, no. 3 (1946), 249–50.
33. Donald Bell, "Leon Blum's American Mission," *Deseret News* (Salt Lake City) (February 5, 1946), http://news.google.com/newspapers?nid=336&dat=19460205&id=tGBSAAAAIBAJ&sjid=x3oDAAAAIBAJ&pg=7004,3719109, accessed on July 18, 2012.
34. Edward Rice-Maximin, "The United States and the French Left, 1945–1949: The View from the State Department," *Journal of Contemporary History* 19, no. 4 (1984), 730.
35. Tony Judt, *Postwar: A History of Europe since 1945* (New York: Random House, 2010), 126, 268.
36. Lewis Joachim Edinger, *Kurt Schumacher: A Study in Personality and Political Behavior* (Stanford, Calif.: Stanford University Press, 1965), 182–86.

37. On de Gaulle and the Americans, see Fenby, *The General*.

38. Yusuf al-Qaradawi, "Islam and Democracy," in Euben and Zaman, *Princeton Readings in Islamist Thought*, 232, 226. But see Qaradawi's frank and extreme anti-Semitism and anti-apostasy, noted earlier in this chapter.

39. Marc Lynch, "Islam Divided between Salafi-Jihad and the Ikhwan." *Studies in Conflict & Terrorism* 33, no. 6 (2010), 467–87.

40. "Over 15 Nations to Join US-Led Military Drill Near Syria Border," *Turkish Weekly* (May 10, 2012), http://www.turkishweekly.net/news/135866/over-15-nations-to-join-us-led-military-drill-near-syria-border.html, accessed on August 24, 2012.

41. Ahmet Davutoğlu, "Turkey's Zero-Problems Foreign Policy," *Foreign Policy* (May 20, 2010), http://www.foreignpolicy.com/articles/2010/05/20/turkeys_zero_problems_foreign_policy?page=0,0&hidecomments=yes, accessed on August 31, 2012.

42. Lynch, "Islam Divided."

43. Combined Joint Task Force Spartan Public Affairs, "Eager Lion Commanders Hold Press Conference," U.S. Central Command (May 15, 2012), http://www.centcom.mil/press-releases/eager-lion-commanders-hold-press-conference.html, accessed on August 31, 2012.

44. Trita Parsi, *Treacherous Alliance: The Secret Dealings of Israel, Iran, and the United States* (New Haven: Yale University Press, 2007), chap. 19.

45. Interviews available at "The 'Grand Bargain' Fax: A Missed Opportunity?," *Frontline*, http://www.pbs.org/wgbh/pages/frontline/showdown/themes/grandbargain.html, accessed on January 29, 2013.

Lesson 3: Foreign Interventions Are Normal

1. CNN/Opinion Research Poll, March 18–20, http://politicalticker.blogs.cnn.com/2011/03/21/cnnopinion-research-poll-march-18-20-libya/, accessed on February 14, 2012.

2. Katia McGlynn, "Jon Stewart Rips U.S. Attack on Libya: 'Don't We Already Have Two Wars?,'" *Huffington Post* (March 22, 2011), http://www.huffingtonpost.com/2011/03/22/jon-stewart-libya_n_838872.html, accessed on February 14, 2012.

3. Patrick Goldstein and James Rainey, "Al Jazeera, Fox Log Biggest Audience Jumps during Egypt Crisis," *LA Times Blogs* (February 17, 2011), http://latimesblogs.latimes.com/the_big_picture/2011/02/al-jazeera-fox-log-biggest-audience-jumps-during-egypt-crisis.html, accessed on January 2, 2012.

4. Michael Desch, "America's Illiberal Liberalism," *International Security* 32, no. 3 (2008), 7–43.

5. Tony Smith, *A Pact with the Devil: Washington's Bid for World Supremacy and the Betrayal of the American Promise* (New York: Routledge, 2012), 199.

6. Owen, *Clash of Ideas*.

7. On this and other Sunni-Shia Islamist ties and fissures, see Bernard Haykel, "Al-Qa'ida and Shiism," in Moghadam and Fishman, *Fault Lines in Global Jihad*, 186–90.

8. Kaveh L. Afrasiabi, "Iran Gets a Mini-Break—in Bahrain," *Asia Times Online* (November 29, 2011), http://www.atimes.com/atimes/Middle_East/MK29Ak03.html, accessed on March 13, 2012.

9. Neil MacFarquhar, "Odd Twist for Elite Unit Guiding Iran's Proxy Wars," *New York Times* (October 11, 2011), http://www.nytimes.com/2011/10/12/world/middleeast /new-plot-is-odd-twist-for-irans-elite-quds-force.html, accessed on March 13, 2012.

10. "Syria Unrest: Arab League Adopts Sanctions in Cairo," *BBC News* (November 27, 2011), http://www.bbc.co.uk/news/world-middle-east-15901360, accessed on March 13, 2012.

11. Vali Nasr, "If the Arab Spring Turns Ugly," *New York Times* (August 27, 2011), http:// www.nytimes.com/2011/08/28/opinion/sunday/the-dangers-lurking-in-the-arab -spring.html?pagewanted=all, accessed on February 14, 2012.

12. Dan Perry, "John McCain, Joe Lieberman, Lindsey Graham Urge to Arm Syria's Rebels," *Huffington Post* (September 7, 2012), http://www.huffingtonpost.com/2012 /09/07/john-mccain-joe-lieberman-syria_n_1865884.html, accessed on January 27, 2013.

13. See Owen, "Why Islamism Is Winning."

14. Joseph S. Nye, *Understanding International Conflicts* (New York: Longman, 1997), 158.

15. Rami G. Khouri, "A Saudi-Iranian Cold War Takes Shape," *Daily Star* (Beirut), October 19, 2011, http://www.dailystar.com.lb/Opinion/Columnist/2011/Oct-19/151642 -a-saudi-iranian-cold-war-takes-shape.ashx#axzz1oSjNVdTN, accessed on March 7, 2012. See also F. Gregory Gause III, *Beyond Sectarianism: The New Middle East Cold War* (Washington: Brookings Institution, 2014).

16. John M. Owen IV and Michael Poznansky, "When Does America Drop Dictators?," *European Journal of International Relations* (2014), doi:10.1177/1354066113508990.

17. I shall not consider what makes foreign interventions and occupations succeed. On that topic, see David M. Edelstein, *Occupational Hazards: Success and Failure in Military Occupation* (Ithaca, N.Y.: Cornell University Press, 2011).

18. Edmund Burke, "Speech of Edmund Burke, Esq., on American Taxation" (April 19, 1774), sec. 1.2.105, http://www.econlib.org/library/LFBooks/Burke/brkSWv1c2. html, accessed on January 2, 2012.

19. Edmund Burke, *Correspondence 3* (1776), in *Oxford Dictionary of National Biography*, 252–53, http://www.oxforddnb.com/view/article/4019, accessed on January 2, 2012.

20. Edmund Burke, "Speech on the Impeachment of Warren Hastings" (February 15, 1788), http://www.civilisationis.com/smartboard/shop/burkee/extracts/chap12.htm, accessed on January 2, 2012.

21. Richard Price, "A Discourse on the Love of Our Country (1789)," *Norton Topics Online*, http://www.wwnorton.com/college/english/nael/romantic/topic_3/price.htm, accessed on May 14, 2014..

22. Jennifer M. Welsh, *Edmund Burke and International Relations: The Commonwealth of Europe and the Crusade Against the French Revolution* (New York: Macmillan, 1995), 102–3.

23. Christopher Hitchens, "Reactionary Prophet," *Atlantic Monthly* (April 2004), http:// www.theatlantic.com/past/docs/issues/2004/04/hitchens.htm, accessed on January 2, 2012.

24. Edmund Burke, *Reflections on the Revolution in France* (Harmondsworth, UK: Penguin, 1969), 185.

25. "In the weakness of one kind of authority," writes Burke, "and in the fluctuation of all, the officers of an army will remain for some time mutinous and full of faction, until some popular general, who understands the art of conciliating the soldiery, and who possesses the true spirit of command, shall draw the eyes of all men upon himself. Armies will obey him on his personal account. There is no other way of securing military obedience in this state of things. But the moment in which that event shall happen, the person who really commands the army is your master; the master (that is little) of your king, the master of your Assembly, the master of your whole republic." As Christopher Hitchens writes, "This is almost eerily exact." Hitchens, "Reactionary Prophet."

26. Quoted in Emma Vincent Macleod, *A War of Ideas: British Attitudes toward the Wars against Revolutionary France 1792-1802* (Burlington, Vt.: Ashgate, 1998), 13. The original is in Burke, "An Appeal from the New to the Old Whigs" (1791).

27. Burke, "Thoughts on French Affairs" (1791), in *The Works of the Right Honourable Edmund Burke*, vol. 3, *Political Miscellanies* (London: Henry G. Bohn, 1855), 359-61, read via Google Books, http://books.google.com/ebooks/reader?id=7U8XAAAAYA AJ&printsec=frontcover&output=reader, accessed on January 3, 2012.

28. Macleod, *War of Ideas*, chaps. 2-4.

29. Owen, *Clash of Ideas*, 140-41.

30. Carl J. Friedrich, "Military Government and Democratization: A Central Issue of American Foreign Policy," in *American Experiences in Military Government in World War II*, ed. Friedrich et al. (New York: Rinehart, 1948), 19.

31. Tony Smith, *America's Mission: The United States and the Worldwide Struggle for Democracy* (Princeton: Princeton University Press, 1994), 152-53.

32. John Lamberton Harper, *American Visions of Europe: Franklin D. Roosevelt, George F. Kennan, and Dean G. Acheson* (New York: Cambridge University Press, 1996), 78-91.

33. Smith, *America's Mission*, 153-54; Carl C. Hodge and Cathal J. Nolan, "'As Powerful as We Are': From the Morgenthau Plan to Marshall Aid," in *Shepherd of Democracy? America and Germany in the Twentieth Century*, ed. Hodge and Nolan (Westport, Conn.: Greenwood, 1992), 55-57.

34. Jean Edward Smith, *Lucius D. Clay: An American Life* (New York: Macmillan, 1990), 368-78.

35. Ibid., 367.

36. Ibid., 381; Marc Trachtenberg, *A Constructed Peace: The Making of the European Settlement 1945-1963* (Princeton: Princeton University Press, 1999), 52-54.

37. Ibid., 378-89; Richard L. Merritt, *Democracy Imposed: U.S. Occupation Policy and the German Public, 1945-1949* (New Haven: Yale University Press, 1995), 64-68. Byrnes's speech built upon a draft by Clay; the actual speech was drafted by John Kenneth Galbraith and Charles Kindleberger.

38. Quoted in Robert Gellately, *Lenin, Stalin, and Hitler: The Age of Social Catastrophe* (New York: Random House, 2007). 588.

39. Quoted in Alessandro Brogi, *A Question of Self-Esteem: The United States and the Cold War Choices in France and Italy, 1944-1958* (Westport, Conn.: Greenwood, 2002), 68.

40. Cathy Lynn Grossman, "Number of U.S. Muslims to Double," *USA Today* (January 27, 2011), http://www.usatoday.com/news/religion/2011-01-27-1Amuslim27_ST_N .htm, accessed on January 13, 2012.

41. See, e.g., Oklahoma's law barring state courts from using Sharia (or international law). Elizabeth Flock, "Sharia Law Ban: Is Oklahoma's Proposal Discriminatory or Needed?," *Washington Post Blog* (January 11, 2012), http://www.washingtonpost.com /blogs/blogpost/post/sharia-law-ban-is-oklahomas-proposal-discriminatory-or -useful/2012/01/11/gIQAGFP1qP_blog.html, accessed on March 12, 2012.

42. For an early analysis that remains a rewarding read, see James Davison Hunter, *Culture Wars: The Struggle to Define America* (New York: Basic Books, 1991).

43. Andrew Sullivan, who coined the term "Christianist," agrees: "My Problem with Christianism," *Time* (May 7, 2006), http://www.time.com/time/magazine/article /0,9171,1191826-1,00.html, accessed on January 17, 2013.

44. Murat Iyigun, "Luther and Suleyman," *Quarterly Journal of Economics* 123, no. 4 (2008), 1470–71.

45. In A.D. 395 the Roman Empire was formally severed into an eastern empire, whose capital was Constantinople (formerly Byzantium), and a western, whose capital was Rome.

46. Stephen A. Fischer-Galati, *Ottoman Imperialism and German Protestantism 1521–1555* (New York: Octagon, 1972), 1–3.

47. Charles A. Frazee, *Catholics and Sultans: The Church and the Ottoman Empire 1453–1923* (New York: Cambridge University Press, 2006), 26.

48. Ibid., 25–28.

49. Halil İnalcık and Donald Quataert, *An Economic and Social History of the Ottoman Empire, 1300–1914* (New York: Cambridge University Press, 1994), 373.

50. A. H. de Groot, *The Ottoman Empire and the Dutch Republic: A History of the Earliest Diplomatic Relations 1610–1630* (Istanbul: Nederlands Historisch-Archaeologisch Instituut, 1978), 84–85.

51. Mustafa Serdar Palabiyik, "Contributions of the Ottoman Empire to the Construction of Modern Europe" (master's thesis, Middle East Technical University, 2005), 79–80.

52. De Groot, *Ottoman Empire and the Dutch Republic*, 85–86. Historians note that these were private actors, not speaking for government officials or public opinion.

53. Palabiyik, "Contributions," 77–78.

54. John W. Bohnstedt, "The Infidel Scourge of God: The Turkish Menace as Seen by German Pamphleteers of the Reformation Era," *Transactions of the American Philosophical Society* 58, no. 9 (1968), 18–22. The bad optics are evident in the relations of Francis I of France, a Catholic monarch but archrival to the Habsburg Charles V. In 1536 Francis and Suleyman signed a commercial and naval treaty, and it included a provision—probably to appease outraged Christian sentiment—that the Turks would tolerate Christianity in their empire. Frazee, *Catholics and Sultans*, 28; William Miller, *The Ottoman Empire and Its Successors 1801–1927: With an Appendix, 1927–1936* (New York: Cambridge University Press, 2013), 2.

55. Philip Schaff, "Augsburg Interim," in *New Schaff-Herzog Encyclopedia of Religious Knowledge*, vol. 6, *Innocents-Liudger*, http://www.ccel.org/s/schaff/encyc/encyc06 /htm/iii.ix.htm, accessed on January 26, 2012.

56. Palabiyik, "Contributions," 64.

57. Bohnstedt, "Infidel Scourge." On the distinction between a crusade and a just war, see James Turner Johnson, *The Holy War Idea in Western and Islamic Traditions* (University Park: Penn State University Press, 1997).

58. Fischer-Galati, *Ottoman Imperialism*, 38–56.

59. Palabiyik, "Contributions," 90.

60. Clive Jones, *Britain and the Yemen Civil War, 1962–1965: Ministers, Mercenaries and Mandarins: Foreign Policy and the Limits of Covert Action* (Eastbourne, UK: Sussex Academic Press, 2010).

61. Owen, *Clash of Ideas*, 218–20.

62. Ibid., 202–4.

63. See, e.g., Jacob Heilbrunn, *They Knew They Were Right: The Rise of the Neocons* (New York: Random House, 2009).

64. Brian C. Schmidt and Michael C. Williams, "The Bush Doctrine and the Iraq War: Neoconservatives versus Realists," *Security Studies* 17, no. 2 (2008), 191–220; Mark L. Haas, "Missed Ideological Opportunities and George W. Bush's Middle Eastern Policies," *Security Studies* 21, no. 3 (2012), 416–54.

Lesson 4: A State May Be Rational and Ideological at the Same Time

1. "Nuclear Weapons."

2. International Institute for Strategic Studies, *Nuclear Programmes in the Middle East: In the Shadow of Iran* (London: IISS, 2008), 132.

3. Dieter Bednarz, Erich Follath, and Georg Mascolo, "Ahmadinejad's Challenge to the World," *Der Spiegel* (December 19, 2005), http://www.spiegel.de/international/spiegel /fanaticism-in-iran-ahmadinejad-s-challenge-to-the-world-a-391199.html, accessed on December 18, 2012.

4. Stephen Walt, "The Arrogance of Power," *Foreign Policy* blogs (May 25, 2012), http:// walt.foreignpolicy.com/category/topic/iran, accessed on December 18, 2012.

5. Flynt Leverett and Hillary Mann Leverett, *Going to Tehran: Why the United States Must Come to Terms with the Islamic Republic of Iran* (New York: Henry Holt, 2013), 15–59.

6. Fareed Zakaria, "Iran Is a Rational Actor," *Fareed Zakaria GPS* (March 8, 2012), http://globalpublicsquare.blogs.cnn.com/2012/03/08/zakaria-iran-is-a-rational-actor/, accessed on December 18, 2012.

7. "Russia to Strengthen Its Caspian Sea Fleet," *RT News* (May 4, 2011), http://rt.com /politics/caspian-fleet-missiles-warships/, accessed on December 18, 2012.

8. Stephen Walt, "Top Ten Media Failures in the Iran Debate," *Foreign Policy* blogs (March 11, 2012), http://walt.foreignpolicy.com/category/topic/iran, accessed on December 18, 2012.

9. Andrew Moravcsik, "Taking Preferences Seriously: A Liberal Theory of International Politics," *International Organization* 51, no. 4 (1997), 513–53.

10. Randall Schweller, "Bandwagoning for Profit: Bringing the Revisionist State Back In," *International Security* 19, no. 1 (1994), 72–107; Charles L. Glaser, *Rational Theory of International Politics: The Logic of Competition and Cooperation* (Princeton: Princeton University Press, 2010), Andrew Kydd refers to *greedy* states; Kydd, "Game Theory and the Spiral Model," *World Politics* 49, no. 3 (April 1997), 371–400.

11. Holborn, *History of Modern Germany*, 221, 260.

12. The *Heidelberg Catechism*, commissioned by Frederick in 1563, remains one of the most widely used statements of Calvinist doctrine. The English text is available at http://www.ccel.org/creeds/heidelberg-cat-ext.txt.

13. Claus-Peter Clasen, *The Palatinate in European History, 1559–1660* (Oxford: Basil Blackwell, 1963), 3.

14. Ibid., 1–2.

15. Ibid.; Holborn, *History of Modern Germany*, 262.

16. Clasen, *Palatinate*, 3–5.

17. Ibid., 6–12.

18. Holborn, *History of Modern Germany*, 296.

19. Ibid., 311.

20. Ibid., 297, 312–17; Clasen, *Palatinate*, 24–26.

21. Holborn, *History of Modern Germany*, 317.

22. Ibid., 320–25.

23. Clasen, *Palatinate*, 25.

24. David Armstrong, *Revolution and World Order: The Revolutionary State in International Society* (Oxford: Clarendon, 1993), 120.

25. Robert Service, *Trotsky: A Biography* (New York: Oxford University Press, 2009), 191–92, quoting from Trotsky, *My Life* (1930).

26. Armstrong, *Revolution and World Order*, 123–24.

27. Owen, *Clash of Ideas*, 173.

28. George Frost Kennan, *Russia and the West under Lenin and Stalin* (Boston: Little, Brown, 1961), 54–59; Armstrong, *Revolution and World Order*, chap. 4.

29. Karl Marx and Friedrich Engels, *The Communist Manifesto* (1848; repr., New York: Oxford University Press, 2008), chap. 2, http://www.marxists.org/archive/marx/works/1848/communist-manifesto/ch02.htm, accessed on December 29, 2012.

30. Owen, *Clash of Ideas*, 173–74.

31. Stephen Walt, *Revolution and War* (Ithaca, N.Y.: Cornell University Press, 1996), 208.

32. Armstrong, *Revolution and World Order*, 139.

33. Moravcsik, "Taking Preferences Seriously."

34. Owen, *Clash of Ideas*, 175–79.

35. Armstrong, *Revolution and World Order*, 144.

36. Mark L. Haas, *The Ideological Origins of Great Power Politics 1789–1989* (Ithaca, N.Y.: Cornell University Press, 2005), 125–26; Armstrong, *Revolution and World Order*, 146–47.

37. Mark L. Haas, "The United States and the End of the Cold War: Reactions to Shifts in Soviet Power, Policies, or Domestic Politics?," *International Organization* 61, no. 1 (2007), 145–79. Ironically, Gorbachev presided over the dissolution of the Soviet Union. Either he pursued status-quo ends irrationally or the Soviet Union could not survive as a status-quo power.

38. Mlada Bukovansky, *Legitimacy and Power Politics: The American and French Revolutions in International Political Culture* (Princeton: Princeton University Press, 2010), 68–77.

39. See James I of England, "The Trew Law of Free Monarchies" (1598), http://www .constitution.org/primarysources/stuart.html; Jean Bodin, *Six Books of the Commonwealth* (1576), trans. M. J. Tooley (Oxford: Basil Blackwell, 1955); Jacques-Bénigne Bossuet, *Politics Drawn from the Very Words of Holy Scripture* (1679), ed. Patrick Riley (New York: Cambridge University Press, 1999).

40. Anne-Robert Jacques Turgot, *Reflections on the Formation and Distribution of Wealth* (1774; repr., London: E. Spragg, 1793), available at http://www.econlib.org /library/Essays/trgRfl1.html, accessed on December 31, 2012; Adam Smith, *An Inquiry into the Nature and Causes of the Wealth of Nations* (1776; repr., London: Methuen, 1904), http://www.econlib.org/library/Smith/smWN.html, accessed on December 31, 2012.

41. Iain McLean and Arnold B. Urken, "Did Jefferson or Madison Understand Condorcet's Theory of Social Choice?," *Public Choice* 73, no. 4 (1992), 445–57.

42. John M. Owen IV, *Liberal Peace, Liberal War: American Politics and International Security* (Ithaca, N.Y.: Cornell University Press, 1997), 69–71.

43. Robert W. Tucker and David C. Hendrickson, *Empire of Liberty: The Statecraft of Thomas Jefferson* (New York: Oxford University Press, 1990).

44. For a magisterial treatment of these years, see R. R. Palmer, *The Age of the Democratic Revolution: A Political History of Europe and America*, vols. 1–2 (Princeton: Princeton University Press, 1959, 1964).

45. France's new republic, in other words, was using very risky means to pursue its radical ends, bypassing a sovereign government to reach its people directly, much as the Russian Bolsheviks were to do 118 years later. For a full treatment, see Walt, *Revolution and War*, chap. 3.

46. Stanley Elkins and Eric McKitrick, *The Age of Federalism: The Early American Republic, 1788–1800* (New York: Oxford University Press, 1994), 330–34.

47. Ibid., 340–47, 356.

48. Owen, *Liberal Peace*, 78–81.

49. Ibid., 69–70. Especially important was Hamilton's *Report on Manufactures* (1791), available at http://constitution.org/ah/rpt_manufactures.pdf, accessed on December 31, 2012.

50. Owen, *Liberal Peace*, 105–13, 119–24; Henry Nau, *Conservative Internationalism: Armed Diplomacy under Jefferson, Polk, Truman, and Reagan* (Princeton: Princeton University Press, 2013), chap. 5.

51. For more on U.S. accommodations to the international system, see Armstrong, *Revolution and World Order*, chap. 2.

52. Elizabeth Borgwardt, *A New Deal for the World: America's Vision for Human Rights* (Cambridge, Mass.: Harvard University Press, 2007).

53. G. John Ikenberry, *Liberal Leviathan: The Origins, Crisis, and Transformation of the American World Order* (Princeton: Princeton University Press, 2012).

54. See Francis Fukuyama, *The End of History and the Last Man* (New York: Free Press, 1992).

55. John Gerard Ruggie, "Multilateralism: The Anatomy of an Institution," *International Organization* 46, no. 3 (1992), 561–98.

56. F. Gregory Gause III, "From 'Over the Horizon' to 'Into the Backyard': The US-Saudi Relationship and the Gulf War," in *The Middle East and the United States*, 5th ed., ed. David W. Lesch and Mark L. Haas (Boulder, Colo.: Westview, 2014), 329.

57. Dehghani Firooz-Abadi, "The Islamic Republic of Iran and the Ideal International System," in *Iran and the International System*, ed. Anoushiravan Ehteshami and Reza Molavi (New York: Routledge, 2011), chap. 4. See also Walt, *Revolution and War*, 223–24.

58. For an argument as to why Iran has remained a revolutionary state rather than being "socialized" into working within the status quo, see Maximilian Terhalle, "Revolutionary Power and Socialization: Explaining the Persistence of Revolutionary Zeal in Iran's Foreign Policy," *Security Studies* 18, no. 3 (2009), 557–86.

59. Suzanne Maloney, "Identity and Change in Iran's Foreign Policy," in *Identity and Foreign Policy in the Middle East*, ed. Shibley Telhami and Michael Barnett (Ithaca, N.Y.: Cornell University Press, 2002), 88–116.

60. Quoted in Owen, *Clash of Ideas*, 227.

61. Of course America is also anti-Hamas, and so the story is complex, but a fundamental reason for the bad relations is that Hamas refuses to recognize Israel's right to exist.

62. Owen, *Clash of Ideas*, 202–4.

63. Said Amir Arjomand, *After Khomeini: Iran under His Successors* (New York: Oxford University Press, 2009), 133–34.

64. Walt, *Revolution and War*, 264–67.

65. Arjomand, *After Khomeini*, 141–42.

66. Ibid., 147.

67. Ibid., 145.

68. Ray Takeyh, *Guardians of the Revolution: Iran and the World in the Age of the Ayatollahs* (New York: Oxford University Press, 2009), 5.

69. Ibid., chap. 11.

70. Louis Charbonneau, "In New York, Defiant Ahmadinejad Says Israel Will Be 'Eliminated'," *Reuters* (September 24, 2012), http://www.reuters.com/article/2012/09/24/us-un-assembly-ahmadinejad-idUSBRE88N0HF20120924, accessed on January 10, 2013.

71. Christine Hauser, "Holocaust Conference in Iran Provokes Outrage," *New York Times* (December 12, 2006), http://www.nytimes.com/2006/12/12/world/middleeast/13holocaustcnd.html?_r=1&oref=slogin, accessed on January 10, 2013.

72. Thomas Erdbrink, "Iran's Vice President Makes Anti-Semitic Speech at Forum," *New York Times* (June 26, 2012), http://www.nytimes.com/2012/06/27/world/middle east/irans-vice-president-rahimi-makes-anti-semitic-speech.html?_r=0, accessed on January 10, 2012. Above both of these presidents sat Ayatollah Ali Khamenei, successor as supreme leader (literally "guardian jurist") to Khomeini. Khamenei is difficult to read, at times supporting moderation, at times militancy. In any case, notwithstanding his ultimate power, it has made a clear difference to Iranian policy whether a moderate or militant is president.

73. Among the many statements from Israel officials is Yolande Knell, "Israeli PM Netanyahu 'Ready' to Order Strike on Iran," BBC News (November 6, 2012), http://www.bbc.co.uk/news/world-middle-east-20220566, accessed on January 10, 2013.

74. Lee Harris, "Is Iran a Rational Actor?" *Weekly Standard* (March 13, 2012), http://www.weeklystandard.com/blogs/iran-rational-actor_633497.html?page=1, accessed on December 19, 2012. For a rigorous treatment of this side of rationality, see Thomas C. Schelling, *Arms and Influence: With a New Preface and Afterword* (New Haven: Yale University Press, 1966), chap. 3, "The Manipulation of Risk," 92–125.

Lesson 5: The Winner May Be "None of the Above"

1. Francis Fukuyama, "The End of History?," *National Interest* 16 (Summer 1989).

2. Fukuyama, *End of History.*

3. Isaac Chotiner, "Thomas Piketty: I Don't Care for Marx," *New Republic*, May 5, 2014, http://www.newrepublic.com/article/117655/thomas-piketty-interview-econo mist-discusses-his-distaste-marx, accessed on May 13, 2014.

4. See, respectively, http://www.socialistworld.net/, http://world.internationalism.org/, http://revcom.us/s/corim.htm, and http://www.internationalsocialist.org/.

5. See http://www.fourthinternational.org/.

6. "I Challenge You to Debate the Truth of Communism, and to Defend Your Distortions about the Cultural Revolution, before the Harvard Community," open letter from Raymond Lotta to Roderick McFarquhar, professor at Harvard, http://revolu tionbookscamb.org/open%20letter%20macfar.html.

7. Jeffrey Goldberg, "Fidel: 'Cuban Model Doesn't Even Work for Us Anymore," *Atlantic*, September 9, 2010, http://www.theatlantic.com/international/archive/2010/09 /fidel-cuban-model-doesnt-even-work-for-us-anymore/62602/.

8. In the early twenty-first century traditional Leftism was resurgent across Latin America, propelled to some extent by Hugo Chávez's regime and example in Venezuela. Chávez's Bolivarism did enjoy demonstration effects but was never the threat to regimes in the region that communism was in the twentieth century. The occupy movement that ran across Western capitalist democracies, although clearly of the political Left, did not formulate the kind of positive program that would have made it a bona fide ideological movement.

9. Willie Thompson, *The Communist Movement since 1945* (Oxford: Blackwell, 1998), 183.

10. Daniel Patrick Moynihan, *Pandaemonium: Ethnicity in International Politics* (New York: Oxford University Press, 1994), 38–40. Moynihan adds, however, "It would take time for this news to reach the Vietnamese jungle, Angolan bush, or Nicaraguan mountains."

11. David S. Lane, *The Rise and Fall of State Socialism: Industrial Society and the Socialist State* (Cambridge: Polity, 1996), 176.

12. Fred Halliday, *Revolution and World Politics: The Rise and Fall of the Sixth Great Power* (Durham, N.C.: Duke University Press, 1999), 217.

13. Zbigniew K. Brzezinski, *The Grand Failure: The Birth and Death of Communism in the Twentieth Century* (New York: Scribner, 1989), 213.

14. Ibid., 215.

15. See, e.g., Peter A. Hall and David Soskice, *Varieties of Capitalism: The Institutional Foundations of Comparative Advantage* (New York: Oxford University Press, 2001).

16. It is important to acknowledge different varieties of secularism. What Pope Benedict XVI called "positive secularism" is the separation of religious from political authority; "negative secularism" is the attempt by the state to control and weaken or even eliminate traditional religion. Positive secularism characterizes most Western countries. The Soviet Union practiced negative secularism. See Daniel Philpott, Timothy Shah, and Monica Duffy Toft, "The Dangers of Secularism in the Middle East," *Christian Science Monitor* (August 11, 2011), http://www.csmonitor.com /Commentary/Opinion/2011/0811/The-dangers-of-secularism-in-the-Middle-East, accessed on January 17, 2013.

17. M. E. H. N. Mout, "Limits and Debates: A Comparative View of Dutch Toleration in the Sixteenth and Early Seventeenth Centuries," in *The Emergence of Tolerance in the Dutch Republic*, ed. C. Berkvens-Stevelinck, J. Israel, and G. H. M. P. Meyjes (Leiden, Netherlands: Brill, 1997), 37.

18. Pettegree, "Religion and the Revolt," 71–72; John Witte Jr., *The Reformation of Rights: Law, Religion and Human Rights in Early Modern Calvinism* (New York: Cambridge University Press, 2007), 143–44.

19. Martin van Gelderen, *The Political Thought of the Dutch Revolt 1555–1590* (New York: Cambridge University Press, 2002), 219–20.

20. Mout, "Limits and Debates," 40.

21. Pettegree, "Religion and the Revolt," 73–80; Geoffrey Parker, *The Dutch Revolt* (Harmondsworth, UK: Penguin, 1979), 148–49.

22. The text of the Act of Abjuration (Plakkaat van Verlatinghe) can be found at http:// www.h4.dion.ne.jp/~room4me/docs/abj_dut.htm. Its preamble is remarkably similar to that of the American Declaration of Independence, drafted more than two centuries later.

23. Willem Frijhoff, "Religious Toleration in the United Provinces: From 'Case' to 'Model,'" in *Calvinism and Religious Toleration in the Dutch Golden Age*, ed. R. P.-C. Hsia and H. Van Nierop (New York: Cambridge University Press, 2002), 48.

24. This deduction from Calvinist theology was stated most explicitly by Johannes Althusius in the mid-seventeenth century but is evident in Dutch writings in the 1570s. On Althusius, see Witte, *Reformation of Rights*, esp. 171–72.

25. Mark Greengrass, *The Longman Companion to the European Reformation, c. 1500–1618* (New York: Longman, 1998), 142.

26. Remonstrants were Reformed believers who followed the theologian Jacobus Arminius in rejecting the orthodox Calvinist doctrine that before he created the world God determined who would be saved. The Remonstrant leader Johann van Oldenbarnevelt was executed in 1619.

27. Jonathan Israel, "The Intellectual Debate about Toleration in the Dutch Republic," in Berkvens-Stevelinck, Israel, and Meyjes, *Emergence of Tolerance*, 21.

28. In Amsterdam, perhaps the most tolerant city, Catholic baptisms increased from 320 in the 1630s to 15,031 in the 1690s; Lutheran baptisms, from 7,600 to 11,778 in the same period. Jonathan Israel, *The Dutch Republic: Its Rise, Greatness, and Fall, 1477–1806* (Oxford: Clarendon, 1995), 641.

29. Israel, "Intellectual Debate," 23. Anti-Trinitarians deny the orthodox Christian doctrine that God is a trinity, or three persons (Father, Son, and Holy Spirit) in one Godhead. Cartesians were followers of the French philosopher René Descartes, who set belief in God on a foundation of reason rather than revelation.

30. Joke Spaans, "Religious Policies in the Seventeenth-Century Dutch Republic," in Hsia and Van Nierop, *Calvinism and Religious Toleration*, 78.

31. Willem Frijhoff, "The Threshold of Toleration: Interconfessional Conviviality in Holland during the Early Modern Period," in *Embodied Belief: Ten Essays on Religious Culture in Dutch History* (Hilversum, Netherlands: Uitgeverij Verloren, 2002), 40–45.

32. Mout, "Limits and Debates," 45.

33. Angus Maddison, *The World Economy: A Millennial Perspective* (Paris: OECD, 2006), 81.

34. Broers, *Europe after Napoleon*, 118.

35. J. A. S. Grenville, *Europe Reshaped: 1848–1878* (Oxford: Blackwell, 2000), 229–60.

36. Edvard Radzinsky, *Alexander II: The Last Great Tsar* (New York: Simon & Schuster, 2005), 361–421.

37. Grenville, *Europe Reshaped*, 9–10.

38. Marx and Engels, *Communist Manifesto*.

39. Christopher Lasch, *The True and Only Heaven: Progress and Its Critics* (New York: Norton, 1991), 212–14.

40. Eric Hobsbawm, *The Age of Capital 1848–1875* (New York: Vintage, 1996), 15.

41. "Iran: Oil, Grandeur and a Challenge to the West."

42. Asef Bayat, "The Post-Islamist Revolutions: What the Revolts in the Arab World Mean," *Foreign Affairs* (April 26, 2011), http://www.foreignaffairs.com/articles/67812/asef-bayat/the-post-islamist-revolutions, accessed on April 9, 2012.

43. Angelique Chrisafis and Ian Black, "Tunisia Elections Winner: 'We're Hardly the Freemasons, We're a Modern Party,'" *Guardian* (Manchester, UK) (October 25, 2011), http://www.guardian.co.uk/world/2011/oct/25/tunisia-elections-islamist-party-winner, accessed on April 6, 2012.

44. Sarah Lynch, "Muslim Brotherhood Top Winner in Egyptian Election," *USA Today* (December 4, 2011), http://usatoday30.usatoday.com/news/world/story/2011-12-04/israel-egypt-elections/51641978/1, accessed on January 25, 2014.

45. Catherine Herridge, "The Islamist Winter: New Report Suggests Extremist Views Winning in Libya," Foxnews.com (January 4, 2012), http://www.foxnews.com/poli tics/2012/01/04/islamist-winter-new-report-suggests-extremist-views-winning-in -libya/, accessed on April 6, 2012.

46. Thomas Hobbes, *Leviathan* (1651), ed. C. B. Macpherson (Harmondsworth, UK: Penguin, 1981), chap. 17, p. 223; chap. 18, p. 612.

47. Nathan Brown, *When Victory Is Not an Option: Islamist Movements in Arab Politics* (Ithaca, N.Y.: Cornell University Press, 2012).

48. The *CIA World Factbook* of 2010 lists the following hybrid regimes: Oman, Bahrain, United Arab Emirates, Iraq, Syria, Yemen, Kuwait, Jordan, Qatar, Afghanistan, Egypt, Libya, Algeria, Tunisia, Morocco, Mauritania, Eritrea (Muslims only), Gambia, Somalia, Turkmenistan, Kazakhstan, Brunei, and Malaysia.

49. Browers, *Political Ideology*.

50. Abdulaziz Sachedina, *The Islamic Roots of Democratic Pluralism* (New York: Oxford University Press, 2000); Sohail H. Hashmi, "Islam, Constitutionalism, and Democracy," in Owen and Owen, *Religion, the Enlightenment*, 221–39.

51. Brown, *When Victory Is Not an Option*.

52. Browers, *Political Ideology*, 55–59.

53. Nicholas Wolterstorff, *Justice: Rights and Wrongs* (Princeton: Princeton University Press, 2010); Jean Bethke Elshtain, "Religion, Enlightenment, and a Common Good," in Owen and Owen, *Religion, the Enlightenment*, 57–76; and John Witte Jr., "Puritan Sources of Enlightenment Liberty," in Owen and Owen, *Religion, the Enlightenment*, 140–73.

Lesson 6: Watch Turkey and Iran

1. Melvyn P. Leffler, *For the Soul of Mankind: The United States, the Soviet Union, and the Cold War* (New York: Macmillan, 2008).

2. Zachary Elkins and Beth A. Simmons, "The Globalization of Liberalization: Policy Diffusion in the International Political Economy," *American Political Science Review* 98 (2004), 171–89.

3. At the time of this writing it is not clear what kind of regime Egypt will have in the long term, but there are signs that it too eventually may settle on some kind of fusion of Islamism and secularism.

4. See the discussion in Lesson 5 of various forms of secularism. By "secular" I simply mean a regime that does not attempt to coerce religious conformity.

5. Paul Kennedy, *The Rise and Fall of the Great Powers: Economic Change and Military Conflict from 1500 to 2000* (New York: Random House, 1987), 99. Immanuel Wallerstein argues that the Netherlands was a hegemon during this period, comparable to Britain in the nineteenth century and the United States since the 1940s. Wallerstein, *The Modern World System*, vol. 1 (Berkeley: University of California Press, 2011).

6. Maddison, *World Economy*, 81–83.

7. In *Mystery of Iniquity*, quoted in Stephen Wright, "Thomas Helwys," in *Oxford Dictionary of National Biography* (2004), http://www.oxforddnb.com/view/article/12880.

8. John Coffey, *Persecution and Toleration in Protestant England, 1558–1689* (London: Longman, 2000), 70.
9. Frijhoff, "Religious Toleration," 31.
10. Steven M. Nadler, *Spinoza: A Life* (New York: Cambridge University Press, 1999), 315–16.
11. Notwithstanding its being a republic, the United Provinces had a Stadholder ("place-keeper"), a noble selected by the states to be a sort of quasi-monarch.
12. Quoted in Robert C. Steensma, *Sir William Temple* (New York: Twayne, 1970), 45.
13. Quoted in Homer E. Woodbridge, *Sir William Temple: The Man and His Work* (New York: Modern Language Association of America, 1940), 134.
14. Maddison, *World Economy*, 82.
15. "Declaration of Indulgence of King James II" (April 4, 1687), http://www.jacobite.ca/documents/16870404.htm.
16. "Declaration of Indulgence of King James II" (April 27, 1688), http://www.jacobite.ca/documents/16880427.htm (italics mine).
17. To counteract Louis's propaganda, William had assured the Holy Roman emperor, prior to invading England, that he would allow English and Scottish Catholics to practice their religion. To prove his goodwill William increased toleration of Catholicism in the Netherlands itself. Jonathan I. Israel, "William III and Toleration," in *From Persecution to Toleration: The Glorious Revolution and Religion in England*, ed. Ole Peter Grell and Jonathan I. Israel (New York: Oxford University Press, 1991), 140–42.
18. Ibid., 140–58.
19. John Morrill, "The Sensible Revolution," in *The Anglo-Dutch Moment: Essays on the Glorious Revolution and Its World Impact*, ed. J. Israel (New York: Cambridge University Press, 2003), 96–98.
20. The text of the Revocation (also known as the Edict of Fontainebleau) is at http://www.historyguide.org/earlymod/revo_nantes.html.
21. Theodor Schott, "Edict of Nîmes," in *The New Schaff-Herzog Religious Encyclopedia*, vol. 8, ed. Samuel Macauley Jackson (New York: Funk and Wagnalls, 1910), 178–79.
22. François Bluche, *Louis XIV*, trans. Mark Greengrass (Oxford: Blackwell, 1990), 630.
23. Philippe Erlanger, *Louis XIV*, trans. Stephen Cox (New York: Praeger, 1970), 213–14.
24. Quoted in Ian Dunlop, *Louis XIV* (New York: Random House, 1999), 281.
25. Voltaire, *Letters on the English (or Lettres philosophiques)*, http://www.fordham.edu/halsall/mod/1778voltaire-lettres.asp, accessed on March 22, 2014.
26. Colin Jones, *The Great Nation: France from Louis XV to Napoleon 1715–99* (New York: Columbia University Press, 2002), 199–204.
27. S. B. Chrimes, *English Constitutional History* (New York: Oxford University Press, 1967). It is important to note that, although Britain was the exemplary constitutional state in Europe, it lacked—then as now—a written constitution. The British constitution consists of the body of law and custom that has built up over the centuries.
28. Broers, *Europe after Napoleon*, 74–75.
29. Harry Hearder, *Cavour* (New York: Routledge, 1994), 22–23.

30. Denis Mack Smith, *Cavour and Garibaldi 1860: A Study in Political Conflict* (New York: Cambridge University Press, 1985), 26–27, 35, 44–45.

31. Ibid., 31–34.

32. In 1990 U.S. dollars.

33. Charles P. Kindleberger, *The World in Depression, 1929–1939* (Berkeley: University of California Press, 1986); Robert Gilpin, *War and Change in World Politics* (New York: Cambridge University Press, 1981).

34. For explanations of the Soviet slowdown, see Paul Krugman, "The Myth of Asia's Miracle," *Foreign Affairs* 73, no. 6 (November–December 1994), 62–78.

35. On the IRA, see Peter Pringle, "KGB Approved 1m Pounds Aid Request by Party with IRA Link: Peter Pringle in Moscow Finds Evidence in Formerly Secret Archives of How Close the Soviet Union Came to Funding Dublin Politicians," *Independent* (October 26, 1992), http://www.independent.co.uk/news/world/europe/kgb-approved-1m-pounds-aid-request-by-party-with-ira-link-peter-pringle-in-moscow-finds-evidence-in-formerly-secret-archives-of-how-close-the-soviet-union-came-to-funding-dublin-politicians-1559647.html, accessed on October 13, 2011.

36. Reprinted from Owen, *Clash of Ideas*, 206.

37. Kepel, *Revenge of God*, 23.

38. Haykel, "Al-Qa'ida and Shiism," 187. I thank Ahmed al-Rahim for directing me to this source.

39. *CIA World Factbook*, https://www.cia.gov/library/publications/the-world-factbook/, accessed on September 15, 2012.

40. Namely, the Supreme Council of Iraq.

41. Vali Nasr, *The Shia Revival: How Conflicts within Islam Will Shape the Future* (New York: Norton, 2007), 247.

42. The alleged Iranian plot to assassinate the Saudi ambassador to the United States and blow up a Washington restaurant was reputed to be planned by the Quds Force. Joby Warrick and Thomas Erdbrink, "Alleged Plot Is Uncharacteristically Bold," *Washington Post* (October 11, 2011), http://articles.washingtonpost.com/2011-10-11/world/35280214_1_alleged-plot-assassination-plot-quds-force, accessed on September 15, 2012.

43. Mike Shuster, "Iran's Nuclear Fatwa: A Policy or a Ploy?," *NPR News* (June 14, 2012), http://www.npr.org/2012/06/14/154915222/irans-nuclear-fatwa-a-policy-or-a-ploy, accessed on January 18, 2013.

44. "Iran Flirts with Breakout Capability," Center of Strategic and International Studies (January 14, 2014), http://csis.org/blog/iran-flirts-breakout-capability, accessed on January 14, 2014.

45. Matthew Fuhrmann, *Atomic Assistance: How Atoms for Peace Programs Cause Nuclear Insecurity* (Ithaca, N.Y.: Cornell University Press, 2012).

46. James Zogby, "Arab Attitudes toward Iran, 2011" (Washington, D.C.: Arab American Institute Foundation), http://www.aaiusa.org/reports/arab-attitudes-toward-iran-2011, accessed on October 17, 2011. The authors include the following qualification: "In previous polls, when Arabs were asked questions about Iran or its nuclear program, and the U.S. and its threats of sanctions or military action were a

part of the question, Arabs would indicate strong support for Iran and its defiance on nuclear issues. The more negative attitudes toward Iran reflected here may be accounted for by the fact that in this survey Arabs are being asked to state their attitudes toward Iran without reference to the U.S. and/or that Iran's regional behavior has succeeded in alienating Arab opinion."

47. Michael Peel and Najmeh Bozorgmehr, "Iran Gives Syria $1bn Credit Line," *Financial Times* (January 16, 2013), http://www.ft.com/intl/cms/s/0/c0266202-600c-11e2 -b657-00144feab49a.html#axzz2IMbfw945, accessed on January 18, 2013.

48. Jumana Al Tamimi, "Poll Shows Iran Has Lost Arab Support," Gulfnews.com (August 3, 2011), http://gulfnews.com/news/region/iran/poll-shows-iran-has-lost-arab -support-1.846469, accessed on October 17, 2011.

49. Adel Guindy, "The Islamization of Egypt," *Middle East Review of International Affairs* 10, no. 3 (2006).

50. Beken Saatçioğlu, "How Does the European Union's Political Conditionality Induce Compliance? Insights from Turkey and Romania" (Ph.D. diss., University of Virginia, 2009).

51. Recep Tayyip Erdoğan, "Conservative Democracy and the Globalization of Freedom," speech before the American Enterprise Institute (Washington, D.C.), January 29, 2004, reprinted in *The Emergence of a New Turkey: Democracy and the AK Parti*, ed. M. Hakan Yavuz (Salt Lake City: University of Utah Press, 2006), 333–41.

52. Marcie J. Patton, "AKP Reform Fatigue in Turkey: What Has Happened to the EU Process?," *Mediterranean Politics* 12, no. 3 (2007), 343.

53. Meltem Müftüler-Baç, "Turkey's Political Reforms and the Impact of the European Union," *South European Society and Politics* 10, no. 1 (March 2005), 21.

54. Neslihan Çevik, "The Theological Roots of Liberalism in Turkey: 'Muslimism' from Islamic Fashion to Foreign Policy," *Hedgehog Review* 13, no. 2 (Summer 2011), 87–93.

55. Beken Saatçioğlu, "Unpacking the Compliance Puzzle: The Case of Turkey's AKP under EU Conditionality," Working paper, Kolleg-Forschergruppe (KFG), Free University of Berlin, June 2010, 15–21.

56. See, for example, Hassan Abou Taleb, "Following the Turkish Model or Forging Our Own?," *Ahram Online* (September 19, 2011), http://english.ahram.org.eg/NewsCon tentP/4/21638/Opinion/Following-the-Turkish-model-or-forging-our-own.aspx, accessed on October 19, 2011; Mark LeVine, "Is Turkey the Best Model for Arab Democracy?" *Al Jazeera* (September 19, 2011), http://english.aljazeera.net/indepth /opinion/2011/09/201191684356995273.html, accessed on October 19, 2011.

57. *CIA World Factbook*, https://www.cia.gov/library/publications/the-world-factbook /geos/tu.html, accessed on May 14, 2014.

58. Mushtak Parker, "Economy Puts Turkey's AKP Way Ahead in Sunday's Election," *Arab News* (June 11, 2011), http://arabnews.com/middleeast/article452649.ece, accessed on October 19, 2011.

59. Ilter Turan, "Turkish Foreign Policy: Interplay between the Domestic and External," Carnegie Endowment for International Peace (September 21, 2011), http://carnegie endowment.org/2011/09/21/turkish-foreign-policy-interplay-between-domestic-and -external/57qd, accessed on October 19, 2011.

60. "Is Turkey Turning?," *Economist* (June 10, 2010), http://www.economist.com/node /16333417, accessed on October 19, 2011; Turan, "Turkish Foreign Policy."

61. Figures 6.3 and 6.4 cover fifteen Arab countries and Iran. Reconstructed from Mensur Akgün and Sabiha Senyücel Gündoğar, *The Perception of Turkey in the Middle East 2012* (Istanbul: TESEV Foreign Policy Program, 2013).

62. Heba Saleh and Daniel Dombey, "Erdoğan Rallies Arab League Against Israel," *Financial Times* (September 13, 2011), http://www.ft.com/intl/cms/s/0/179e80d4-de11 -11e0-a115-00144feabdc0.html#axzz1bLgTorY7, accessed on October 20, 2011.

63. Selcan Hacaoglu, "Turkey: Kurds Attack Largest in 3 Years, Military Says," *Huffington Post* (October 20, 2011), http://www.huffingtonpost.com/2011/10/20/turkey-at tack-kurds_n_1021671.html, accessed on October 20, 2011.

64. "Erdogan v Gulen," *Economist*, December 14, 2013, http://www.economist.com /news/europe/21591645-who-will-prevail-erdogan-v-gulen, accessed on May 14, 2014.

65. Pinar Tremblay, "Can Erdogan Take Cover behind Turkish Military?," *Al Monitor/ Turkey Pulse*, March 2014, http://www.al-monitor.com/pulse/originals/2014/03 /erdogan-hides-behind-military.html, accessed on May 14, 2014.

66. Soner Cagaptay and Jim Jeffrey, "The Islamist Feud behind Turkey's Turmoil," *Wall Street Journal* (December 29, 2013), http://online.wsj.com/news/articles/SB10001424 05270230334510457928408302047774, accessed on December 31, 2013.

Conclusion

1. Michael Beckley, "China's Century? Why America's Edge Will Endure," *International Security* 26, no. 3 (2011), 41–78.

2. "Text of Bush Inaugural Speech," CBS News (February 11, 2009), http://www.cbsnews .com/news/text-of-bush-inaugural-speech/, accessed on January 20, 2013.

3. For a robust defense see Nau, *Conservative Internationalism.*

4. Jonathan Monten, "The Roots of the Bush Doctrine: Power, Nationalism, and Democracy Promotion in U.S. Strategy," *International Security* 29, no. 4 (2005), 112–56.

5. Eugene Gholz and Daryl Press, "Protecting the Prize: Oil and the US National Interest," *Security Studies* 19, no. 3 (2010), 453–85; Michael Levi, "The Enduring Vulnerabilities of Oil Markets," *Security Studies* 22, no. 1 (2013), 132–38; Gholz and Press, "Enduring Resilience: How Oil Markets Handle Disruptions," *Security Studies* 22, no. 1 (2013), 139–47; Caitlin Talmadge and Joshua Rovner, "Hegemony, Force Posture, and the Provision of Public Goods: The Once and Future Role of Outside Powers in Securing Persian Gulf Oil," *Security Studies* 23, no. 3 (2014).

6. Joseph S. Nye Jr., *Soft Power: The Means to Success in World Politics* (New York: Public Affairs, 2004).

7. Lisa Blaydes and Drew A. Linzer, "Elite Competition, Religiosity, and Anti-Americanism in the Islamic World," *American Political Science Review* 106, no. 2 (2012), 225–43.

8. Hashmi, "Islam, Constitutionalism, and Democracy," 221–39.

9. Sachedina, *Islamic Roots.*

10. For a general strategy, see John M. Owen IV, "Democracy, Realistically," *National Interest* 83 (Spring 2006), 35–42.

11. Peter G. Peterson, "Public Diplomacy and the War on Terrorism," *Foreign Affairs* 81, no. 5 (2002), 74–94.

12. Richard Wike, "Karen Hughes' Uphill Battle," Pew Research Global Attitudes Project (November 1, 2007), http://www.pewglobal.org/2007/11/01/karen-hughes-uphill -battle/, accessed on February 5, 2013.

13. Joseph S. Nye Jr., "Public Diplomacy and Soft Power," *Annals of the American Academy of Political and Social Science* 616, no. 1 (2008), 94–109, 102.

14. Thomas Jefferson to John B. Colvin (September 20, 1810), *The Founders' Constitution*, art. 2, sec. 3, http://press-pubs.uchicago.edu/founders/documents/a2_3s8.html, accessed on February 5, 2013.

15. Alex Kane, "5 Ways Obama Is Just Like George W. Bush," *Salon* (January 9, 2013), http://www.salon.com/2013/01/09/5_ways_obama_has_doubled_down_on_george _w_bushs_policies/, accessed on February 5, 2013; "Barack Obama, Civil Liberties Nightmare," Cato Institute (March 28, 2012), http://www.cato.org/multimedia /events/barack-obama-civil-liberties-nightmare, accessed on February 5, 2013.

16. As far back as the early 1990s: see Hunter, *Culture Wars.*

17. See Philpott et al., "Dangers of Secularism."

18. Wolterstorff, *Justice.* Madison, writing in 1785, is quoted in William Galston, "Claims of Conscience: Religious Freedom and State Power," *Commonweal* (April 19, 2013), https://www.commonwealmagazine.org/claims-conscience, accessed on July 29, 2014.

19. "X" (George F. Kennan), "The Sources of Soviet Conduct," *Foreign Affairs* (July 1947).

BIBLIOGRAPHY

Aboul-Enein, Y. N. *Militant Islamist Ideology: Understanding the Global Threat*. Annapolis, Md.: Naval Institute Press, 2010.

Ackoff, R. L., and J. P. Strümpfer. "Terrorism: A Systemic View." *Systems Research and Behavioral Science* 20, no. 3 (2003), 287–94.

"After Earlier Growth, Decline in Freedom Seen in Middle East in 2007." Press release, Freedom House (January 18, 2008). Retrieved November 18, 2010, from http://www.freedomhouse.org/template.cfm?page=70&release=613

Akgün, M., and S. S. Gündoğar. *The Perception of Turkey in the Middle East 2012*. Istanbul: TESEV Foreign Policy Program, 2013.

Al-Qaradawi, Y. "Islam and Democracy." In R. L. Euben and M. Q. Zaman (Eds.), *Princeton Readings in Islamist Thought: Texts and Contexts from al-Banna to bin Laden*. Princeton: Princeton University Press, 2009: 224–48.

al-Rahim, A. H. "Whither Political Islam and the 'Arab Spring'?" *Hedgehog Review* 13, no. 3 (2011), 8–22.

"And the Winner Is. . . ." *Economist* (December 20, 2011). Retrieved January 14, 2014, from http://www.economist.com/node/21541404.

Arjomand, S. A. *After Khomeini: Iran under His Successors*. New York: Oxford University Press, 2009.

Armstrong, D. *Revolution and World Order: The Revolutionary State in International Society*. Oxford: Clarendon, 1993.

Artz, F. B. *Reaction and Revolution, 1814–1832*. New York: Harper, 1934.

Ashworth, S., J. D. Clinton, A. Meirowitz, and K. W. Ramsay. "Design, Inference, and the Strategic Logic of Suicide Terrorism." *American Political Science Review* 102, no. 2 (2008), 269–73.

Baer, R. *Sleeping with the Devil: How Washington Sold Our Soul for Saudi Crude*. New York: Random House, 2004.

Barkey, K. "Islam and Toleration: Studying the Ottoman Imperial Model." *International Journal of Politics, Culture, and Society* 19, nos. 1–2 (2005), 5–19.

Bashir, H. "How the Roots of Revolution Began to Grow." In H. Bashir and S. G. Safavi (Eds.), *The Roots of the Islamic Revolution in Iran: Economical, Political, Social and Cultural Views*. London: Book Extra, 2002: 9–20.

Bayat, A. "The Post-Islamist Revolutions: What the Revolts in the Arab World Mean." *Foreign Affairs* (April 26, 2011). Retrieved April 9, 2012, from http://www.foreignaffairs.com/articles/67812/asef-bayat/the-post-islamist-revolutions

Beckley, M. "China's Century? Why America's Edge Will Endure." *International Security* 26, no. 3 (2011), 41–78.

Berger, P. L. "The Desecularization of the World: A Global Overview." In P. L. Berger (Ed.), *The Desecularization of the World: Resurgent Religion and World Politics*. Grand Rapids, Mich.: Eerdmans, 1999: 1–18.

Berlin, I. *The Hedgehog and the Fox: An Essay on Tolstoy's View of History*. New York: Simon & Schuster, 1951.

Berman, S. "Islamism, Revolution, and Civil Society." *Perspective on Politics* 1, no. 2 (2003), 257–72.

———. "Marx's Lesson for the Muslim Brothers." *New York Times* (August 10, 2013), SR6.

Birnbaum, N. *After Progress: American Social Reform and European Socialism in the Twentieth Century*. New York: Oxford University Press, 2001.

Blaydes, L., and D. A. Linzer. "Elite Competition, Religiosity, and Anti-Americanism in the Islamic World." *American Political Science Review* 106, no. 2 (2012), 225–43.

Bloom, M. *Dying to Kill: The Allure of Suicide Terror*. New York: Columbia University Press, 2005.

Bluche, F. *Louis XIV*. Translated by Mark Greengrass. Oxford: Blackwell, 1990.

Bodin, J. *Six Books of the Commonwealth* (1576). Translated by M. J. Tooley. Oxford: Basil Blackwell, 1955. Retrieved March 22, 2014, from http://www.constitution.org/bodin/bodin_.htm

Bohnstedt, J. W. "The Infidel Scourge of God: The Turkish Menace as Seen by German Pamphleteers of the Reformation Era." *Transactions of the American Philosophical Society* 58, no. 9 (1968), 1–58.

Borgwardt, E. *A New Deal for the World: America's Vision for Human Rights*. Cambridge, Mass.: Harvard University Press, 2007.

Bossuet, J.-B. *Politics Drawn from the Very Words of Holy Scripture* (1679). Edited by Patrick Riley. New York: Cambridge University Press, 1999.

Broers, M. *Europe after Napoleon: Revolution, Reaction, and Romanticism, 1814–1848*. Manchester: Manchester University Press, 1996.

Brogi, A. *A Question of Self-Esteem: The United States and the Cold War Choices in France and Italy, 1944–1958*. Westport, Conn.: Greenwood, 2002.

Browers, M. *Political Ideology in the Arab World: Accommodation and Transformation*. New York: Cambridge University Press, 2009.

Browers, M., and C. Kurzman (Eds.). *An Islamic Reformation?* Lanham, Md.: Lexington Books, 2004.

Brown, D. "The Influence of Religion on Armed Conflict Onset." Ph.D. dissertation, University of Virginia, 2012.

Brown, N. J. *When Victory Is Not an Option: Islamist Movements in Arab Politics*. Ithaca, N.Y.: Cornell University Press, 2012.

Brzezinski, Z. K. *The Grand Failure: The Birth and Death of Communism in the Twentieth Century*. New York: Scribner, 1989.

Bukovansky, M. *Legitimacy and Power Politics: The American and French Revolutions in International Political Culture*. Princeton: Princeton University Press, 2010.

Burke, E. *Correspondence 3* (1776). In *Oxford Dictionary of National Biography*. Retrieved January 2, 2012, from http://www.oxforddnb.com/view/article/4019

———. *Reflections on the Revolution in France* (1790). Harmondsworth, UK: Penguin, 1969.

———. "Speech of Edmund Burke, Esq., on American Taxation" (April 19, 1774). Library of Economics and Liberty. Retrieved January 2, 2012, from http://www.econlib.org /library/LFBooks/Burke/brkSWv1c2.html

———. "Speech on the Impeachment of Warren Hastings" (February 15, 1788). Retrieved January 2, 2012, from http://www.civilisationis.com/smartboard/shop/burkee/extracts /chap12.htm

———. "Thoughts on French Affairs" (1791). In *The Works of the Right Honourable Edmund Burke*, vol. 3, *Political Miscellanies*. London: Henry G. Bohn, 1855: 359–61. Retrieved January 3, 2012, from http://books.google.com/books/reader?id=7U8XAA AAYAAJ&printsec=frontcover&output= reader

Bush, G. W. "Text of Bush Inaugural Speech." CBS News (February 11, 2009). Retrieved January 20, 2013, from http://www.cbsnews.com/news/text-of-bush-inaugural-speech/

Butterfield, H. *The Whig Interpretation of History.* New York: Norton, 1965.

Carr, E. H. *The Twenty Years' Crisis, 1919–1939: An Introduction to the Study of International Relations* (1946). London: Macmillan, 2001.

Cassels, A. *Ideology and International Relations in the Modern World.* New York: Routledge, 2002.

Caute, D. *The Fellow-Travellers: Intellectual Friends of Communism.* New Haven: Yale University Press, 1988.

Cavanaugh, W. T. *The Myth of Religious Violence: Secular Ideology and the Roots of Modern Conflict.* New York: Oxford University Press, 2009.

Çevik, N. "The Theological Roots of Liberalism in Turkey: 'Muslimism' from Islamic Fashion to Foreign Policy." *Hedgehog Review* 13, no. 2 (Summer 2011), 87–93.

Chotiner, I. "Thomas Piketty: I Don't Care for Marx." *New Republic*, May 5, 2014. Retrieved May 12, 2014, from http://www.newrepublic.com/article/117655/thomas -piketty-interview-economist-discusses-his-distaste-marx

Chrimes, S. B. *English Constitutional History.* New York: Oxford University Press, 1967.

CIA World Factbook. Langley, Va.: Central Intelligence Agency, 2012. Retrieved September 15, 2012, from https://www.cia.gov/library/publications/the-world-factbook/geos/le .html

Clasen, C. P. *The Palatinate in European History, 1559–1660.* Oxford: Basil Blackwell, 1963.

Coffey, J. *Persecution and Toleration in Protestant England, 1558–1689.* London: Longman, 2000.

Cohen, D. "Violence Is Inherent in Islam—It Is a Cult of Death." *Evening Standard* (London) (February 7, 2007). Retrieved November 8, 2010, from http://www.islamophobia -watch.com/islamophobia-watch/2007/2/7/violence-is-inherent-in-islam-it-is-a-cult -of-death.html

Combined Joint Task Force Spartan Public Affairs. "Eager Lion Commanders Hold Press Conference." U.S. Central Command (May 15, 2012). Retrieved August 31, 2012, from http://www.centcom.mil/press-releases/eager-lion-commanders-hold-press-conference .html

Conquest, R. *The Harvest of Sorrow: Soviet Collectivization and the Terror-Famine.* New York: Oxford University Press, 1987.

———. *Reflections on a Ravaged Century.* New York: Norton, 2001.

Cook, D. *Martyrdom in Islam.* New York: Cambridge University Press, 2007.

Coolsaet, R. "Anarchist Outrages." *Le Monde Diplomatique* (September 2004). Retrieved December 14, 2010, from http://mondediplo.com/2004/09/03anarchists

Coupland, P. "H.G. Wells's Liberal Fascism." *Journal of Contemporary History* 35, no. 4 (2000), 541–58.

Crawford, T. W. "Preventing Enemy Coalitions: How Wedge Strategies Shape Power Politics." *International Security* 35, no. 4 (2011), 155–89.

Crawley, C. W. "International Relations, 1815–1830." In *The New Cambridge Modern History,* vol. 9, *War and Peace in an Age of Upheaval, 1793–1830.* New York: Cambridge University Press, 1965: 668–90.

Crenshaw, M. "Explaining Suicide Terrorism: A Review Essay." *Security Studies* 16, no. 1 (2007), 133–62.

Darwish, N. *The Devil We Don't Know: The Dark Side of Revolutions in the Middle East.* New York: John Wiley, 2012.

Davutoğlu, A. "Turkey's Zero-Problems Foreign Policy." *Foreign Policy* (May 20, 2010). Retrieved August 31, 2012, from http://www.foreignpolicy.com/articles/2010/05/20 /turkeys_zero_problems_foreign_policy?page=0,0&hidecomments=yes

De Groot, A. H. *The Ottoman Empire and the Dutch Republic: A History of the Earliest Diplomatic Relations 1610–1630.* Istanbul: Nederlands Historisch-Archaeologisch Instituut, 1978.

Desch, M. "America's Illiberal Liberalism." *International Security* 32, no. 3 (2008), 7–43.

Dogan, P., and D. Rodrik. "How Turkey Manufactured a Coup Plot." *Foreign Policy* (April 6, 2010). Retrieved October 20, 2011, from http://www.foreignpolicy.com/articles/2010/04 /06/how_turkey_manufactured_a_coup_plot

Dunlop, I. *Louis XIV.* New York: Random House, 1999.

Edelstein, D. M. *Occupational Hazards: Success and Failure in Military Occupation.* Ithaca, N.Y.: Cornell University Press, 2011.

Edinger, L. J. *Kurt Schumacher: A Study in Personality and Political Behavior.* Stanford, Calif.: Stanford University Press, 1965.

Elkins, S., and E. McKitrick. *The Age of Federalism: The Early American Republic, 1788–1800.* New York: Oxford University Press, 1994.

Elkins, Z., and B. A. Simmons. "The Globalization of Liberalization: Policy Diffusion in the International Political Economy." *American Political Science Review* 98 (2004), 171–90.

Elshtain, J. B. "Religion, Enlightenment, and a Common Good." In J. M. Owen IV and J. J. Owen (Eds.), *Religion, the Enlightenment, and the New Global Order.* New York: Columbia University Press, 2011: 57–76.

Encyclopædia Britannica (1997). Retrieved April 30, 1999, from http://www.eb.com:180

Erdoğan, R. T. "Conservative Democracy and the Globalization of Freedom." American Enterprise Institute (January 29, 2004). Retrieved October 25, 2011, from http://www .aei.org/EMStaticPage/735?page=Summary

Erlanger, P. *Louis XIV.* Translated by Stephen Cox. New York: Praeger, 1970.

Euben, R. L., and M. Q. Zaman (Eds.). *Princeton Readings in Islamist Thought: Texts and Contexts from al-Banna to bin Laden*. Princeton: Princeton University Press, 2009.

Fenby, J. *The General: Charles de Gaulle and the France He Saved*. New York: Simon & Schuster, 2010.

Firooz-Abadi, D. "The Islamic Republic of Iran and the Ideal International System." In A. Ehteshami and R. Molavi (Eds.), *Iran and the International System*. New York: Routledge, 2011: 223–24.

Fischer-Galati S. A. *Ottoman Imperialism and German Protestantism 1521–1555*. New York: Octagon, 1972.

Fox, J. "Two Civilizations and Ethnic Conflict: Islam and the West." *Journal of Peace Research* 38, no. 4 (2001), 459–72.

Frazee, C. A. *Catholics and Sultans: The Church and the Ottoman Empire 1453–1923*. New York: Cambridge University Press, 2006.

Frederick III, Elector Palatinate. *Heidelberg Catechism* (1563). Retrieved March 22, 2014, from http://www.ccel.org/creeds/heidelberg-cat-ext.txt

Friedrich, C. J. "Military Government and Democratization: A Central Issue of American Foreign Policy." In C. J. Friedrich et al. (Eds.), *American Experiences in Military Government in World War II*. New York: Rinehart, 1948: 3–22.

Frijhoff, W. "Religious Toleration in the United Provinces: From 'Case' to 'Model.'" In R. P.-C. Hsia and H. Van Nierop (Eds.), *Calvinism and Religious Toleration in the Dutch Golden Age*. New York: Cambridge University Press, 2002: 27–52.

———. "The Threshold of Toleration: Interconfessional Conviviality in Holland during the Early Modern Period." In *Embodied Belief: Ten Essays on Religious Culture in Dutch History*. Hilversum, Netherlands: Uitgeverij Verloren, 2002: 40–45.

Fuhrmann, M. *Atomic Assistance: How Atoms for Peace Programs Cause Nuclear Insecurity*. Ithaca, N.Y.: Cornell University Press, 2012.

Fukuyama, F. "The End of History?" *National Interest* 16 (1989): 15–25.

———. *The End of History and the Last Man*. New York: Free Press, 1992.

Galston, W. "Claims of Conscience: Religious Freedom and State Power." Retrieved July 29, 2014, from *Commonweal* (April 19, 2013), https://www.commonwealmagazine.org/claims-conscience.

Gause, F. G., III. *Beyond Sectarianism: The New Middle East Cold War*. Brookings Doha Center Analysis Paper Number 11 (July 2014).

———. "From 'Over the Horizon' to 'Into the Backyard': The US-Saudi Relationship and the Gulf." In D. W. Lesch and M. L. Haas (Eds.), *The Middle East and the United States*, 5th ed. Boulder, Colo.: Westview, 2014: 326–40.

Gellately, R. *Lenin, Stalin, and Hitler: The Age of Social Catastrophe*. New York: Random House, 2007.

Gholz, E., and D. G. Press. "Enduring Resilience: How Oil Markets Handle Disruptions." *Security Studies* 22, no. 1 (2013), 139–47.

———. "Protecting the Prize: Oil and the US National Interest." *Security Studies* 19, no. 3 (2010), 453–85.

Gilpin, R. *War and Change in World Politics*. New York: Cambridge University Press, 1981.

Glaser, C. L. *Rational Theory of International Politics: The Logic of Competition and Cooperation*. Princeton: Princeton University Press, 2010.

Goldstein, Patrick, and James Rainey. "Al Jazeera, Fox Log Biggest Audience Jumps during Egypt Crisis." *LA Times Blogs* (February 17, 2011). Retrieved January 2, 2012, from http://latimesblogs.latimes.com/the_big_picture/2011/02/al-jazeera-fox-log-biggest -audience-jumps-during-egypt-crisis.html

Goodman, J. David. "Police Arrest 5 in Danish Terror Plot." *New York Times* (December 29, 2010). Retrieved January 16, 2014, from http://www.nytimes.com/2010/12/30 /world/europe/30denmark.html?ref=danishcartooncontroversy

Gorka, K. C., and P. Sookhdeo (Eds.). *Fighting the Ideological War: Winning Strategies from Communism to Islamism*. McLean, Va.: Westminster Institute, 2012.

Greengrass, M. *The Longman Companion to the European Reformation, c. 1500–1618*. New York: Longman, 1998.

Grenville, J. A. S. *Europe Reshaped: 1848–1878*. Oxford: Blackwell, 2000.

Guindy, A. "The Islamization of Egypt." *Middle East Review of International Affairs* 10, no. 3 (2006), 92–102.

Haas, M. L. *The Clash of Ideologies: Middle Eastern Politics and American Security*. New York: Oxford University Press, 2012.

———. *The Ideological Origins of Great Power Politics 1789–1989*. Ithaca, N.Y.: Cornell University Press, 2005.

———. "Missed Ideological Opportunities and George W. Bush's Middle Eastern Policies." *Security Studies* 21, no. 3 (2012), 416–54.

———. "The United States and the End of the Cold War: Reactions to Shifts in Soviet Power, Policies, or Domestic Politics?" *International Organization* 61, no. 1 (2007), 145–79.

Haass, R. N. "The New Thirty Years' War." *Project Syndicate* (July 21, 2014). Retrieved July 24, 2014, from http://www.project-syndicate.org/richard-n--haas-argues-that-the -middle-east-is-less-a-problem-to-be-solved-than-a-condition-to-be-managed

Hall, P. A., and D. Soskice. *Varieties of Capitalism: The Institutional Foundations of Comparative Advantage*. New York: Oxford University Press, 2001.

Halliday, F. *Revolution and World Politics: The Rise and Fall of the Sixth Great Power*. Durham, N.C.: Duke University Press, 1999.

Halperin, S. W. "Leon Blum and Contemporary French Socialism." *Journal of Modern History* 18, no. 3 (1946), 241–50.

Hamid, Shadi. "Did Religious Parties Really Lose the Iraqi Elections?" *Democracy Arsenal* (blog) (April 4, 2010). Retrieved October 15, 2010, from http://www.democracyarsenal .org/2010/04/did-religious-parties-really-lose-the-iraqi-elections-.html

———. "Underestimating Religious Parties." *Democracy Arsenal* (blog) (April 5, 2010). Retrieved October 15, 2010, from http://www.democracyarsenal.org/2010/04/under estimating-religious-parties.html

Hamzawy, Amr. "Two Sorrowful Scenes at a Church Funeral." *Atlantic Council* (November 8, 2013). Retrieved December 30, 2013, from http://www.atlanticcouncil.org/blogs /egyptsource/two-sorrowful-scenes-at-a-church-funeral

Harper, J. L. *American Visions of Europe: Franklin D. Roosevelt, George F. Kennan, and Dean G. Acheson*. New York: Cambridge University Press, 1996.

Harris, L. "Is Iran a Rational Actor?" *Weekly Standard* (March 13, 2012). Retrieved December 19, 2012, from http://www.weeklystandard.com/blogs/iran-rational-actor_633497.html?page=1

Hashmi, S. H. "Islam, Constitutionalism, and Democracy." In J. M. Owen IV and J. J. Owen (Eds.), *Religion, the Enlightenment, and the New Global Order.* New York: Columbia University Press, 2010: 221–39.

Haykel, B. "Al-Qa'ida and Shiism." In A. Moghadam and B. Fishman (Eds.), *Fault Lines in Global Jihad: Organizational, Strategic, and Ideological Fissures.* New York: Routledge, 2011: 184–202.

Hearder, H. *Cavour.* New York: Routledge, 1994.

Hegel, G. W. F. *Lectures on the Philosophy of World History.* Translated by H. B. Nisbet. New York: Cambridge University Press, 1975.

Heilbrunn, J. *They Knew They Were Right: The Rise of the Neocons.* New York: Random House, 2009.

Henry IV of France. *The Edict of Nantes* (April 13, 1598). Retrieved March 22, 2014, from http://www2.stetson.edu/~psteeves/classes/edictnantes.html

Herman, A. *Metternich.* London: Allen & Unwin, 1932.

Hitchens, C. "Reactionary Prophet." *Atlantic Monthly* (April 2004), 130–38. Retrieved January 2, 2012, from http://www.theatlantic.com/past/docs/issues/2004/04/hitchens.htm

Hobbes, T. *Leviathan* (1651). Edited by C. B. Macpherson. Harmondsworth, UK: Penguin, 1981.

Hobsbawm, E. *The Age of Capital 1848–1875.* New York: Vintage, 1996.

———. *The Age of Revolution 1789–1848.* New York: Vintage, 1996.

Hodge, C. C., and C. J. Nolan (Eds.). *Shepherd of Democracy? America and Germany in the Twentieth Century.* Westport, Conn.: Greenwood, 1992.

Holborn, H. *A History of Modern Germany: The Reformation.* New York: Knopf, 1961.

Horowitz, M. C. "Nonstate Actors and the Diffusion of Innovations: The Case of Suicide Terrorism." *International Organization* 64, no. 1 (2010), 33–64.

Hunter, I. *Malcolm Muggeridge: A Life.* Vancouver: Regent College Publishing, 2003.

Hunter, J. D. *Culture Wars: The Struggle to Define America.* New York: Basic Books, 1991.

Huntington, S. P. *The Clash of Civilizations and the Remaking of World Order.* New York: Simon & Schuster, 1996.

Ikenberry, G. J. *Liberal Leviathan: The Origins, Crisis, and Transformation of the American World Order.* Princeton: Princeton University Press, 2012.

İnalcık, H., and D. Quataert. *An Economic and Social History of the Ottoman Empire, 1300–1914.* New York: Cambridge University Press, 1994.

International Institute for Strategic Studies. *Nuclear Programmes in the Middle East: In the Shadow of Iran.* London: IISS, 2008.

"Iran: Oil, Grandeur and a Challenge to the West." *Time* (November 4, 1974). Retrieved April 9, 2012, from http://www.time.com/time/magazine/article/0,9171,945047,00.html

Israel, J. *The Dutch Republic: Its Rise, Greatness, and Fall, 1477–1806.* Oxford: Clarendon, 1995.

———. "The Intellectual Debate about Toleration in the Dutch Republic." In C. Berkvens-Stevelinck, J. Israel, and G. H. M. P. Meyjes (Eds.), *The Emergence of Tolerance in the Dutch Republic*. Leiden, Netherlands: Brill, 1997: 3–36.

———. "William III and Toleration." In O. P. Grell and J. I. Israel (Eds.), *From Persecution to Toleration: The Glorious Revolution and Religion in England*. New York: Oxford University Press, 1991: 129–70.

Iyigun, M. "Luther and Suleyman." *Quarterly Journal of Economics* 123, no. 4 (2008), 1465–94.

Izumikawa, Y. "To Coerce or Reward? Theorizing Wedge Strategies in Alliance Politics." *Security Studies* 22, no. 3 (2013), 498–531.

James I of England. "The True Lawe of Free Monarchies" (1598). Retrieved March 22, 2014, from http://www.constitution.org/primarysources/stuart.html

James II of England. "Declaration of Indulgence of King James II" (April 4, 1687). The Jacobite Heritage. Retrieved March 17, 2014, from http://www.jacobite.ca/documents /16870404.htm

———. "Declaration of Indulgence of King James II" (April 27, 1688). Retrieved May 15, 2014, from http://www.jacobite.ca/documents/16880427.htm.

Jefferson, T. "Thomas Jefferson to John B. Colvin" (September 20, 1810). Retrieved March 22, 2014, from http://press-pubs.uchicago.edu/founders/documents/a2_3s8.html

Jervis, R. *System Effects: Complexity in Political and Social Life*. Princeton: Princeton University Press, 1998.

———. *Why Intelligence Fails: Lessons from the Iranian Revolution and the Iraq War*. Ithaca, N.Y.: Cornell University Press, 2011.

Johnson, J. T. *The Holy War Idea in Western and Islamic Traditions*. University Park: Penn State University Press, 1997.

Jones, C. *Britain and the Yemen Civil War, 1962–1965: Ministers, Mercenaries and Mandarins: Foreign Policy and the Limits of Covert Action*. Eastbourne, UK: Sussex Academic Press, 2010.

———. *The Great Nation: France from Louis XV to Napoleon 1715–99*. New York: Columbia University Press, 2002.

Judt, T. *Postwar: A History of Europe since 1945*. New York: Random House, 2010.

Juergensmeyer, M. *Global Rebellion: Religious Challenges to the Secular State, from Christian Militias to al Qaeda*. Berkeley: University of California Press, 2009.

Kant, I. "Idea for a Universal History with Cosmopolitan Intent" (1784). In T. Humphrey (Ed.), *Perpetual Peace and Other Essays*. Indianapolis: Hackett Press, 1981: 29–40.

Karabell, Z. *Architects of Intervention: The United States, the Third World, and the Cold War, 1946–1962*. Baton Rouge: Louisiana State University Press, 1999.

Kennan, G. F. "The Charge in the Soviet Union (Kennan) to the Secretary," also known as "The Long Telegram" (February 22, 1946). Retrieved February 5, 2013, from http:// www.gwu.edu/~nsarchiv/coldwar/documents/episode-1/kennan.htm

———. *Russia and the West under Lenin and Stalin*. Boston: Little, Brown, 1961.

———. "The Sources of Soviet Conduct." *Foreign Affairs* 25, no. 4 (July 1947): 566–82.

Kennedy, P. *The Rise and Fall of the Great Powers: Economic Change and Military Conflict from 1500 to 2000*. New York: Random House, 1987.

Kepel, G. *Jihad: The Trail of Political Islam.* London: I.B. Tauris, 2006.

———. *The Revenge of God: The Resurgence of Islam, Christianity, and Judaism in the Modern World.* University Park: Penn State University Press, 1994.

Keynes, J. M. *General Theory of Employment, Interest, and Money.* London: Macmillan, 1936.

"Khatami Condemns 9/11 Terror Attacks." *Reuters* (September 10, 2006). Retrieved November 9, 2010, from http://gulfnews.com/news/world/usa/khatami-condemns-9-11 -terror-attacks-1.254539

Khong, Y. F. *Analogies at War: Korea, Munich, Dien Bien Phu, and the Vietnam Decisions of 1965.* Princeton: Princeton University Press, 1992.

Kindleberger, C. P. *The World in Depression, 1929–1939.* Berkeley: University of California Press, 1986.

Kissinger, H. A. *A World Restored: Metternich, Castlereagh and the Problems of Peace, 1812–22.* Boston: Houghton Mifflin, 1957.

Krieger, T., and D. Meierrieks. "What Causes Terrorism?" *Public Choice* 147, nos. 1–2 (2011), 3–27.

Krueger, A. B., and J. Malečková. "Education, Poverty, and Terrorism: Is There a Causal Connection?" *Journal of Economic Perspectives* 17, no. 4 (2003), 119–44.

Krugman, P. "The Myth of Asia's Miracle." *Foreign Affairs* 73, no. 6 (November–December 1994), 62–78.

Kurzman, C. *The Missing Martyrs: Why There Are So Few Muslim Terrorists.* New York: Oxford University Press, 2011.

Kurzman, C., and I. Naqvi. "The Islamists Are Not Coming." *Foreign Policy* (January– February 2010). Retrieved October 20, 2010, from http://www.foreignpolicy.com /articles/2010/01/04/the_islamists_are_not_coming

Kydd, A. "Game Theory and the Spiral Model." *World Politics* 49, no. 3 (1997), 371–400.

Lane, D. S. *The Rise and Fall of State Socialism: Industrial Society and the Socialist State.* Cambridge: Polity, 1996.

Lapidus, I. *A History of Islamic Societies.* 2nd ed. New York: Cambridge University Press, 2002.

Lasch, C. *The True and Only Heaven: Progress and Its Critics.* New York: Norton, 1991.

Ledeen, M. A. *West European Communism and American Foreign Policy.* Piscataway, N.J.: Transaction, 1987.

Leffler, M. P. *For the Soul of Mankind: The United States, the Soviet Union, and the Cold War.* New York: Macmillan, 2008.

Legro, J. W. *Rethinking the World: Great Power Strategies and International Order.* Ithaca, N.Y.: Cornell University Press, 2005.

Leurdijk, J. H. *Intervention in International Politics.* Leeuwarden, Netherlands: Eisma BV, 1986.

Leverett, F., and H. M. Leverett. *Going to Tehran: Why the United States Must Come to Terms with the Islamic Republic of Iran.* New York: Henry Holt, 2013.

Levi, M. "The Enduring Vulnerabilities of Oil Markets." *Security Studies* 22, no. 1 (2013), 132–38.

Lindbergh, A. M. *The Wave of the Future: A Confession of Faith.* New York: Harcourt, Brace, 1940.

Linz, J. "The Crisis of Democracy after the First World War." In R. Griffin (Ed.), *International Fascism: Theories, Causes, and the New Consensus*. London: Arnold, 1988: 175–85.

Lipset, S. M., and G. W. Marks. *It Didn't Happen Here: Why Socialism Failed in the United States*. New York: Norton, 2000.

Lynch, M. "Islam Divided between Salafi-Jihad and the Ikhwan." *Studies in Conflict & Terrorism* 33, no. 6 (2010), 467–87.

Mackey, Robert. "Israeli Minister Agrees that Ahmadinejad Never Said Israel 'Must Be Wiped off the Map.'" *New York Times* (April 17, 2012). Retrieved January 16, 2014, from http://thelede.blogs.nytimes.com/2012/04/17/israeli-minister-agrees-ahmadinejad-never-said-israel-must-be-wiped-off-the-map/

Mackintosh, J. *The Story of Scotland from the Earliest Times to the Present Century*. New York: G.P. Putnam's Sons, 1890.

Macleod, E. V. *A War of Ideas: British Attitudes toward the Wars against Revolutionary France 1792–1802*. Burlington, Vt.: Ashgate, 1998.

Maddison, A. *The World Economy: A Millennial Perspective*. Paris: OECD, 2006.

Maddison Project. Retrieved September 21, 2010, from http://www.ggdc.net/maddison/maddison-project/home.htm

Malament, B. C. "British Labour and Roosevelt's New Deal: The Response of the Left and the Unions." *Journal of British Studies* 17, no. 2 (1978), 136–67.

Maloney, S. "Identity and Change in Iran's Foreign Policy." In S. Telhami and M. Barnett (Eds.), *Identity and Foreign Policy in the Middle East*. Ithaca, N.Y.: Cornell University Press, 2002: 88–116.

Marshall, P. *The Magic Circle of Rudolf II: Alchemy and Astrology in Renaissance Prague*. New York: Bloomsbury, 2009.

Marx, K., and F. Engels. *The Communist Manifesto* (1848). New York: Oxford University Press, 2008.

McLean, I., and A. B. Urken. "Did Jefferson or Madison Understand Condorcet's Theory of Social Choice?" *Public Choice* 73, no. 4 (1992), 445–57.

Merritt, R. L. *Democracy Imposed: U.S. Occupation Policy and the German Public, 1945–1949*. New Haven: Yale University Press, 1995.

Miller, J. E. *The United States and Italy, 1940–1950: The Politics and Diplomacy of Stabilization*. Chapel Hill: University of North Carolina Press, 1986.

Miller, W. *The Ottoman Empire and Its Successors 1801–1927: With an Appendix, 1927–1936*. New York: Cambridge University Press, 2013.

Moghadam, A., and B. Fishman. "Introduction: Jihadi 'Endogenous Problems.'" In A. Moghadam and B. Fishman (eds.), *Fault Lines in Global Jihad: Organizational, Strategic, and Ideological Fissures*. New York: Routledge, 2011: 1–22.

Monten, J. "The Roots of the Bush Doctrine: Power, Nationalism, and Democracy Promotion in U.S. Strategy." *International Security* 29, no. 4 (2005), 112–56.

Moravcsik, A. "Taking Preferences Seriously: A Liberal Theory of International Politics." *International Organization* 51, no. 4 (1997), 513–53.

Morrill, J. "The Sensible Revolution." In J. Israel (Ed.), *The Anglo-Dutch Moment: Essays on the Glorious Revolution and Its World Impact*. New York: Cambridge University Press, 2003: 73–104.

"Most Muslims Want Democracy, Personal Freedoms, and Islam in Political Life." Pew Research Center, July 10, 2012. Retrieved December 19, 2012, from http://www.pew global.org/2012/07/10/most-muslims-want-democracy-personal-freedoms-and -islam-in-political-life/

Mout, M. E. H. N. "Limits and Debates: A Comparative View of Dutch Toleration in the Sixteenth and Early Seventeenth Centuries." In C. Berkvens-Stevelinck, J. Israel, and G. H. M. P. Meyjes (Eds.), *The Emergence of Tolerance in the Dutch Republic.* Leiden, Netherlands: Brill, 1997: 37–48.

Moynihan, D. P. *Pandaemonium: Ethnicity in International Politics.* New York: Oxford University Press, 1994.

Muasher, M. *The Arab Center: The Promise of Moderation.* New Haven: Yale University Press, 2008.

Müftüler-Baç, M. "Turkey's Political Reforms and the Impact of the European Union." *South European Society and Politics* 10, no. 1 (2005), 17–31.

Muggeridge, M. "The Soviet and the Peasantry." *Manchester Guardian* (March 25, 1933). Retrieved March 19, 2014, from http://www.garethjones.org/soviet_articles/soviet_and _the_peasantry_1.htm

"Muslim Publics Share Concern about Extremist Groups." Pew Research Global Attitudes Project, September 10, 2013. Retrieved January 14, 2014, from http://www.pewglobal .org/2013/09/10/muslim-publics-share-concerns-about-extremist-groups/

"Muslims Believe U.S. Seeks to Undermine Islam." World Public Opinion (April 24, 2007). Retrieved December 13, 2010, from http://www.worldpublicopinion.org/pipa/articles /brmiddleeastnafricara/346.php?lb=brme&pnt=346&nid=&id=

Nadler, S. M. *Spinoza: A Life.* New York: Cambridge University Press, 1999.

Nasr, V. "If the Arab Spring Turns Ugly." *New York Times* (August 27, 2011). Retrieved February 14, 2012, from http://www.nytimes.com/2011/08/28/opinion/sunday/the -dangers-lurking-in-the-arab-spring.html?pagewanted=all

———. *The Shia Revival: How Conflicts within Islam Will Shape the Future.* New York: Norton, 2007.

Nau, H. *Conservative Internationalism: Armed Diplomacy under Jefferson, Polk, Truman, and Reagan.* Princeton: Princeton University Press, 2013.

Nenni, Pietro. "Where the Italian Socialists Stand." *Foreign Affairs* 40, no. 2 (1962), 216–18.

Neustadt, R. E., and E. R. May. *Thinking in Time: The Uses of History for Decision Makers.* New York: Simon & Schuster, 2011.

Nexon, D. H. *The Struggle for Power in Early Modern Europe: Religious Conflict, Dynastic Empires, and International Change.* Princeton: Princeton University Press, 2009.

Nisbet, R. A. *History of the Idea of Progress.* Piscataway, N.J.: Transaction, 1980.

Nordsieck, W. *Parties and Elections in Europe* (2006). Retrieved August 15, 2012, from http://www.parties-and-elections.eu/

"Nuclear Weapons: Who Has What at a Glance." Washington, D.C.: Arms Control Association, November 2012. Retrieved January 19, 2013, from http://www.armscontrol.org /factsheets/Nuclearweaponswhohaswhat

Nye, J. S. "Public Diplomacy and Soft Power." *Annals of the American Academy of Political and Social Science* 616, no. 1 (2008), 94–109.

——. *Soft Power: The Means to Success in World Politics*. New York: Public Affairs, 2004.

——. *Understanding International Conflicts*. New York: Longman, 1997.

O'Driscoll, G. P., Jr., K. R. Holmes, and M. A. O'Grady. *Index of Economic Freedom*. Washington, D.C.: Heritage Foundation, 2002.

O'Reilly, B. "The False Monolith of Political Islam." *Asia Times* (December 17, 2011). Retrieved July 19, 2012, from http://www.atimes.com/atimes/Middle_East/ML17Ak01.html

Owen, J. M., IV. *The Clash of Ideas in World Politics: Transnational Networks, States, and Regime Change, 1510–2010*. Princeton: Princeton University Press, 2010.

——. "Democracy, Realistically." *National Interest* 83 (Spring 2006), 35–42.

——. *Liberal Peace, Liberal War: American Politics and International Security*. Ithaca, N.Y.: Cornell University Press, 1997.

——. "Why Islamism Is Winning." *New York Times* (January 7, 2012), A19.

Owen, J. M., IV, and J. J. Owen (Eds.). *Religion, the Enlightenment, and the New Global Order*. New York: Columbia University Press, 2011.

Owen, J. M., IV, and M. Poznansky. "When Does America Drop Dictators?" *European Journal of International Relations* (2014), doi:10.1177/1354066113508990.

Palabiyik, M. S. "Contributions of the Ottoman Empire to the Construction of Modern Europe." Master's thesis, Middle East Technical University, 2005.

Palmer, R. R. *The Age of the Democratic Revolution: A Political History of Europe and America*. Vols. 1–2. Princeton: Princeton University Press, 1959, 1964).

Pape, R. A. *Dying to Win: The Strategic Logic of Suicide Terrorism*. New York: Random House, 2005.

Pape, R. A., and J. K. Feldman. *Cutting the Fuse: The Explosion of Global Suicide Terrorism and How to Stop It*. Chicago: University of Chicago Press, 2010.

Parker, G. *The Dutch Revolt*. Harmondsworth, UK: Penguin, 1979.

Parker, G., and S. Adams (Eds.). *The Thirty Years' War*. New York: Routledge, 1997.

Parsi, T. *Treacherous Alliance: The Secret Dealings of Israel, Iran, and the United States*. New Haven: Yale University Press, 2007.

Patton, M. J. "AKP Reform Fatigue in Turkey: What Has Happened to the EU Process?" *Mediterranean Politics* 12, no. 3 (2007), 339–58.

Peterson, P. G. "Public Diplomacy and the War on Terrorism." *Foreign Affairs* 81, no. 5 (2002), 74–94.

Pettegree, A. "Religion and the Revolt." In G. Darby (Ed.), *The Origins and Development of the Dutch Revolt*. New York: Routledge, 2001: 67–83.

Philpott, D., T. S. Shah, and M. D. Toft. "The Dangers of Secularism in the Middle East." *Christian Science Monitor* (August 11, 2011). Retrieved January 17, 2013, from http://www.csmonitor.com/Commentary/Opinion/2011/0811/The-dangers-of-secularism-in-the-Middle-East.

Pinker, S. *The Better Angels of Our Nature: Why Violence Has Declined*. New York: Viking, 2011.

Pipes, D. "The Scandal of U.S.-Saudi Relations." *National Interest* (Winter 2003), 66–78. Retrieved July 20, 2012, from http://www.danielpipes.org/995/the-scandal-of-us-saudi-relations

Podhoretz, N. *World War IV: The Long Struggle Against Islamofascism*. New York: Random House, 2007.

Pridham, G. *Political Parties and Coalitional Behaviour in Italy*. New York: Routledge, 2013.

"Qaradawi's Ruling on Major and Minor Apostasy," *Islamopedia Online* (October 22, 2010). Retrieved July 28, 2014, from http://www.islamopediaonline.org/fatwa/ al-qaradawis-200-7-ruling-apostasy.

"Quintus Fabius Maximus Verrucosus." In *Encyclopædia Britannica*. Retrieved November 4, 2010, from http://www.britannica.com/EBchecked/topic/199706/Quintus-Fabius -Maximus-Verrucosus

Rabasa, A., and F. S. Larrabee. *The Rise of Political Islam in Turkey*. Santa Monica, Calif.: RAND, 2008.

Radzinsky, E. *Alexander II: The Last Great Tsar*. New York: Simon & Schuster, 2005.

Religious Peace of Augsburg (1555/1905). Edited by E. Reich. Retrieved October 20, 2010, from http://pages.uoregon.edu/sshoemak/323/texts/augsburg.htm

Rice-Maximin, E. "The United States and the French Left, 1945–1949: The View from the State Department." *Journal of Contemporary History* 19, no. 4 (1984), 729–47.

Rodgers, D. T. *Atlantic Crossings: Social Politics in a Progressive Age*. Cambridge, Mass.: Harvard University Press, 1998.

Roy, O. *The Failure of Political Islam*. Cambridge, Mass.: Harvard University Press, 1994.

———. "Islamism's Failure, Islamists' Future." *Open Democracy* (October 30, 2006). Retrieved October 12, 2010, from http://www.opendemocracy.net/faith-europe_islam /islamism_4043.jsp

———. "This Is Not an Islamic Revolution." *New Statesman* (February 15, 2011). Retrieved January 14, 2014, from http://www.newstatesman.com/religion/2011/02/egypt-arab -tunisia-islamic

Ruggie, J. G. "Multilateralism: The Anatomy of an Institution." *International Organization* 46, no. 3 (1992), 561–98.

Saatçioğlu, B. "How Does the European Union's Political Conditionality Induce Compliance? Insights from Turkey and Romania." Ph.D. dissertation, University of Virginia, 2009.

———. "Unpacking the Compliance Puzzle: The Case of Turkey's AKP under EU Conditionality." Working paper, Kolleg-Forschergruppe (KFG), Free University of Berlin, 2010.

Sachedina, A. *The Islamic Roots of Democratic Pluralism*. New York: Oxford University Press, 2000.

Salem, P. *Bitter Legacy: Ideology and Politics in the Arab World*. Syracuse: Syracuse University Press, 1994.

"Saving Faith." *Economist* (July 15, 2010). Retrieved December 23, 2013, from http://www .economist.com/node/16564186

Schaff, P. "Augsburg Interim." In *New Schaff-Herzog Encyclopedia of Religious Knowledge*. Vol. 6, *Innocents-Liudger*. Retrieved January 26, 2012, from http://www.ccel.org/s /schaff/encyc/encyc06/htm/iii.ix.htm

Schelling, T. C. *Arms and Influence: With a New Preface and Afterword*. New Haven: Yale University Press, 1966.

Schmidt, B. C., and M. C. Williams. "The Bush Doctrine and the Iraq War: Neoconservatives versus Realists." *Security Studies* 17, no. 2 (2008), 191–220.

Schott, T. "Edict of Nîmes." In *The New Schaff-Herzog Religious Encyclopedia*. Vol. 8, edited by Samuel Macauley Jackson. New York: Funk and Wagnalls, 1910: 178–79.

Schroeder, P. W. *The Transformation of European Politics 1763–1848*. New York: Oxford University Press, 1994.

Schweller, R. L. "Bandwagoning for Profit: Bringing the Revisionist State Back In." *International Security* 19, no. 1 (1994), 72–107.

Service, R. *Trotsky: A Biography*. New York: Oxford University Press, 2009.

Shalev, Chemi. "With New BFFs Like Saudi Arabia, Who Needs Anti-Semitic Enemies?" *Haaretz* (October 27, 2013). Retrieved January 18, 2014, from http://www.haaretz.com /blogs/west-of-eden/.premium-1.554722

Smith, A. *An Inquiry into the Nature and Causes of the Wealth of Nations* (1776). London: Methuen, 1904. Retrieved December 31, 2010, from http://www.econlib.org/library /Smith/smWN.html

Smith, D. M. *Cavour and Garibaldi 1860: A Study in Political Conflict*. New York: Cambridge University Press, 1985.

Smith, J. E. *Lucius D. Clay: An American Life*. New York: Macmillan, 1990.

Smith, T. *America's Mission: The United States and the Worldwide Struggle for Democracy*. Princeton: Princeton University Press, 1994.

———. *A Pact with the Devil: Washington's Bid for World Supremacy and the Betrayal of the American Promise*. New York: Routledge, 2012.

Spaans, J. "Religious Policies in the Seventeenth-Century Dutch Republic." In R. P.-C. Hsia and H. Van Nierop (Eds.), *Calvinism and Religious Toleration in the Dutch Golden Age*. New York: Cambridge University Press, 2002: 72–86.

Spencer, R. *Religion of Peace? Why Christianity Is and Islam Isn't*. Washington, D.C.: Regnery, 2007.

———. *The Truth about Muhammad: Founder of the World's Most Intolerant Religion*. Washington, D.C.: Regnery, 2006.

Stauffer, R. "Calvin." In M. Prestwich (Ed.), *International Calvinism, 1541–1715*. Oxford: Clarendon, 1985: 15–38.

Steensma, R. C. *Sir William Temple*. New York: Twayne, 1970.

Steffens, L. *The Autobiography of Lincoln Steffens*. Vol. 1. New York: Harcourt Brace, 1931.

Steinberg, J. "1848 and 2011: Bringing Down the Old Order Is Easy; Building a New One Is Tough." *Foreign Affairs* (September 28, 2011). Retrieved May 15, 2014, from http:// www.foreignaffairs.com/articles/68306/jonathan-steinberg/1848-and-2011

Stringer, D. "Poverty Fueling Muslim Anti-West Tendencies: Study." *Huffington Post* (May 7, 2009). Retrieved November 11, 2010, from http://www.huffingtonpost.com/2009/05 /07/poverty-fueling-muslim-an_n_199192.html#

Sullivan, A. "My Problem with Christianism." *Time* (May 7, 2006). Retrieved January 17, 2013, from http://www.time.com/time/magazine/article/0,9171,1191826-1,00.html

Takeyh, R. *Guardians of the Revolution: Iran and the World in the Age of the Ayatollahs.* New York: Oxford University Press, 2009.

Taleb, H. A. "Following the Turkish Model or Forging Our Own?" *Ahram Online* (September 19, 2011). Retrieved October 19, 2011, from http://english.ahram.org.eg/News ContentP/4/21638/Opinion/Following-the-Turkish-model-or-forging-our-own.aspx

Talmadge, C., and J. Rovner. "Hegemony, Force Posture, and the Provision of Public Goods: The Once and Future Role of Outside Powers in Securing Persian Gulf Oil." *Security Studies* 23, no. 3 (2014), 548–81.

Tassel, J. "Militant about 'Islamism.'" *Harvard Magazine*, January–February 2005, 38–47.

Terhalle, M. "Revolutionary Power and Socialization: Explaining the Persistence of Revolutionary Zeal in Iran's Foreign Policy." *Security Studies* 18, no. 3 (2009), 557–86.

"Terrorism, Poverty, and Islam." *Indonesia Matters* (October 6, 2006). Retrieved November 11, 2010, from http://www.indonesiamatters.com/742/terrorism-poverty-islam/

Thompson, W. *The Communist Movement since 1945.* Oxford: Blackwell, 1998.

Toft, M. D., D. Philpott, and T. S. Shah. *God's Century: Resurgent Religion and Global Politics.* New York: Norton, 2011.

"Tolerance and Tension: Islam and Christianity in Sub-Saharan Africa." Pew Forum on Religion and Public Life, April 2010. Retrieved May 16, 2014, from http://www.pew forum.org/files/2010/04/sub-saharan-africa-full-report.pdfhttp://www.pewforum.org /files/2010/04/sub-saharan-africa-full-report.pdf

Trachtenberg, M. *A Constructed Peace: The Making of the European Settlement 1945–1963.* Princeton: Princeton University Press, 1999.

Tucker, R. W., and D. C. Hendrickson. *Empire of Liberty: The Statecraft of Thomas Jefferson.* New York: Oxford University Press, 1990.

Turan, I. "Turkish Foreign Policy: Interplay between the Domestic and External." Washington, D.C.: Carnegie Endowment for International Peace, September 21, 2011. Retrieved October 19, 2011, from http://carnegieendowment.org/2011/09/21/turkish -foreign-policy-interplay-between-domestic-and-external/57qd

Turchetti, M. "Jean Bodin." In E. N. Zalta (Ed.), *Stanford Encyclopedia of Philosophy* (2010). Retrieved August 14, 2012, from http://plato.stanford.edu/entries/bodin/#4

Turgot, A.-R. J. *Reflections on the Formation and Distribution of Wealth* (1774). London: E. Spragg, 1793. Retrieved December 31, 2012, from http://www.econlib.org/library /Essays/trgRfl1.html

United Nations Development Program. *Arab Human Development Report: Human Security.* New York: United Nations, 2009. Retrieved March 17, 2014, from http://www .arab-hdr.org/contents/index.aspx?rid=5

Van Gelderen, M. *The Political Thought of the Dutch Revolt 1555–1590.* New York: Cambridge University Press, 2002.

Voltaire. *Letters on the English (or Lettres philosophiques)* (1733). Fordham University. Retrieved March 22, 2014, from http://www.fordham.edu/halsall/mod/1778voltaire -lettres.asp

Wallace, M. *The American Axis: Henry Ford, Charles Lindbergh, and the Rise of the Third Reich.* New York: Macmillan, 2004.

Wallace-Wells, B. "The Lonely Battle of Wael Ghonim." *New York* (January 22, 2012). Retrieved December 28, 2013, from http://nymag.com/news/features/wael-ghonim
-2012-1

Wallerstein, I. *The Modern World System.* Vol. 1. Berkeley: University of California Press, 2011.

Walt, S. "The Arrogance of Power." *Foreign Policy* blogs (May 25, 2012). Retrieved December 18, 2012, from http://www.foreignpolicy.com/posts/2012/05/25/the_arrogance_of
_power

———. *Revolution and War.* Ithaca, N.Y.: Cornell University Press, 1996.

———. "Top Ten Media Failures in the Iran War Debate." *Foreign Policy* blogs (March 11, 2012). Retrieved December 18, 2012, from http://www.foreignpolicy.com/posts/2012
/03/11/top_ten_media_failures_in_the_iran_war_debate

Walzer, M. *The Revolution of the Saints: A Study in the Origins of Radical Politics.* Cambridge, Mass.: Harvard University Press, 1965.

Webb, S., and B. Webb. *The Decay of Capitalist Civilisation.* London: Fabian Society, 1923.

———. *Soviet Communism: A New Civilisation?* 3rd ed. New York: Longmans, Green, 1944.

Weber, E., and L. L. Snyder. *Varieties of Fascism: Doctrines of Revolution in the Twentieth Century.* New York: Van Nostrand, 1964.

Welsh, J. M. *Edmund Burke and International Relations: The Commonwealth of Europe and the Crusade Against the French Revolution.* New York: Macmillan, 1995.

Weyland, K. "The Arab Spring: Why the Surprising Similarities with the Revolutionary Wave of 1848?" *Perspectives on Politics* 10, no. 4 (2012), 917–34.

Wike, R. "Karen Hughes' Uphill Battle." Pew Research Global Attitudes Project (November 1, 2007). Retrieved February 5, 2013, from http://www.pewglobal.org/2007/11/01
/karen-hughes-uphill-battle/

Wilders, G. *Speech of Geert Wilders, New York, Four Seasons* (February 23, 2009). Retrieved December 1, 2010, from http://www.geertwilders.nl/index.php/component
/content/article/87-news/1535-speech-geert-wilders-new-york-four-seasons-monday
-feb-23-2009

Witte, J., Jr. "Puritan Sources of Enlightenment Liberty." In J. M. Owen IV and J. J. Owen (Eds.), *Religion, the Enlightenment, and the New Global Order.* New York: Columbia University Press, 2011: 140–73.

———. *The Reformation of Rights: Law, Religion and Human Rights in Early Modern Calvinism.* New York: Cambridge University Press, 2007.

Wolterstorff, N. *Justice: Rights and Wrongs.* Princeton: Princeton University Press, 2010.

Woodbridge, H. E. *Sir William Temple: The Man and His Work.* New York: Modern Language Association of America, 1940.

World Bank. "Replicate the World Bank's Regional Aggregation." Retrieved November 19, 2010, from http://iresearch.worldbank.org/PovcalNet/povDuplic.html

Wright, S. "Thomas Helwys." In *Oxford Dictionary of National Biography.* 2004. Retrieved from http://www.oxforddnb.com/view/article/12880

Yavuz, M. H. "Cleansing Islam from the Public Sphere." *Journal of International Affairs* 54, no. 1 (2000), 21–42.

Zakaria, F. "Egypt's Real Parallel to Iran's Revolution." *Washington Post* (February 7, 2011). Retrieved January 14, 2014, from http://www.washingtonpost.com/wp-dyn/content /article/2011/02/06/AR2011020603398.html

———. "The Politics of Rage: Why Do They Hate Us?" *Newsweek* (October 14, 2001). Retrieved January 16, 2014, from http://www.newsweek.com/politics-rage-why-do -they-hate-us-154345

Zogby, J. "Arab Attitudes toward Iran, 2011." Washington, D.C.: Arab American Institute Foundation. Retrieved October 17, 2011, from http://www.aaiusa.org/reports/arab -attitudes-toward-iran-2011

INDEX

Page numbers in *italics* refer to figures and tables